THE TAN.

CHURCHILL TANK
VEHICLE HISTORY AND SPECIFICATION

David Fletcher

© The Tank Museum 2022.

All rights reserved. No part of this publication may be reproduced or stored in a retrieval system or transmitted, in any form or by any means, electronic, mechanical, photocopying, recording or otherwise, without prior permission in writing from The Tank Museum.

First published in 1983 by HMSO.
This edition published in 2022 by The Tank Museum.

British Library Cataloguing in Publication Data.

A catalogue record for this book is available from the British Library.

Printed book ISBN 978 1916355972

Designed and produced for The Tank Museum by JJN Publishing Ltd.
Printed and bound in Malta.

MIX
Paper from responsible sources
FSC® C022612

CONTENTS

INTRODUCTION
SERIES INTRODUCTION 4
THE CHURCHILL TANK 6

THE MANUAL
LAYOUT AND SPECIFICATION 25
GENERAL DESCRIPTION 26
DRIVER'S CONTROLS 29
HOW TO DRIVE 36
ENGINE AND CLUTCH 41
TRANSMISSION 58
TRACKS AND SUSPENSION 68
BRAKES 72
THE TURRET 75
ARMAMENT 83
QF 75MM GUN 84
75MM AMMUNITION 90
QF 95MM HOWITZER 99
95MM AMMUNITION 105
7.92MM BESA MACHINE-GUN 111
7.92MM AMMUNITION 122
2IN BOMB-THROWER 128
2IN BOMB-THROWER AMMUNITION 131
THE GUN MOUNTINGS 135
INTERNAL STOWAGE DIAGRAMS 149
EXTERNAL STOWAGE DIAGRAMS 155
PLATE THICKNESS DIAGRAMS 158
SCALE DRAWINGS 160

CHURCHILL TANK

SERIES INTRODUCTION

Surely no British tank of the Second World War is better known than the Churchill. The name alone echoes the spirit of the time, and the squat, pugnacious look of the tank does nothing to detract from its reputation for invincibility.

This handbook deals with the final production models, the Marks VII and VIII, which were only distinguished from one another by variations in the main armament. Despite a basic similarity in appearance they differed considerably from the earlier marks, being of welded construction. In this they represented a belated attempt by British designers to adopt techniques that the Germans had employed for years, although they still failed to match the enemy in terms of gun power.

The book is arranged in three sections. The first is a newly written introduction to the type, telling the troubled story of its development, from an unreliable beginning to a successful conclusion in some of the hardest fighting of the war. The main body of the book is taken from the Official War Office Handbook, carefully edited to exclude unnecessary detail and repetition without destroying the essence of the original. The final part contains a selection of other official documents associated with the type, while the

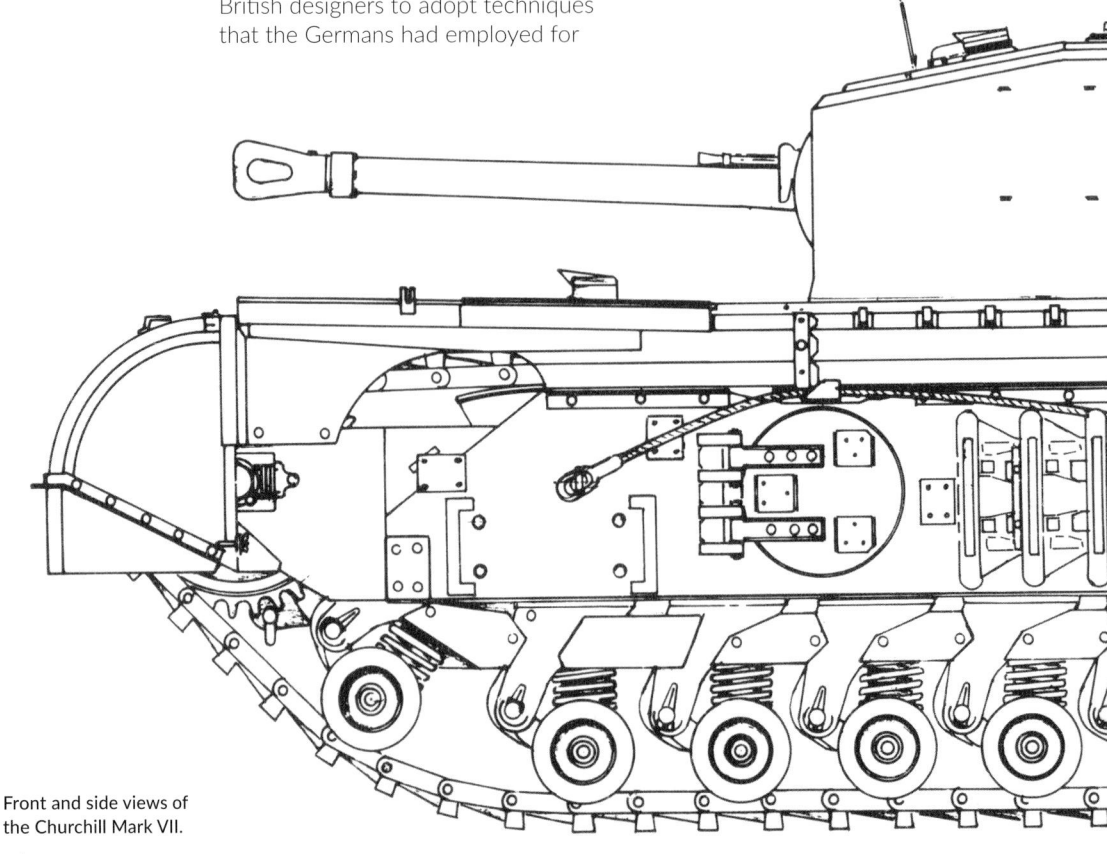

Front and side views of the Churchill Mark VII.

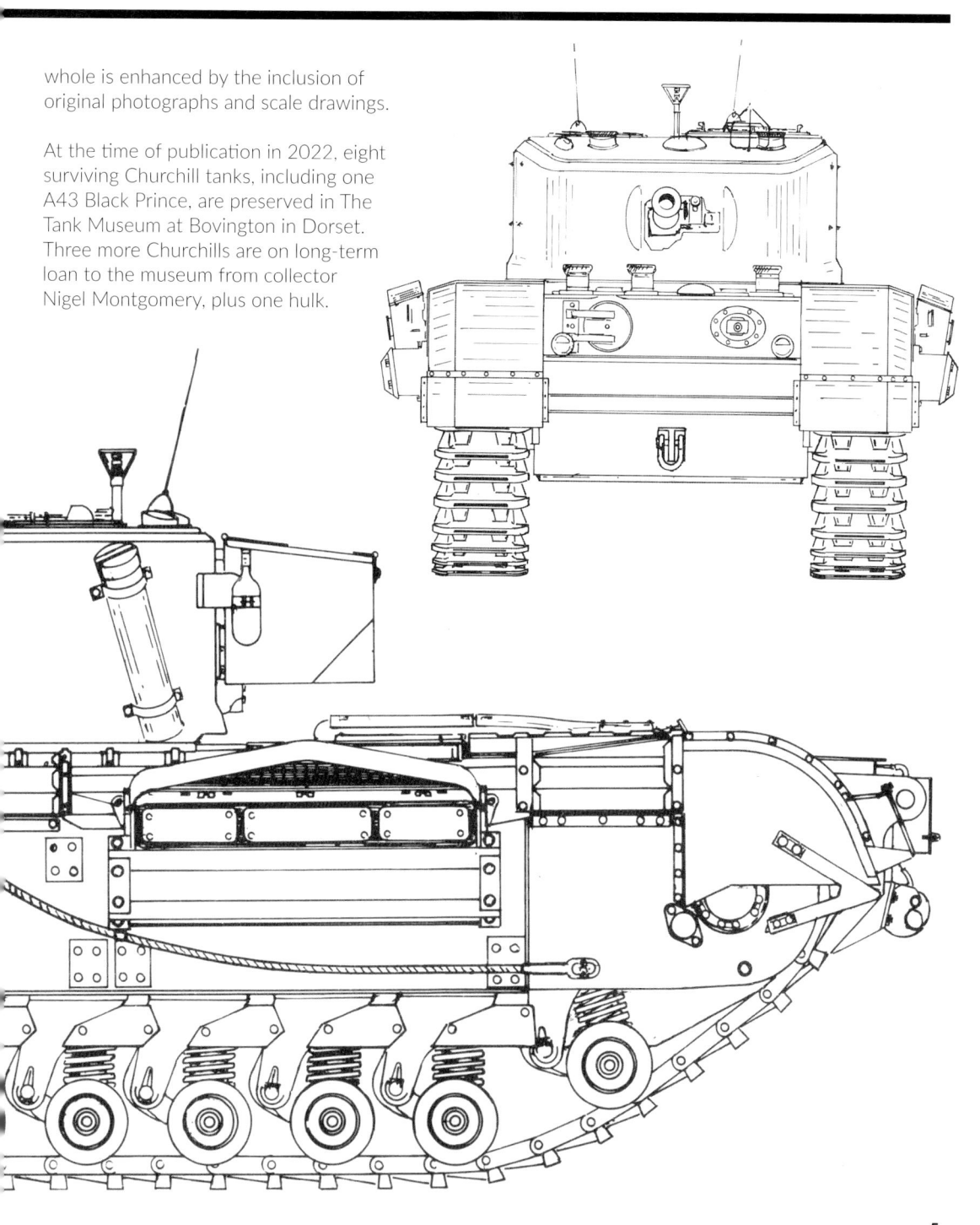

INTRODUCTION

whole is enhanced by the inclusion of original photographs and scale drawings.

At the time of publication in 2022, eight surviving Churchill tanks, including one A43 Black Prince, are preserved in The Tank Museum at Bovington in Dorset. Three more Churchills are on long-term loan to the museum from collector Nigel Montgomery, plus one hulk.

THE CHURCHILL TANK

From the first landings on the Normandy beaches, through the many hard battles fought across France, to the mud of the Reichswald Forest and the final German surrender, the Churchill tank was there. At almost every stage in that bitter struggle the British infantryman, and often his Allied counterpart, could count on the reassuring bulk of a Churchill close by. In addition to the conventional gun tanks, there were numerous special purpose variants, laying bridges, filling gaps and squirting liquid fire. Some blew pillboxes apart with Petard mortars while others acted as close support artillery with their 95mm howitzers. The name Churchill became a byword for solid, rugged reliability, with a superb ability to move through mud and up steep slopes that often defeated lighter and ostensibly more agile machines.

But it had not always been that way; the tanks that earned the laurels in North West Europe did not represent the happy conclusion to a long-running success story. Instead, they were the fortunate heirs to a tale of woe that highlights the confused state that Britain's tank designers had got themselves into at the beginning of the war. In spite of the lessons so clearly taught by the evolutions of the Mechanised Force and the Tank Brigades of the late twenties and early thirties, the immediate pre-war view was that three basic types of tanks were needed to fight a war: the light tanks, with two machine-guns apiece, that served as scouts; the Cruiser tanks, with high-velocity 2-pounder guns, that used their speed and range to carry out long

INTRODUCTION

A column of Churchills awaiting the order to move forward in early 1945. Note the extra track carried for added protection and the worn whitewash applied to the turret and track guards.

distance strikes; the infantry tank, slow, heavily armoured, pugnacious, which worked alongside the infantry and absorbed on its tough hide much of the punishment directed at them.

Britain began the war with two varieties of infantry tank, the Mark I and Mark II. The latter is usually better known by its official nickname Matilda, although in fact it had inherited this from the Mark I, which bore it unofficially. The Mark I was a small two-man tank equipped with a single machine-gun. It was well armoured and reliable but it was used out of context when the war failed to take the course that the tank's designers had expected, and it has received a lot of criticism on that account ever since. In contrast, the Mark II was a classic; in its day it was one of the best protected and best armed tanks fielded by any army. Unfortunately, it required much individual attention and skill in its construction, and it never appeared in the right quantities until it had been outclassed. During the early battles in France it suffered many of the vicissitudes endemic in a new design, although it came into its own a short time later in the desert and, as the Australians found, was still more than a match for Japanese armour at the end of the war. The infantry tank Mark III was the Valentine. This tank was produced by Vickers in answer to a War Office request for an effective but simple infantry tank to make up what the Matilda lacked in numbers. The Valentine was based upon a previous design of adequate quality, the A10 or Cruiser Mark II, and as such began

Heavy Tank A20 with Matilda turret.

INTRODUCTION

life with a better pedigree. Despite the limitations of a small turret and cramped hull it was relatively easy to produce, reliable in service and a good deal more agile than the Matilda. For this reason in particular it seems to have gradually taken upon itself the mantle of the Cruiser tank, which was probably just as well since its armour protection was inferior to that of Matilda, and indeed little better than the Infantry Tank Mark I.

Thus, it was that by the middle of 1940 the War Office, while realising the need for a bigger and better infantry tank, had no idea where it might come from. None of the existing designs were really suitable as a basis for improvement, and the time required to build a new design from scratch, with that design not yet established, was unacceptable at a time when the future looked so bleak on all fronts. No doubt, in their minds was the image of an improved model of the Matilda and the nearest thing to that in 1940 was the A20.

Although the three types of tank – light, cruiser and infantry – were considered suitable for most facets of modern warfare as it was imagined in 1939, there were those who preferred the concrete evidence of the last great struggle as a basis for their ideas, rather than the less substantial results of peacetime war-gaming. To these men the confrontation in France between the Germans and the Allies was where they left off in 1918. The long period of the 'Phoney War' gave them time

T30971, a Churchill Mark I, and production technicians, patiently await the arrival of a military delegation.

to think, and the static lines of British and French defenders facing west served to confirm in many minds the image of 1918 over again. It is not surprising to find that the results of their deliberations on tanks were likewise an extension of First World War thinking.

There is no doubt that Winston Churchill was one of the leading lights of this movement, as he had been in 1915, but it is odd to see the dissipation of effort that resulted, in marked contrast to 1915. On one hand, at the behest of the General Staff, in September 1939 the Belfast engineering firm Harland and Wolff began to design an extra-large infantry tank based on First World War principles, the A20. On the other Churchill established, through the Ministry of Supply, the Special Vehicle Development Committee (SVDC), a team of all the talents, composed of the almost legendary men who had first forged the tank in 1915, Stern, Tritton, Wilson, Swinton, Ricardo and D'Eyncourt. A month after the A20 design was mooted this body began work on an alternative, the specifications for which are so little different that one wonders at the wasted effort. Unlike the A20, the SVDC tank did not have the direct blessing of the General Staff (and therefore no specification number) and it became known instead by the initials of the catchphrase applied to its design team, The Old Gang – TOG. In the event, both designs were short lived. No doubt in time the technical problems could have been overcome, but the war could not be changed to suit, and

INTRODUCTION

the Panzer Divisions rendered them as obsolete as the Mechanised Force had proved 1918 thinking to be in 1928.

Of the TOG designs we will hear no more, although they soldiered on for an untoward time to little or no avail. The A20 on the other hand held latent promise, but it had to go to Luton to discover it. By the summer of 1940 at least one A20 pilot model had been built. There would be no production machines, an order for 100 had been cancelled in May when the Germans attacked France, and all immediate thoughts of assaulting the Siegfried Line evaporated. This pilot was almost completed to the point of wanting a turret and guns fitted. It was powered by a Meadows flat twelve engine rated at 300bhp driving through a five-speed Merritt transmission. In this respect it had something in common with the Cruiser tank Convenanter, although this later entered production with a simpler transmission. But the Covenanter only weighed 18 tons, whereas the A20 tipped the scales at 43 tons – little wonder that it was considered to be underpowered. Hence the trip to Luton. Vauxhall Motors had developed a new 12-cylinder engine based on two Bedford lorry engines and it was hoped that this would prove a more suitable power unit for the massive tank.

In the event the new engine was never fitted. Indeed, the only thing that seems to have been done to A20 at Luton was the reversal of the tracks. In the meantime, it had been decided that the crying need was for something a bit smaller, less complicated and easier to transport by rail or road. This soon resolved itself into General Staff specification A22 with a plea from the Prime Minister that a simplified heavy tank be available in quantity by 3 March 1941. Vauxhall Motors became the main contractors and since

Extruding mud from its tracks, INDUS, a Churchill Mark I of B Squadron 9th RTR, manoeuvres during an exercise on Salisbury Plain.

CHURCHILL TANK

time was not on their side they chose to use as many features of the A20 as might be practicable. Just to what extent this was done was revealed to members of the Tank Board when they met at the Vauxhall works on 25 November 1940 to inspect the pilot mock-up. It revealed a tank that, besides A20 itself, seems to have owed little or nothing to previous British experience and precious little to anyone else, although the French Char B is thought to have been an influence. Despite the Prime Minister's desire to have the tanks rolling off the production lines by March 1941 the programme was soon two months behind schedule. Serious faults had developed in the suspension components and the engine heads during early trials. But in April the Prime Minister and the Tank Board pressed Vauxhall to have 100 tanks ready in May and 400 more by the end of August. The manufacturers felt that the time had already arrived to rethink the entire design in view of an increasing list of problems, but they accepted the pleas of urgency and expediency on the understanding that such later modifications as had been agreed would be incorporated as soon as possible.

Welcome or not, the interest shown by the Prime Minister in the new tank assured it of a name, and one which happily coincided with the curious British practice of giving the majority of their tanks names beginning with the third letter of the alphabet. Thus, early production models of the A22 were known as the Churchill I. The hull was in the shape of a long, low box with a step at the front. It was of riveted construction with the crew at the front and the engine and transmission in the rear. The suspension on each side of the

A Churchill Mark II at Lulworth. Note the Lakeman anti-aircraft Bren gun mounting.

hull comprised of small steel rollers on short coil springs housed between inner and outer plates, which protected it externally and increased the available stowage space within. The tracks ran right around this section, exposed on their upper run. Beside the driver at the front was a 3in howitzer of very limited traverse while a 2-pounder gun and a Besa machine-gun occupied the small cast turret. The tank weighed 38½ tons and carried a crew of five. The Bedford engine was of course employed along with a modified form of transmission known as the Merritt-Brown.

Before long the supply of 3in howitzers had fallen behind schedule and a number of tanks were completed with a second Besa machine-gun in the hull mounting instead. These were designated Churchill II. In July the War Office were pressing for a new turret design to take the 6-pounder gun, which had finally been decided upon. A roomier turret was therefore designed of box shape and built from flat welded plates. When it appeared towards the end of the year it carried the Churchill on to the Mark III stage. A shortage of suitable plate for welding then led to yet another design of cast turret to take the 6-pounder and in this form the tank was known as the Churchill IV.

A top-down view of a Churchill Mark II. Shovels, a pick and hammer are stowed on the rear deck behind the twin exhaust mufflers.

Fresh off the production line this Churchill Mark III features a welded armour-plated turret to accommodate the new 6-pounder gun.

CHURCHILL TANK

Turretless A22F Churchills await the fitting of engines on the production line at Vauxhall. Note the floor rails along which the bogie wheels run.

Fitted with 6ft wading trunking for trials, this Churchill also has weights bolted to the turret.

Even so, all through this period of development the incidents of unreliability and the root causes multiplied. Faults were manifest in the cooling, the suspension, the transmission and the engine itself – indeed, everything that was connected with making the tank function. But with the Germans just across the Channel it had already been decreed that an immobile Churchill would at least serve as a formidable Pill Box! In August 1941 a tank was even sent to Fosters of Lincoln, builders of the very first tanks, for their expert advice, but after a thorough examination they could offer no helpful suggestions. In December 1941, the blow fell. The War Office announced that they did not intend to develop the A22 beyond the present 6-pounder model and they had it in mind to arrange for the design of a new type of infantry tank instead. As if to knock in the final nail a report dated 15 January 1942 stated that 42 per cent of service Churchills were off the road at that time with one problem or another.

On the credit side, production was now well underway and a parallel rework programme had been instituted whereby tanks were systematically returned to the makers to have some of the more glaring faults corrected and, in some cases, a 6-pounder turret substituted for the original 2-pounder type. A further

INTRODUCTION

move that altered the appearance of the tank considerably was the fitting of sheet metal guards to cover the top run of the tracks. It was hoped that by the summer a new style of rubber suspension would be available, in which much hope was placed, but the delays were such that it was announced in June that the final batch of 500 machines then on order would be completed with the regular suspension. The following month the Tank Board affirmed that Churchill production was to end after 3,500 tanks had been completed and that Vauxhalls would then be expected to join the A27 Cruiser tank production team, to which end they soon began to build a pilot. Then at the end of the month the final decision to cease Churchill production was put to its namesake the Prime Minister. He in turn referred it to the War Cabinet. A short while before this the Director of Tank Design had reported on the results of the rework programme. Three sample tanks had been tested and all turned out to be unsatisfactory in terms of reliability with faults in the tracks, suspension, engine and transmission, which in due course led to a decision to limit the reworking to 1,205 tanks. This programme then being in the hands of Vauxhall Motors and Messrs Broom and Wade.

In the meantime, despite these sorry reports the Churchill had seen action. The first occasion was the Dieppe Raid of August 1942 but it was a poor test. The landing was heavily opposed and the majority of tanks that got ashore remained immobile on the steep beach, their tracks flailing

Wearing brown and black-shaded camouflage, this A22D Churchill 3-inch Gun Carrier should have an 'S' prefix rather than a 'T', being a self-propelled gun.

Reworked Churchill T68831R (the 'R' designating that it has been through the re-work programme). The tank is wading (with a slightly apprehensive looking driver) to test its newly applied waterproofing. Recently fitted track guards and air louvres can also be seen. The lorry in the background carries two Churchill engines on the back.

CHURCHILL TANK

One of six reworked Churchill Mark IIIs, which arrived in Egypt in October 1942 as part of Kingforce. Note the canvas sand dodger screen on the front horns, which was fitted to keep the dust down.

impotently on the loose shingle. A few did manage to scramble over the sea wall but they were gradually put out of action, for although the thick armour was rarely penetrated the exposed tracks were an easy mark. Following the withdrawal or surrender of the survivors, the Germans found themselves the proud owners of samples of one of Britain's latest tanks. Marks I and III were involved.

Six more tanks went out to Egypt later in the year and took a minor part in Second Alamein at the end of October. These were Mark IIIs and by all accounts they survived a veritable hail of anti-tank gun fire. They also served to prove that a tank designed specifically for European climes could operate in warmer regions without undue difficulty and it paved the way for later successes in Tunisia.

Back in Britain, the War Cabinet took their time in deciding the future of the Churchill; so long in fact that a bridging order for 500 more was permitted to keep the production lines active. Of these 300 were to be adapted to mount a 95mm close support howitzer in place of the 6-pounder gun and these would become the Churchill Mark V. A new 75mm gun was also in the process of being

A Churchill Mark III from 145 Regiment RAC leads a column of infantry in Tunisia. Note the sand camouflage applied to the tank to disrupt its green outline.

INTRODUCTION

adopted and with this in place the tank would be known as the Churchill Mark VI. The announcement from the War Cabinet came on 20 April 1943. This was to the effect that the Churchill would remain in production throughout 1944 at least and an immediate order was placed for a further 1,000, bringing the total of A22s built or building to 5,000. A further announcement in May assured the future of the tank when it was announced that 200 examples of a new type, the A22F, were to be built. These would have the frontal armour increased to 6in with a commensurate increase in weight to 40 tons. The sacrifice involved was a reduction in top speed from 18 to 13mph.

Indeed, in many respects this new 'Heavy Churchill' was almost a new tank. For the first time on a British vehicle of this size, welded rather than riveted construction was to be employed. In fact, the idea of applying welding techniques for major components had been considered when the Churchill was first mooted, but it was felt at the time that not enough was known about the effect of battle damage on heavy welded structures so the designers had played it safe and stuck to riveting. Then in July 1940, one experimental hull was welded up and subjected to firing trials, which

Sgt Reg Mead, 11 Troop, C Squadron, 9th RTR, stares at the camera as his tank INTENSIVE sits atop 'London Bridge' in Roosendaal, late in October 1944.

A Churchill Mk VI crosses the river Reno beside a destroyed railway bridge near Bastia Umbra in Italy on 18 April 1945.

CHURCHILL TANK

A nice overhead shot showing great detail. Just visible on the right side of the turret is the red, yellow and black cannon, the marking of the Gunnery School.

produced a satisfactory result and in November Messrs Babcock and Wilcox were ordered to produce a welded Mark IV hull. This was followed by a second in January 1942. A number of alternative techniques were tried until the optimum result was achieved, but nothing more was done while the future of the Churchill hung in the balance. We have already seen that a welded 6-pounder turret appeared in mid-1941. This, too, was the result of an order placed with Babcock and Wilcox in the April. It was then subjected to firing trials while another 21 experimental turrets were ordered from other steelmakers.

It had been estimated that the effect of welding against riveting would save 20 per cent in man hours, 4 per cent in weight, but require 50 per cent more factory space. In the event the first figure proved to be underrated, the last exaggerated and the matter of weight was swallowed up in the thicker armour. Even so it proved to be a considerable advance in British tank design, although it should be remembered that both the Germans and Russians had been welding tank hulls since before the war.

Another feature that contrasted A22F with its predecessors was the shape of the crew access doors in

INTRODUCTION

Fitting the rear top-plate to the cast shell of an A22F Churchill turret at the Babcock & Wilcox foundry.

A22F Churchill Mark VII. Note the first aid box affixed to rear.

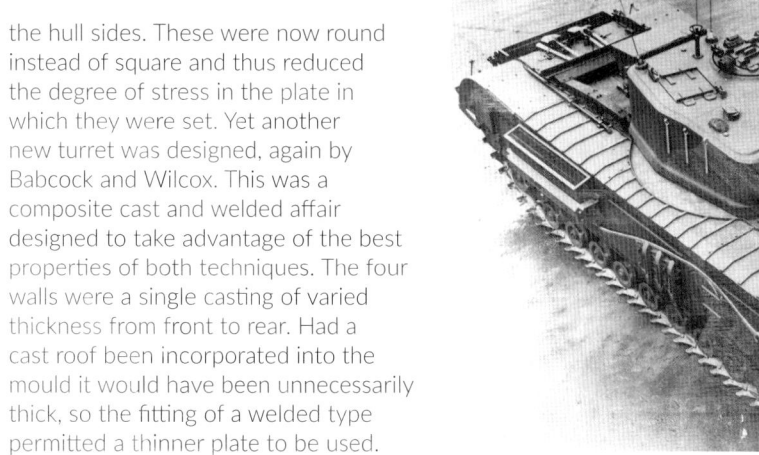

the hull sides. These were now round instead of square and thus reduced the degree of stress in the plate in which they were set. Yet another new turret was designed, again by Babcock and Wilcox. This was a composite cast and welded affair designed to take advantage of the best properties of both techniques. The four walls were a single casting of varied thickness from front to rear. Had a cast roof been incorporated into the mould it would have been unnecessarily thick, so the fitting of a welded type permitted a thinner plate to be used.

The A22F entered the lists in two

A Churchill Mark VIII featuring a 95mm howitzer. Note the three-blade vane sight positioned in front of the commander's hatch for indirect fire.

19

BUGLER is guided onto its transporter. The central track guard section has been removed to avoid jamming the turret when traversing.

A Churchill Mark VII Crocodile demonstrates the fearsome effect of its flamethrower on a suspected enemy position.

of 7 October 1943 mentions that 730 tanks of the proposed 1944 production should be of the heavy type and something over a month later a further 500 were ordered. The tanks saw active service from D-Day onwards. Many of their older brethren were converted to a variety of special-purpose roles but the one reserved for the Mark VII was probably the most famous of all Churchill variants, the Crocodile flamethrower.

With the ending of the war most of the earlier Churchills were taken to the scrapheap and the Marks VII and VIII took over the mantle of the 'Funnies' as AVRE bridge-layers and ARKs. They served again as gun tanks and Crocodiles during the Korean War but once that conflict was over they were steadily replaced by the Centurions, which later took over

GNAT, a Churchill Mark VII, fitted out with a spaced meshed steel armour kit, which was being investigated for its ability to defeat hollow charge weapons.

separate forms. As the Churchill Mark VII mounting a 75mm gun or as a Mark VIII with a 95mm howitzer. A curious minute from the Tank Board, dated just nine days after D-Day, discusses the possibility of mounting the 6-pounder gun in the heavy Churchill and mentions that one tank has been so modified at FVPE, but the reason for this apparently retrograde move is not known. Surviving records do not reveal exactly how many Churchill VII/VIIIs were built, but a Tank Board meeting

INTRODUCTION

the special purpose roles as well. Although from the production point of view the VII and VIII were the last of the line, three subsequent marks are recorded, the IX, X and XI. However, these were all rebuilds to varying degrees of earlier types, which equated to Mark VII standard.

There is no doubt that the Churchill vindicated itself from the Tunisian battles onwards, but it was already obsolete by international standards as were many of its British contemporaries. It also helped to prolong the now discredited idea of building different classes of tanks for different functions. For all that, it seems to have been a popular tank with its crews and a great source of comfort to the infantry it assisted, its qualities often being associated with the man whose name it bore. A creditable number survive in museums and private collections all over the world and its unique outline makes it one of the easiest tanks to identify of all time.

The end of an era. Covered in chalk slogans, names and even a lucky horseshoe, a Churchill Mark VII gets a send-off from some of the production team.

CHURCHILL TANK

RESTRICTED

The information given in this document is not to be communicated, either directly or indirectly, to the press or to any person not authorised to receive it.

SERVICE INSTRUCTION BOOK

CHURCHILL VII & VIII

This book has been prepared to the instructions of the Chief Inspector of Fighting Vehicles, to whom all communications should be addressed.

FIRST EDITION,
June, 1944.

Note: The Service Instruction Book is an abridged version of the original and therefore any cross-references to pages and figure numbers contained in the text are no longer relevant.

FOREWORD

THE object of this instruction book is to present a clear and concise picture of the Churchill VII and Churchill VIII, and of the routine maintenance operations necessary to maintain these vehicles in fighting trim.

The first part of the book contains a brief outline of the vehicles, followed by details of the controls and comprehensive driving and handling instructions.

The second part consists of general specifications and complete descriptions of the various sections of the vehicle. These sections are dealt with in the order given on page 9.

The third part of the book is devoted to running adjustments and maintenance operations. The maintenance operations are numbered and bear the prefix letters " A " and " B." " A " jobs are those which are to be performed periodically as maintenance routine. " B " jobs are those which are carried out as and when necessary.

All tools required for the " A " (routine) operations are carried on the vehicle. For some of the " B " operations, however, special tools are required in addition to the normal spanners, etc. These special tools are listed on page 114.

Major operations, for which *workshop* equipment is necessary, are not included in this instruction book.

It is essential that this service instruction book be read in conjunction with the instructions given in the appropriate Military Training Pamphlet for the vehicle and the relative Crew Maintenance Insert in A.B. 413. Information in this insert regarding lubricants and periods of maintenance will be taken as the ruling guide should it differ from the schedule on the lubrication chart in the pocket of this book.

Maintenance and repair operations must be carried out in accordance with the provisions set out in R.E.M.E. Echelon Repair Schedules for Fighting Vehicles. These Schedules, it should be noted, are written as a guide for active service conditions, and the ruling factors of time and the tactical situation will determine whether the permissive limits of work are curtailed or extended.

The Armament chapters are inserted in a separate section at the end of the book.

Frost Precautions—see page 181.

Driver's Controls and Driving Instructions—see pages 16 to 25.

LAYOUT AND SPECIFICATION

GENERAL SPECIFICATION

Overall Length	25 ft. 2 in.
" Width (with air louvres)	10 ft. 8 in.
" " (without air louvres)	9 ft. 2 in.
" Height	8 ft. 2 in.
Length of Tracks on Ground	12 ft. 6 in.
Width over Tracks	9 ft. 1 in.
Clearance under Hull	1 ft. 8 in.
Gross Weight	41 tons approx.

(More detailed dimensions are given on the Transport Diagram inserted in the pocket at the back of this Instruction Book.)

ENGINE

Bedford Twin-Six 12-Cyl. Horizontally Opposed.
Bore—5 in. Stroke—5½ in. R.A.C. Rating—120 h.p. Nominal B.H.P.—350 at 2,200 r.p.m.

WEIGHTS

Weight of Engine (Dry)	3,376 lbs. (approx.)
" " Gearbox (Dry)	1,939 lbs. "
" " Final Drive Unit	1,100 lbs. "
" " Idler Unit	674 lbs. "

CAPACITIES

Oil in Engine	11 gallons (approx.)
Water in Cooling System	26 gallons "
	(13 gallons each side)
Petrol Tank Capacity	150 gallons
Oil in Gearbox—Quantity for Dry Box	3 gallons
Refill Quantity after Draining	2½ gallons
Oil in each Final Drive Unit	1¾ gallons

NOTE.—Detailed specifications of the various units are printed immediately before the general descriptions of the units, and will be found on the following pages:

	Page		Page
Engine and Clutch	29	Idler Unit	65
Engine Electrical System	45	Tracks and Suspension	66
Fuel System	48	Brakes	70
Cooling System	52	Air Pressure System	73
Gearbox	56	Turret	82
Final Drive Unit	62	Electrical Equipment	89

GENERAL DESCRIPTION

The Churchill Infantry Tank is a heavily armoured vehicle, powered by a 350 brake horse power, 12-cylinder horizontally opposed engine.

The hull is divided into four compartments. At the front is the driving compartment, which also houses the front gunner. Immediately behind is the fighting compartment containing the electrically-operated three-man turret. Behind this again is the engine compartment, and behind the engine compartment is the rear compartment, which houses the gearbox, the steering brakes and main brakes, the air compressor and the power traverse generator.

The engine is designed to be as compact as possible, and particular care has been taken to ensure accessibility and to provide long life of such components as valves, cylinder bores and bearings.

The radiators and petrol tanks are placed alongside the engine, and are housed behind the heavy armour. The horizontal tanks are also protected by armour plating against splash.

A conventional single plate clutch transmits the power to the gearbox, which lies transversely across the rear compartment. This unit carries the steering brakes and contains the steering mechanism.

The gearbox output shafts are connected to the final drive units, which provide the necessary speed reduction and carry the double sprockets for the tracks. The main brakes are adjacent to the final drive units.

The tank is carried on 22 bogies, 11 on each side. Each bogie is independently sprung with the exception of No. 11 on each side which are unsprung. Bogies number 1, 4, 5, 6, 7, 8, 9 and 10 on each side are all similar in construction and may be removed as units, complete with all suspension details, for service or replacement. Numbers 2 and 3 on each side are mounted on a common bracket and can be removed as an assembly, complete with all suspension details. Number 11 on each side can be removed independently for servicing.

The tracks are of the steel articulated link type. Flanged steel wheels on the bogies carry the vehicle on the double rail section of the track links.

A 7.92 mm. Besa gun equipped with a sighting telescope is fitted in the driving compartment. The *Churchill VII* turret is provided with a 75 mm. gun and the *Churchill VIII* with a 95 mm. howitzer, each being mounted co-axially with a 7.92 mm. Besa and a sighting telescope.

The radio equipment is of the two wave-length type, a special short wave set being incorporated for short distance work. There is also an intercommunication set for the crew, so arranged that each member can establish contact with any one of the others.

Adequate provision is made for stowage of ammunition and equipment.

Driving and general handling are made as easy as possible with power-assisted clutch and steering operation and an easy gear change.

HULL

The hull is constructed of heavy B.P. plates and is of all-welded construction. The floor is flat and free from projections, and panniers are provided at each side, between the upper and lower runs of the track, for storage of equipment. The whole structure is braced by cross girders and by the bulkheads which separate the various compartments.

GENERAL DESCRIPTION

Escape Hatches

Double-hinged doors are provided in the roof above the driver and front gunner. They are fastened from the inside, but can be opened or fastened from the outside by using a suitable key. Each door frame is provided with a gutter and drain hole to prevent the ingress of water.

In each pannier a door is provided, opening into the driving compartment. These doors can be fastened or opened only from the inside, but the locking handles are so designed that the doors are automatically secured when they are pulled to.

Fig. 4. View of circular pannier door, showing locking handle.

The Turret

The rotating turret is electrically driven and has also provision for manual control. It is dealt with in detail on pages 82 to 88.

The Vision Port

The driver is provided with a round vision aperture, which can be closed by a door operated from inside the vehicle. Full details are given on page 19.

Driver and Front Gunner's Seats.

The driver's seat is readily adjustable for height as well as for reach. The front gunner's seat is adjustable for reach only.

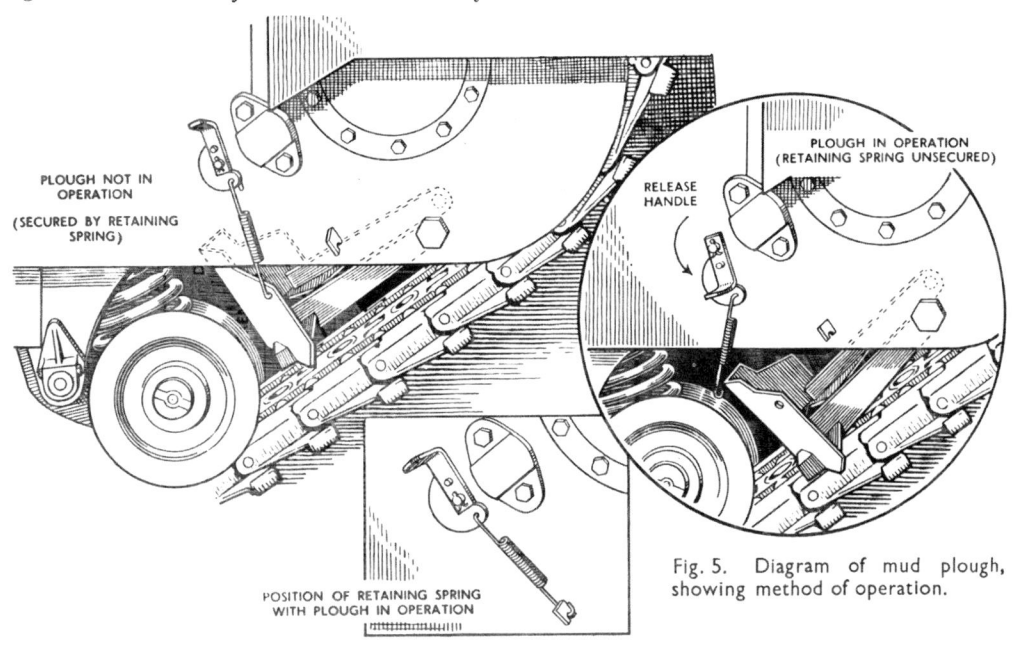

Fig. 5. Diagram of mud plough, showing method of operation.

27

HULL FLOOR TRAPS

Periscopes
Two periscopes are provided for the driver and one for the front gunner. There are also two periscopes in the front of the turret and two in the commander's cupola.

Mud Plough
To minimise "mud packing" between the pannier top plates and the tracks, a mud plough is provided on each side of the vehicle. It is carried on two hinge pins, one located in the final drive carrier and one in the hull side plate, and is located between No. 11 suspension unit and the final drive. When in operation it is held in contact with the track by its own weight, and when not in use, held out of engagement by a spring and toggle lever.

HULL FLOOR TRAPS

Several apertures are provided in the floor of the hull (*see list below*) to give access to the units located inside. They are closed in different ways, but all the covers are arranged so that there is no projection below the hull floor. Cover plates removable from underneath the vehicle are recessed and are retained by recessed bolts.

Inspection Plate No. on Plan	Cover Plates Secured By	Tool Needed	For Access To
1	6—$\frac{3}{8}$ in. B.S.F. Bolts or 6—$\frac{1}{2}$ in. B.S.F. Bolts with $\frac{3}{8}$ in. W. heads.	Medium Ratchet Wrench, TP.10147, Coupler TP.10148 with $\frac{5}{16}$ in. W. Socket TP.10158, or $\frac{3}{8}$ in. W. Socket TP.10159.	Gearbox drain plug. Clutch control pipe unions.

Fig. 6. Inspection plates in hull floor. 1. Gearbox compartment plate. 2. Rectangular inspection cover, engine compartment. 3. Centre large inspection cover, engine compartment. 4. Right centre inspection cover, engine compartment. 5. Right rear inspection cover, engine compartment. 6. Petrol dump valve, engine compartment. 7. Emergency disposal hatch, driving compartment. 8. Drain hole for left-hand water system, fighting compartment. 9. Drain hole for right-hand water system, fighting compartment. 10. Drain plug for rotary base junction, fighting compartment. 11. Hull floor drain plug, engine and gearbox compartments.

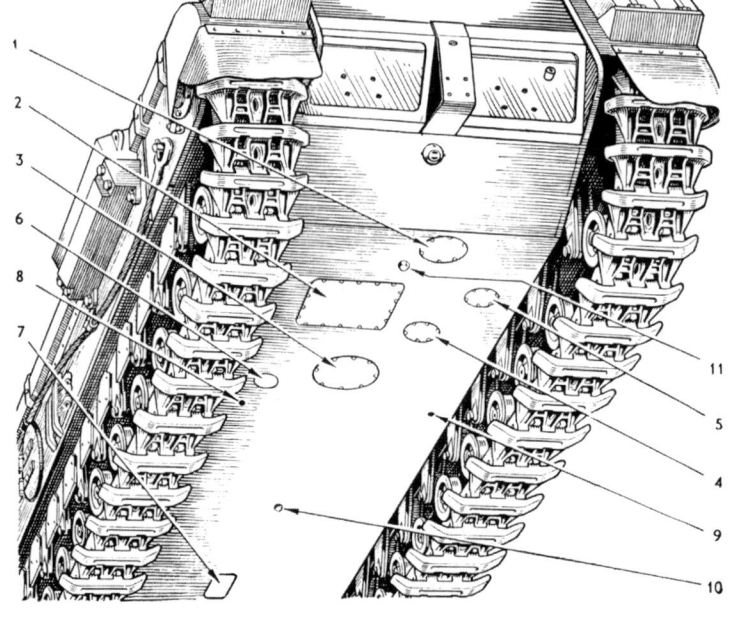

DRIVER'S CONTROLS

ENGINE CONTROLS

Controls for the Electrical Circuits

A master switch is provided in the battery recess to cut off all battery current from the vehicle. Before the engine can be started, this master switch must be turned to the " on " position. A green warning light (in the cover of the panel light for the petrol gauges) serves as a reminder if the switch is inadvertently left on when the vehicle is parked.

On the instrument panel, which is located to the right of the driver, a switch is provided for the ignition circuit. When this is turned on a warning light adjacent to it glows red and continues to glow all the time the switch is on. If the red light does not come on when the switch is turned, either the circuit is broken—the master switch not on, for instance—or the bulb has burned out. Any fault of this type should be rectified immediately.

In the centre of the instrument panel there is a press-type switch to operate the starter motor for the engine. On the left of the panel, an ammeter records the charging rate when the engine is running. This ammeter shows only the charge and not the discharge. It will be noticed that the charging rate varies considerably, beginning with a high rate immediately after starting the engine and falling away as the battery is charged. This is normal, the generator being controlled so that the charging rate is automatically suited to the condition of the battery.

Two electric petrol gauges are provided on the instrument panel to indicate the level in the petrol tanks. These gauges record only when a push-button switch on the panel is pressed. A separate panel—mounted above the instrument panel—contains two push buttons to operate the smoke screen generators.

Controls for Engine Operation

On the left-hand side of the driving compartment a lever is fitted to control the petrol supply from the two sets of main tanks. The lever can be moved to three positions—to shut off both tank sets ; to turn on the left-hand set—marked " L.H."—and to turn on the right-hand set—marked " R.H."

A hand control is fitted in the right-hand top corner of the fighting compartment rear bulkhead to ensure that the float chambers of the carburettors are filled. This is pulled out to operate the petrol pump manually, and several strokes should be given before attempting to start the engine from cold. The control should be pulled out to the fullest extent each time, as only the end portion of the stroke operates the pump.

The normal method of starting from cold is to use the " Ki-gass " system, the control of which is bolted to the rear bulkhead of the fighting compartment. Three or four strokes of the " Ki-gass " plunger is sufficient to start the engine under almost all conditions. In front of the driver and fastened to the side wall of the vehicle, is a control to operate the choke valves of the four carburettors. Careful use of this control enables the engine to be run at slow speed immediately after starting. It should be returned to the " off " position as soon as possible.

The instrument panel also has **an oil gauge which records** the oil pressure while the

DRIVER'S CONTROLS

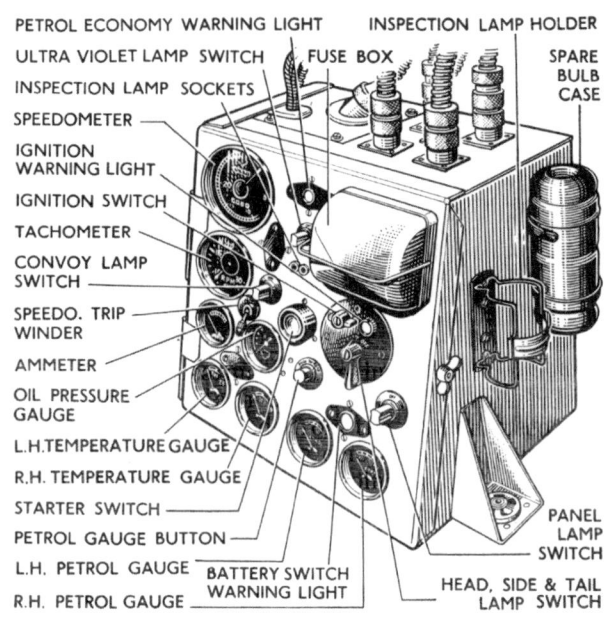

Fig. 7 (*Right*). The instrument panel—located in the right-hand pannier, forward of the driver.

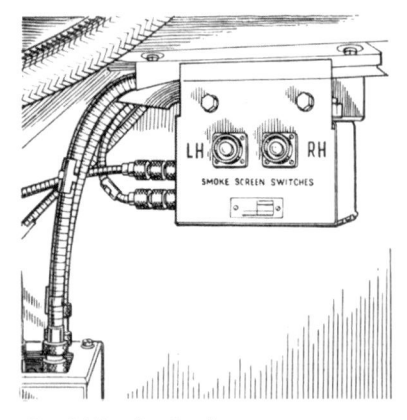

Labels on instrument panel: PETROL ECONOMY WARNING LIGHT, INSPECTION LAMP HOLDER, ULTRA VIOLET LAMP SWITCH, FUSE BOX, SPARE BULB CASE, INSPECTION LAMP SOCKETS, SPEEDOMETER, IGNITION WARNING LIGHT, IGNITION SWITCH, TACHOMETER, CONVOY LAMP SWITCH, SPEEDO. TRIP WINDER, AMMETER, OIL PRESSURE GAUGE, L.H. TEMPERATURE GAUGE, R.H. TEMPERATURE GAUGE, STARTER SWITCH, PETROL GAUGE BUTTON, L.H. PETROL GAUGE, BATTERY SWITCH WARNING LIGHT, R.H. PETROL GAUGE, PANEL LAMP SWITCH, HEAD, SIDE & TAIL LAMP SWITCH.

Fig. 8 (*Above*). Smoke screen generator push buttons. This panel is mounted above the instrument panel.

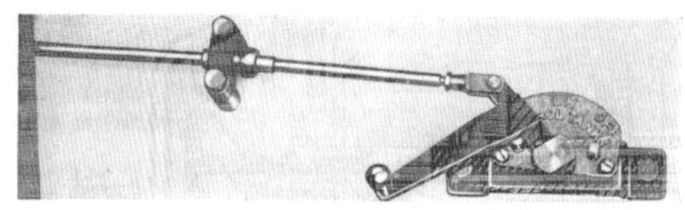

Fig. 9 (*Left*). Lever controlling right-hand and left-hand petrol tanks.

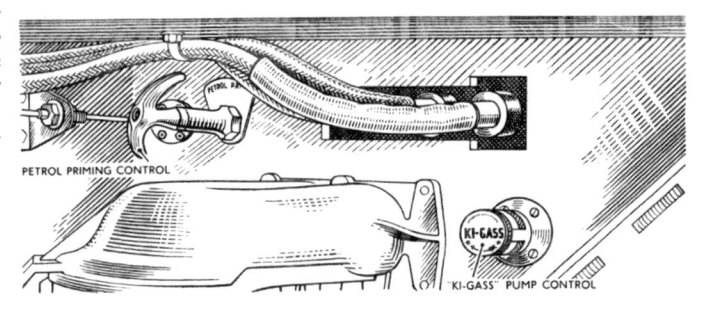

Fig. 10 (*Below*). Petrol hand-priming control, and "Ki-gass" plunger control.

engine is running, and a revolution indicator is provided to show the engine speed. Two water temperature indicators, one for each of the water cooling systems, are located at the bottom of the instrument panel. At the top of the panel, a warning light labelled " petrol " lights up when the engine is working really hard, and therefore using an excessive amount of petrol. Every endeavour should be made to " keep the light out," at all times when circumstances permit. On later vehicles an oil pressure warning light is fitted instead of the petrol economy light.

DRIVING CONTROLS

The three pedals in front of the driver's seat operate the clutch, foot-brake and engine acceleration in the normal way. The left-hand pedal operates the clutch hydraulically, and is provided with an air pressure servo to give a light pedal action. On the right of the clutch pedal is the foot brake pedal, which operates the main brakes

VEHICLE HISTORY AND SPECIFICATION

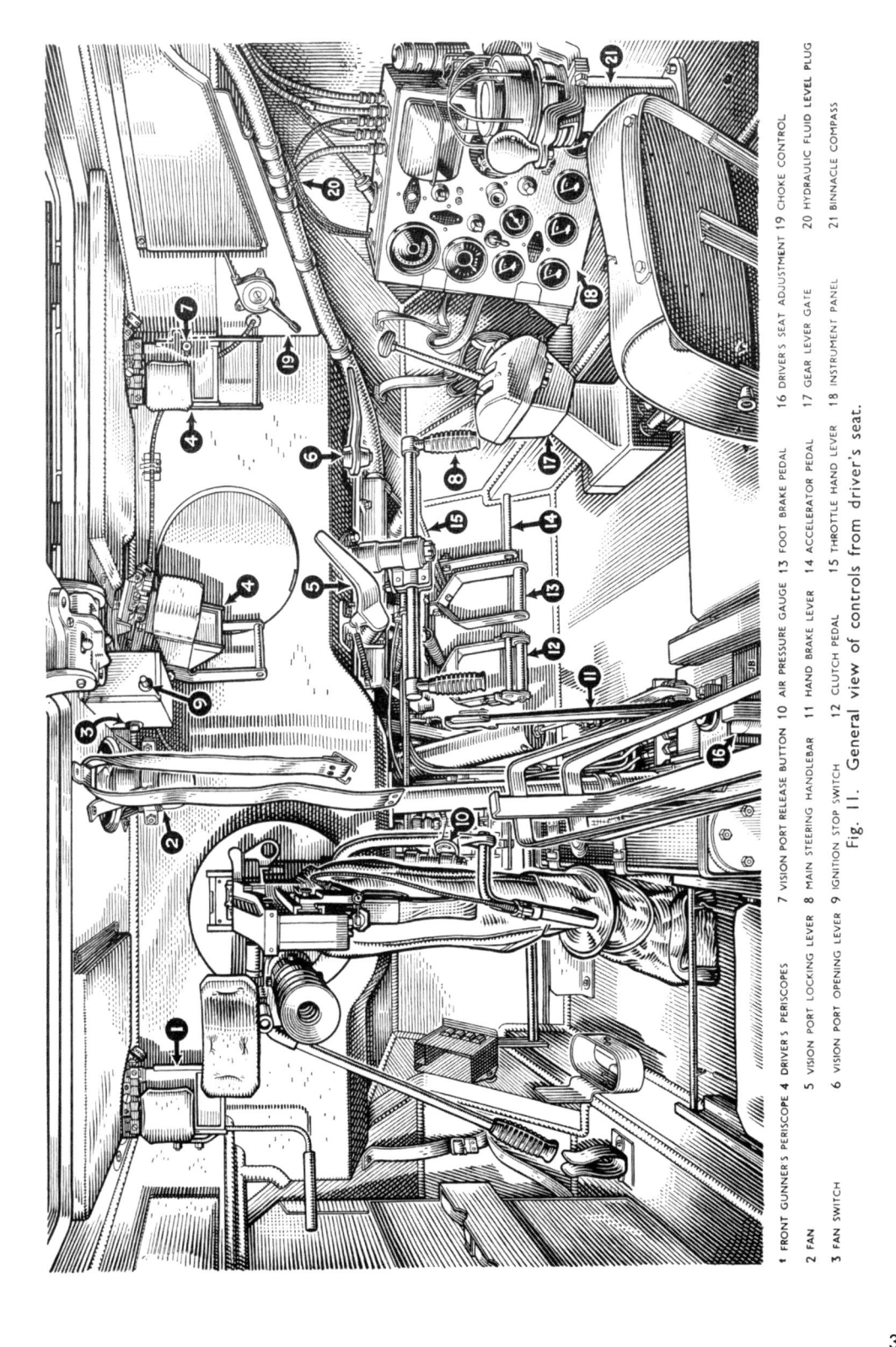

Fig. 11. General view of controls from driver's seat.

1 FRONT GUNNER'S PERISCOPE 2 FAN 3 FAN SWITCH 4 DRIVER'S PERISCOPES 5 VISION PORT LOCKING LEVER 6 VISION PORT OPENING LEVER 7 VISION PORT RELEASE BUTTON 8 MAIN STEERING HANDLEBAR 9 IGNITION STOP SWITCH 10 AIR PRESSURE GAUGE 11 HAND BRAKE LEVER 12 CLUTCH PEDAL 13 FOOT BRAKE PEDAL 14 ACCELERATOR PEDAL 15 THROTTLE HAND LEVER 16 DRIVER'S SEAT ADJUSTMENT 17 GEAR LEVER GATE 18 INSTRUMENT PANEL 19 CHOKE CONTROL 20 HYDRAULIC FLUID LEVEL PLUG 21 BINNACLE COMPASS

31

CHURCHILL TANK

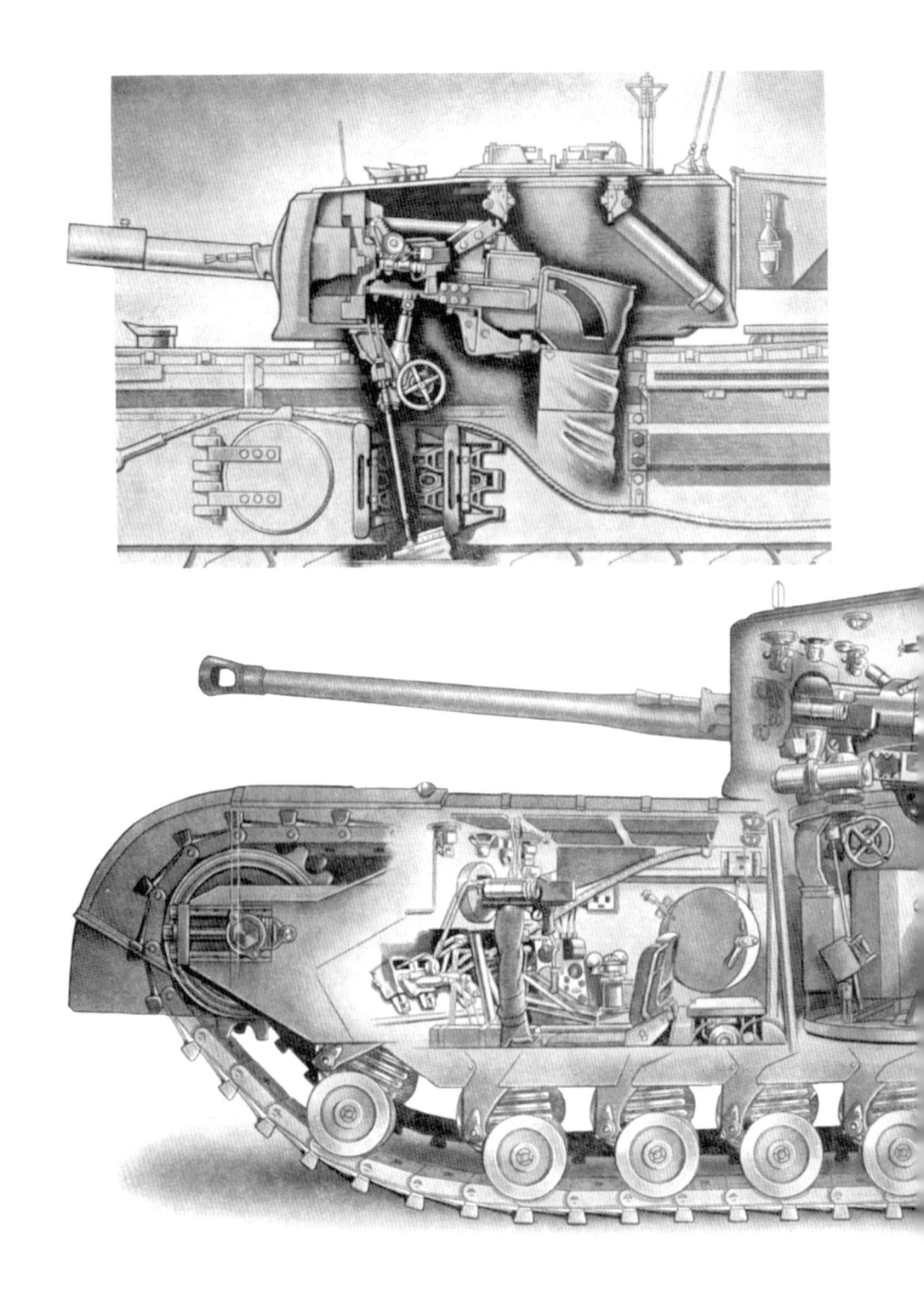

(To face page 10)   Fig. 1. " Ghosted " drawing of Churchill VII, showing general layout.

VEHICLE HISTORY AND SPECIFICATION

general layout. (Inset shows turret and armament differences on Churchill VIII).

DRIVER'S CONTROLS

by the normal hydraulic system. The right-hand pedal of the three is the accelerator pedal. This pedal operates the throttles of the four carburettors through a hydraulic control to the engine compartment where the hydraulic pressure is transferred to a system of inter-connected rods and levers. A right-angled lever is connected to the accelerator pedal for hand throttle operation.

To the left of the pedals a hand lever is fitted to apply the main brakes and thus hold the vehicle when it is stationary.

The steering is operated by a handlebar. The handlebar operates the steering brakes through a normal hydraulic system, but is equipped with air pressure servos to render the control easy. A separate system is fitted for each of the two steering brakes, so that, as the steering handlebar is swung, the corresponding brake is applied. As the right-hand end is pulled, the left-hand brake is applied, and the vehicle turns to the right. As the left-hand end of the bar is pulled, the right-hand brake is operated and a turn to the left is made. (See page 61 for explanation of steering through gearbox epicyclics.)

Fig. 12. Gear lever change-speed positions.

The change speed lever is placed to the right front of the driver. It has a conventional gate, but a stop is placed in the reverse speed slot, to prevent accidental engagement. Connecting rods from the gate operate the selectors in the gearbox.

A speedometer is provided on the instrument panel. It includes a mileage recorder, both for cumulative mileage and for " trip " mileages.

CONTROL OF LIGHTS

A combined switch on the instrument panel controls the headlamps, side lamps and tail lamp. The four positions are " Off," " Tail lamp," " Side and tail lamps " and " Headlamp, side and tail lamps." A separate switch operates the convoy lamp and another separate switch is provided for the ultra-violet headlamp.

The instrument panel is illuminated by three lamps, two of which are operated by a separate switch.

A two-pin plug socket is provided on the panel for an inspection lamp, and a fuse board is also located on the panel.

CONTROLS FOR AUXILIARY PETROL DRIVEN GENERATOR

The ignition switch for this unit is on the side of the battery recess, together with its warning light. The warning light remains alight all the time the ignition switch is on. Both the choke control and the starter switch are on the unit. A stop cock operated by a lever on the floor on the left-hand side of the fighting compartment controls the petrol supply.

CONTROL OF VISION DEVICES

The Driver's Vision Port

Direct vision for the driver is provided through a large round hole, which can be closed by a heavy B.P. steel door.

DRIVER'S CONTROLS

The door is locked in the closed position by a plunger operated by a lever, located on the front plate facing the driver.

The door can be opened after turning the locking handle from its locked position and turning a lever near the driver's right knee.

To close the port it is necessary first to push the spring-loaded catch release button (which is inside facing the driver, to the rop right-hand side of the vision port), thereby releasing the door catch. Then, by operating the lever placed adjacent to the driver's right knee, the door is returned to the closed position, and finally locked in place by turning the locking handle.

Periscopes

When the vision port is completely closed, the vehicle can be handled with the aid of the driver's periscopes. These are adjustable to give the best vision, and will be found to give clear definition.

EMERGENCY CONTROLS

Engine Control

An emergency ignition switch is provided on the left-hand side of the driving compartment fan switch box. This is provided so that the front gunner can switch off the engine should such an action be necessary. *In the normal course of events, this switch should not be operated.*

Petrol Release Control

If the engine compartment should be flooded by petrol, due to a serious leak, the escaped petrol can be quickly jettisoned through a large trap in the floor of the engine compartment. This trap can be opened rapidly by a pull-out handle located in the fighting compartment. A turn of the handle, by bringing a catch into use, will keep the trap open.

Emergency Disposal Hatch

A hatch is provided behind the front gunner's seat for disposal—through the floor —of unwanted material. This hatch is unfastened by a large-handled screw, and can be swung to one side, leaving a hole for jettisoning anything not required.

Towing Hook Remote Control

A remote control is provided so that the towing hook can be operated from inside the vehicle. A pull type control handle is fitted in the driving compartment and is located on the left-hand side member near the roof.

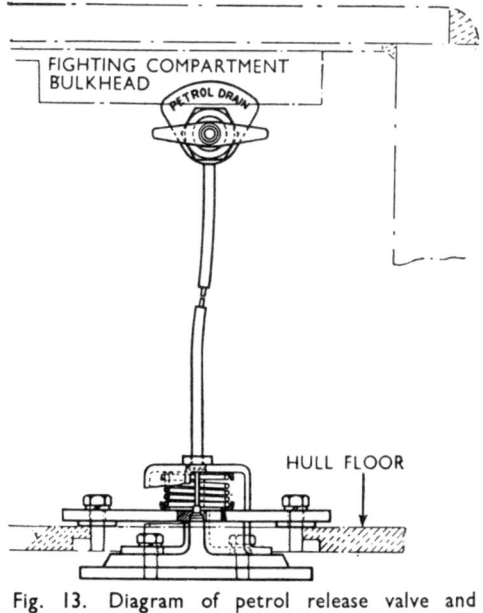

Fig. 13. Diagram of petrol release valve and control.

35

HOW TO DRIVE

The object of the following notes is not to teach a novice to drive a tank, but to give a trained driver some hints and tips about the particular vehicle covered by this Instruction Book. It is advisable to study also the information and instructions given in the " Driver's Controls " chapter on page 16.

IMPORTANT.—Always make sure, before starting the engine or driving the vehicle, that the various levels are checked as detailed in Maintenance Operation A.1 (page 124).

Starting the Engine

Two methods are adopted to provide a rich mixture for starting the engine. The first consists of a normal choke on each carburettor air inlet, connected to a lever in the driving compartment. The choke valves are provided with an automatic partial release when the engine starts, but although this provision weakens the mixture to some extent as soon as the engine fires, the choke control should be *fully* released as soon as possible.

The second method is provided by a complete " Ki-gass " system, consisting of a hand pump which draws petrol from the petrol distribution box and sprays it into the induction pipes through a series of jets. Three or four strokes of the pump will be found sufficient to ensure a ready start, and the use of the choke will ensure steady running immediately after starting. When the engine is warm, it should fire and run without the use of either the " Ki-gass " pump or the choke.

The procedure for starting the engine from cold is as follows :—

1. Make sure that the battery master switch is on. (The switch is located in the battery recess. A green warning light on the instrument panel glows all the time the master switch is on).
2. Set the main tank control to " R.H." or " L.H." (The control is on the left-hand side of the driving compartment).
3. Prime the carburettors by giving several strokes to the petrol priming control. (This control is located in the right-hand top corner of the fighting compartment rear bulkhead).
4. Prime the engine with three or four strokes of the " Ki-gass " pump. (This is near the petrol priming control. Unscrew the " Ki-gass " plunger before pumping, and remember to lock the " Ki-gass " plunger after using the pump by screwing the handle home firmly).
5. Switch on the ignition (the switch is on the instrument panel) and note whether both the ignition warning light and the oil pressure warning light glows.
6. Press the starter switch. (The switch is on the instrument panel). If the engine does not fire at the first attempt, wait a few seconds before pressing the starter switch again—*i.e.*, until all engine movement has ceased. *This is important*.
7. Do NOT exceed 1,000 r.p.m. until the engine is warm enough to run freely.

When the Engine Starts

Check the oil pressure by the gauge on the instrument panel. This should show not less than 35 lbs. per sq. in. at 1,000 r.p.m. when hot.

Check the engine revolution counter on the instrument panel.

Check the charging rate—it will probably be about 60 amps.—by the ammeter on the instrument panel.

HOW TO DRIVE

Check the air pressure—by the gauge to the left of the clutch pedal. The pressure should rise from 0 to 75 lbs. per sq. in. in approximately 30 seconds with the engine running at 1,000 r.p.m.

It will be observed that the ignition warning light remains alight, but this is a normal condition and should cause no alarm.

If the choke has been used, return the lever to the fully open position as soon as possible. Never drive with the choke partially closed.

With the engine cover doors open, arrange for one or two observers to inspect for possible oil or water leaks. This is important, as an oil leak may result in oil being blown into the steering brakes. If a leak is discovered, stop the engine immediately and do not restart until the leak is rectified.

Three Important Points to Watch
1. Always make absolutely certain that no one is standing on, in or under the vehicle, before starting the engine. This must be a strict and never-broken part of driving routine.
2. *Remember that light pressure on the steering bar will swing the vehicle in neutral, particularly if the hand-brake is off.*
3. Always close the engine cover doors and the bulkhead ventilator door before moving off. The air for cooling is drawn through the radiators by the flywheel fan and the air flow is seriously diminished when the engine cover doors are open. The bulkhead ventilator door should be opened only when firing the gun.

When Driving

Make quite sure that the hand-brake is fully off. Start in second gear. First gear should be used only for obstacle crossing, freak hills, towing, or where an extremely low speed or small turning circle is required. The first gear reduction is more than one hundred to one, giving a maximum speed of under two miles per hour. After using reverse gear make sure that the stop is returned to its slot. Third gear can be used for starting on a down grade on the road, or in similar favourable conditions.

Make a habit of referring frequently to the gauges, particularly to those recording oil pressure, air pressure and charging rate, and to the revolution counter.

Gear Changing

As the vehicle is fitted with a crash gearbox, a certain amount of skill is necessary to achieve quiet changes, but this will be acquired fairly easily after a little practice.

A quick change is essential, due to the high rolling resistance of the vehicle. If the operation is not carried out quickly, particularly on grass or heavy going, the vehicle may have time to come to rest while the change is being made. It is therefore necessary to learn to use the clutch stop correctly when changing up.

The gear ratio steps are such that it is unwise to change up until road conditions have eased sufficiently for the engine to pull in the higher gear. If you can, choose a moment when the ground conditions are favourable.

Keep the engine revolutions well up just before changing, and never steer while making the change, or immediately after making it. Always wait until the engine revolutions have risen again.

A very rapid change of the racing type can be made once the driver has mastered the amount of travel and pressure necessary on the clutch pedal to ensure the right amount of clutch stop. The actions of moving the lever out of gear and depressing the

HOW TO DRIVE

clutch pedal should be synchronised as nearly as possible. If the clutch is depressed fully *before* the gear is disengaged, the gear will be " nipped."

The top gear performance is exceptionally good for this type of vehicle, but top gear should not be used for heavy going or for turns on grass. With the double declutching method it is possible to effect a very rapid and silent change down, and the intermediate gears give more power for turning on heavy ground.

Always make sure when changing that the gear goes right home, as running on a partially engaged gear will cause excessive wear and a tendency to jump out.

Steering

It is essential to understand how the steering works and to know how to use it to the best advantage. The important points to remember in steering a Churchill tank are as follows :—

1. The steering brakes must be stopped—not merely slowed—at each and every turn. The steering bar should, therefore, be moved firmly, but it should not be " snatched." A firm steady movement is all that is necessary. Only a moderate amount of steering effort is required for all normal conditions, but additional effort is called for when (*a*) turning in neutral on heavy ground ; (*b*) operating without air assistance ; (*c*) the steering brake linings are oily.

2. Always return the steering bar to the dead straight position after steering.

3. A turn in any gear except reverse provides what might be called a " geared " turn. That is to say, there is a definite ratio between the speeds of the inner and outer tracks when steering. The difference between the speed of the outer track and the speed of the inner track varies with the gear ratio, the disparity being greatest in bottom gear and least in top. There is thus a small turning circle in the low gears and a large turning circle in top gear.

4. One of the most useful features of the steering mechanism is its ability to turn the vehicle in neutral. When this manœuvre is carried out the tracks rotate in opposite directions, so that on level ground the vehicle can be turned in little more than its own length.

   To carry out a neutral turn, the hand-brake should be off, the engine should be accelerated slightly and the steering bar should be moved slowly but firmly in the required direction. Do not speed up the engine unduly in a

Fig. 14. Pictorial guide to steering in forward gears and reverse.

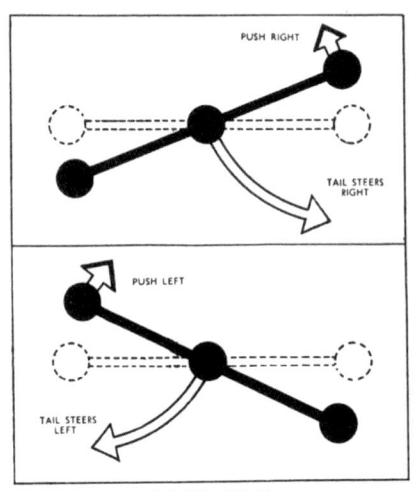

HOW TO DRIVE

congested space as the vehicle swings very rapidly, particularly on a hard surface.
5. Do not attempt a neutral turn on heavy ground, or in any place where damage to turf is undesirable.
6. When making a normal turn in open country, or on a wide road, try to complete the manœuvre with one or two applications of the steering brake rather than a number of movements. Each time the steering brake is applied, power is consumed in heating the drums and wearing the brake linings.
7. Always endeavour to steer the vehicle when the engine revolutions are high. Considerably more power is required to drive the vehicle on a curve, and if an attempt is made to steer when the engine revolutions are low, a gear change will be necessary. If you have to manœuvre on uneven ground, endeavour to steer when on a hump rather than when in a hollow.
8. Whenever possible, avoid steering while negotiating an obstacle such as a shell-hole or a river bed. In general, choose hard rather than soft patches for changes in direction.
9. When crossing a shell-hole proceed slowly and steadily in bottom gear, and make sure that the gear is fully engaged. Cross the hole squarely, because if it is taken at an acute angle the resultant side thrust may push off one of the tracks.
10. Obstacles such as vertical walls and sleepers should be approached squarely and slowly. If they are taken steadily the vehicle will ride over the point of balance smoothly and without jar.

Remember that, when travelling forward, the steering bar operates in the same way as the handlebars of a bicycle, but when travelling backwards, the process is reversed. A simple way of remembering this difference is to apply the following rules.

Travelling Forward

Pull the right-hand end of the handlebar to turn to the right. *Pull* the left-hand end of the handlebar when you want to turn to the left.

Travelling in Reverse

Push the right-hand end of the handlebar if you want the tail of the tank to swing to the right. *Push* the left-hand end of the handlebar if you want the tail to swing to the left.

Manoeuvring in Confined Spaces

If you have to manœuvre the vehicle in a confined space it is advisable to enlist the assistance of observers. The vehicle takes up a lot of road space, and it is possible, when the tail is swung over, for damage to be done without the driver's knowledge. For the same reason it is imperative when passing through a narrow gateway to make sure that the whole of the vehicle is through before turning.

Track Tension

When the tracks are new the track stretch will be comparatively rapid. Do not neglect adjustment, because this slackness may cause the tracks to jump the sprockets, and thus seriously affect the steering. On the other hand, take care not to *over*-tension the tracks as this will impose unnecessary loads and increase the rolling resistance. The correct tension is given on page 133.

Do not drive fast on frozen, bumpy ground unless circumstances make it essential to do so. Maximum speeds may be indulged in on good hard roads or on grass.

HOW TO DRIVE

Some Points to Remember

Adjust the steering and main brakes before the travel of the controls becomes excessive.

Make a habit of checking the clutch free travel at the end of each day's run. It should be adjusted if it is down to an inch or less. Running with less than an inch of free travel may cause clutch burn-out or at least a hold-up during a run. And the effects will almost certainly be felt when negotiating stiff obstacles.

Get into the habit also of carrying out a brief inspection after each run. Examine the petrol, oil and water connections. Try the temperature of brake drums, final drive, suspension and bogies with the hand. Inspect the tracks and suspension for looseness and damage.

VEHICLE HISTORY AND SPECIFICATION

ENGINE AND CLUTCH

GENERAL DATA

Number of Cylinders	12
Bore	5 in.
Stroke	5½ in.
Compression Ratio	5.5 to 1
Capacity	1,296 cu. in.
R.A.C. Rating	120 h.p.
Nominal B.H.P.	350 at 2,200 r.p.m.
Nominal Torque	960 lb. ft. at 800-1,600 r.p.m.
Arrangement of Cylinders—	
Front of Engine	2 4 6 8 10 12 R.H. Bank
	1 3 5 7 9 11 L.H. Bank
Firing Order	1 6 9 12 5 4 11 8 3 2 7 10
Exhaust Valves	Sodium-cooled with Stellite inserted valve seats
Nominal Governed Speed	2,200 r.p.m.
Petrol Consumption	.57 lbs. per B.H.P./hr.
Carburettors	4—46 mm. Solex Model 46 F.N.H.E.
Air Cleaners	2—AC 2-stage, centrifugal and oil-bath type
Tachometer	Smith electrical type
Lubrication	Dry sump type with de-aerating and oil cooling systems
Oil Coolers	Finned tube type combined with rear radiator on each side

CLUTCH

Diameter of Plate	18 in.
Number of Springs	24
Throw-out Bearing	Ball bearing
Spigot Bearings	2 Ball bearings

DESCRIPTION

The power unit is a 12-cylinder, four-stroke, water-cooled petrol engine of the horizontally opposed type. It develops a nominal 350 B.H.P. at 2,200 r.p.m., and maintains its rated torque from 800 to 1,600 r.p.m.

Apart from the virtue of compactness, the " flat twelve " layout results in smooth running. The smoothness is assisted by the use of a counter-balanced seven-bearing crankshaft of rigid design, and light aluminium alloy pistons.

The combustion chambers are of the " L Head " type and are specially shaped for efficient combustion control in relation to two sparking plugs. The cylinder heads are designed to control the rate of pressure rise, thus ensuring smooth running and freedom from detonation.

ENGINE AND CLUTCH

The major components are all arranged for access from above with the engine installed in the hull. Sodium-filled exhaust valves, separately inserted valve seats in the cylinder block, short cylinder liners and hardened crankpins and journals are among the special features which make for durability.

The cooling water is circulated by two pumps and is directed by ducts in the cylinder jackets to the hottest parts of the engine. Thermostats ensure a quick warm-up to an efficient working temperature. A dry sump lubrication system provides an efficient oil supply at the extreme angles at which the vehicle will have to operate, and these special conditions of operation are also provided for in the design of the carburettors and fuel system.

Installation

The engine is mounted on three malleable cast iron brackets, located one at the front and two at the rear, which in turn rest on two channel section girders welded to the engine compartment floor. The mounting bolts, one per bracket, are hexagon-headed one-inch diameter bolts of alloy steel.

In plan, the engine centre line is at right angles to the final drive. Viewed in side elevation, the crankshaft and transmission centre line is arranged at an angle of

Fig. 16. View of front of engine out of hull.

ENGINE AND CLUTCH

Fig. 17. View of left-hand side of engine out of hull.

3° 56' to the horizontal, the slope being downwards to the front of the engine. With the transmission line tilted in this way, the dynamo and other auxiliary units located on top of the engine are brought well within the predetermined roof level. Flanking each side of the engine are the radiators and petrol tanks. Air is drawn through louvres in the sides of the vehicle by a fan carried on the clutch, passes through the radiators, the engine compartment and fan into the gearbox, and is finally expelled through apertures at the rear of the hull.

The rear bulkhead carries a cowling for the cooling fan, and this cowling is made in halves to permit assembly. The carburettors, distributors, governor, tachometer generator and controls are all located on the top of the engine, and in this position are readily accessible from above.

Cylinders and Crankcase

The cylinders are arranged in two blocks, each of which is cast in one piece with a half-crankcase. The right-hand half-case carries the crankshaft in seven main bearings. To allow one connecting rod from each block to operate on one crankpin the L.H. block has the cylinders slightly forward of the R.H. block. The joint faces of the halves of the crankcase are arranged at the centre line of the crankshaft.

The two cylinder blocks are bolted together by bolts and studs of high tensile steel. To ensure the maximum of structural rigidity, these bolts are arranged in three longitudinal rows.

ENGINE AND CLUTCH

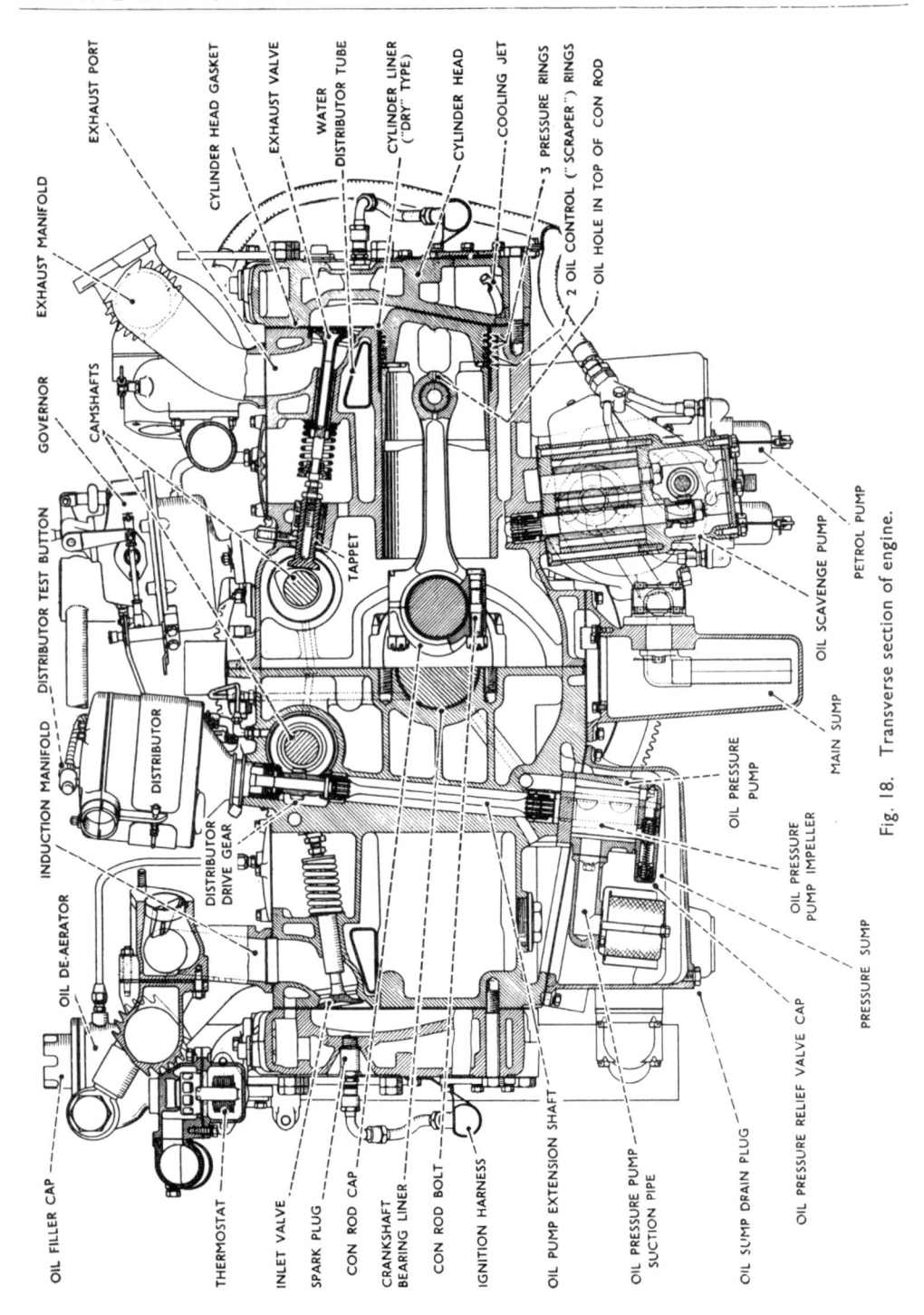

Fig. 18. Transverse section of engine.

ENGINE AND CLUTCH

The top end of each cylinder bore is fitted with a " dry " type liner, 3 in. long. The liners are centrifugally cast from high grade close-grained cast iron and honed to finished size after assembly.

Cylinder Heads

There are four detachable cylinder heads, each serving three cylinders. The cylinder head material is high tensile molybdenum cast iron.

The internal shape of the cylinder head has been designed to keep the pressure rise within limits to ensure smoothness of running and freedom from detonation. The positions of the two sparking plugs fitted in each combustion chamber have been decided with the same object in view. The water flow through the cylinder head is directed to the best advantage by nozzles fitted in the gasket plate of the head. These nozzles receive their water supply through feed holes in the cylinder block.

Crankshaft and Bearings

The crankshaft is of the seven-bearing six-throw type and is forged, with integral counter-weights, from high tensile steel. The crankpins and journals are surface-hardened by the " Tocco " electric process.

At its rear end, the crankshaft is formed with a large diameter flywheel flange and is bored out to house the two ball bearings for the clutch shaft driving dog. In addition to an oil thrower ring to prevent oil leakage from the rear of the crankshaft, a special piston ring type of oil seal is fitted.

Oil leakage past the front end of the crankshaft is prevented by means of a felt oil seal which is housed in a groove machined in the timing chain cover.

Keyed to the front end of the crankshaft are the timing chain sprocket and the triple-grooved belt driving pulley.

The main bearing caps are of cast iron, attached by hexagon-headed bolts of nickel chrome steel and positively located by dowels.

Each main bearing consists of two half-shells of steel, lined with white metal. The upper and lower halves are each formed with a locating tab, and these tabs engage with slots machined in the crankcase and the main bearing caps. Fitted on each side of the centre main bearing is a steel thrust washer faced with white metal. These thrust washers, each of which is made in two pieces to permit assembly, fit in shallow recesses machined in the bearing housing. Rotation of the thrust washers is prevented by projecting tabs which fit into slots machined in the end faces of the bearing cap.

Flywheel

The cast-iron alloy flywheel is spigoted on to the crankshaft rear flange, to which it is secured by means of six high tensile steel bolts. Fitted around each of these bolts is a short tubular dowel which is recessed half into the crankshaft flange and half into the flange face of the flywheel. One bolt is offset $\frac{1}{8}$ in. from the regular spacing to ensure that the flywheel can only be assembled with its timing mark in the correct angular position relative to the crank throws.

The rear face of the flywheel forms one friction face for the single plate clutch.

The starter ring gear is a separate unit. It is of alloy steel, spigoted to the flywheel and secured by eight bolts.

Connecting Rods

Two connecting rods, one from each bank of cylinders, operate on each crankpin. They are of " H " section, machined from stampings of nickel chrome steel.

ENGINE AND CLUTCH

Each rod is drilled throughout its length for pressure oil feed to the small end bearings, and the continuation of this hole through the top of the rod also provides a cooling jet of oil to the underside of the piston crown.

The cap is secured to the rod by two bolts, slotted nuts and cotter pins. Each bolt-head is dowelled to the rod to prevent rotation.

Pressed into the small end are two bronze bushes, the gap between these bushes forming an oil groove whereby oil is fed to the cooling jet oil hole in the top of the rod.

The big end bearings are removable steel shells, faced with copper-lead alloy. A locating tab on each half shell prevents endwise and rotational movement.

Pistons, Piston Rings and Gudgeon Pins

The pistons are of aluminium alloy, and are of special design.

Each piston is fitted with three pressure rings and two scraper rings, all located

Fig. 19. View of rear of engine showing two of the four carburettors.

ENGINE AND CLUTCH

above the gudgeon pin. The piston skirts are tin-plated to prevent " scuffing " during the running-in period.

As the piston crowns are specially shaped for combustion control in combination with a skirt slotted on the non-thrust side only, they are not interchangeable. It is not possible therefore to fit a left-hand piston to the right-hand bank of cylinders, or *vice versa*.

The gudgeon pins are of the fully-floating type. They are hollow, made from special chrome steel, case-hardened on the outer diameter only, and are located in the pistons by circlips.

Camshafts

Two camshafts, made of case-hardened nickel steel, are employed, each carried in four white-metal-lined steel shell bearings which are pressed into the crankcase and line-reamed in position, and each camshaft operates the twelve valves in its respective cylinder block. Formed integrally with the camshaft are spiral gears for driving the distributors (one from each shaft), the governor (spiral gear on L.H. shaft only) and the tachometer generator. End thrust of each camshaft is taken by a bronze thrust plate which is fitted between the hub of the chain sprocket and the front face of the camshaft journal and is bolted to the crankcase.

Camshaft Drive

Two Duplex roller chains, operating as a single triangular drive, drive the two camshafts from a four-row sprocket keyed to the front end of the crankshaft.

Operating on the " slack " side of the chain, viz., on the lower run of the chain to the R.H. side of the crankshaft, is an adjustable chain tensioner sprocket. This is fitted with a white-metal-lined steel shell bearing, and is mounted on a flanged spindle attached to the front wall of the crankcase by means of two setscrews.

The timing case cover is of cast iron.

Valves

The valves (two per cylinder) are disposed side by side, above the cylinders, at an angle of approximately $7\frac{1}{2}°$ to the horizontal. Each valve is controlled by a single spring, retained by cup and split collar, and operates in a replaceable guide which forms part of the cylinder block and crankcase assembly. Cast iron guides are fitted for the inlet valves, and bronze valve guides for the exhaust valves. Seat inserts of " Brimochrome " or Stellited steel are provided for the exhaust valves, the heads and stems of which are sodium-filled.

Adjustable mechanical tappets are used and the adjustment is by adjusting screw and lock-nut. The tappet bodies are provided with flats so that each pair can be held by a special twin spanner to prevent rotation while adjustment is made. The tappet clearance for the inlet valves is .012" and for the exhaust valves—.020" with the engine cold.

Adjustment is not required between major engine overhauls.

The crankcase tappet chambers are fitted with detachable covers of cast iron, two such covers being provided for each cylinder block.

Lubrication System

A dry sump system is used, with full pressure lubrication to the main bearings, camshaft bearings, connecting rod big ends, gudgeon pins and tappets. The cylinder walls are lubricated by oil thrown from the big ends. Subsidiary oil feeds are provided

CHURCHILL TANK

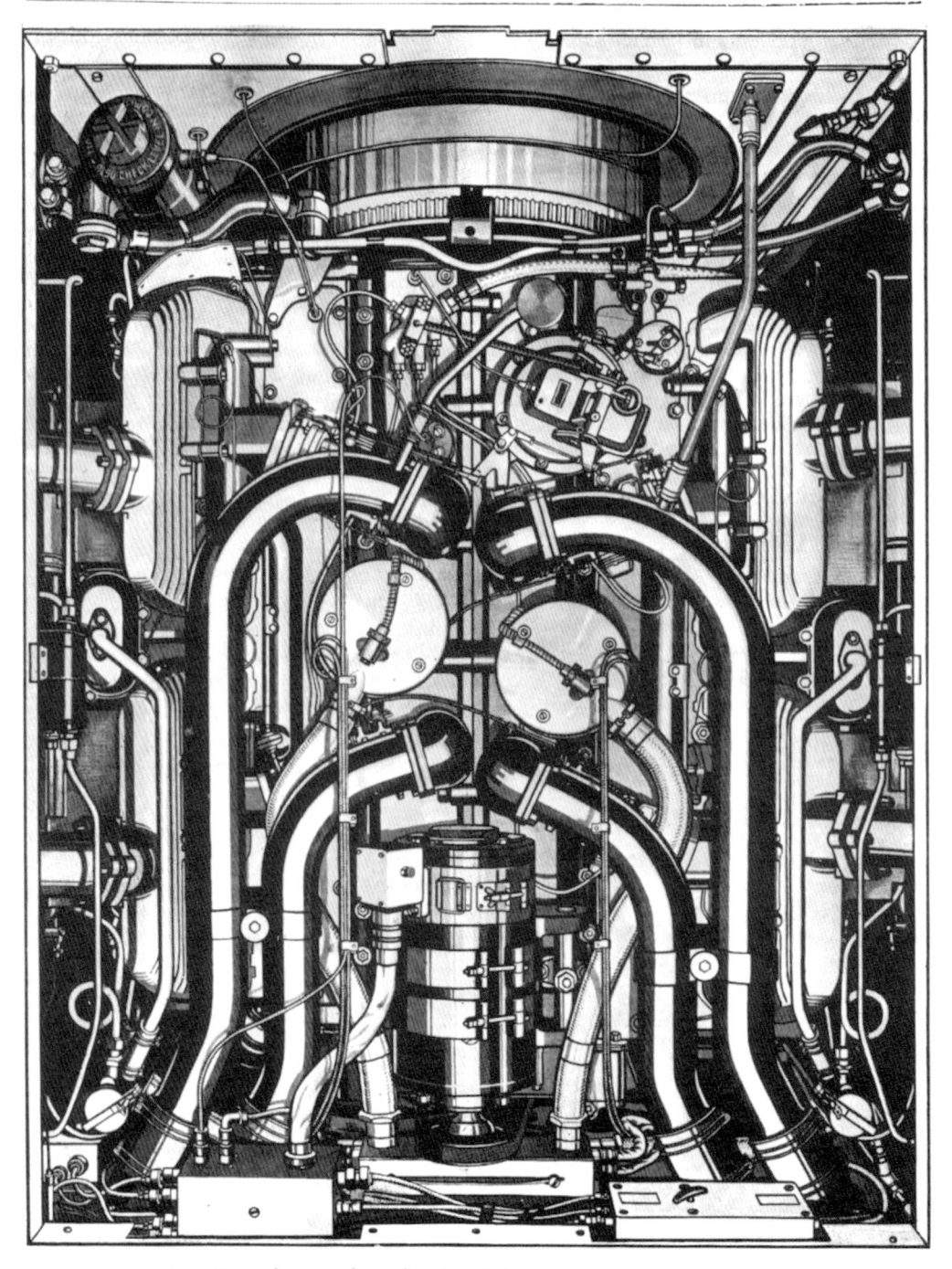

ENGINE AND CLUTCH

Fig. 20. View of engine (from above) with deck removed. (See Fig. 21 for key.)

ENGINE AND CLUTCH

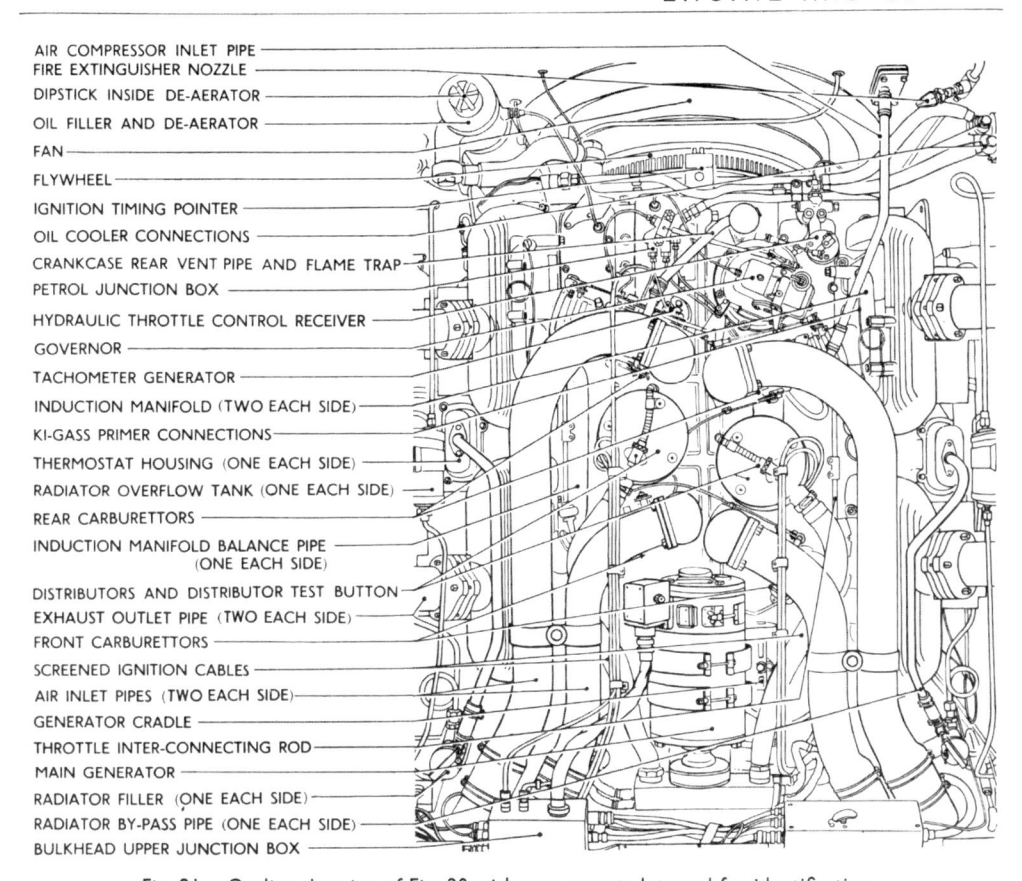

AIR COMPRESSOR INLET PIPE
FIRE EXTINGUISHER NOZZLE
DIPSTICK INSIDE DE-AERATOR
OIL FILLER AND DE-AERATOR
FAN
FLYWHEEL
IGNITION TIMING POINTER
OIL COOLER CONNECTIONS
CRANKCASE REAR VENT PIPE AND FLAME TRAP
PETROL JUNCTION BOX
HYDRAULIC THROTTLE CONTROL RECEIVER
GOVERNOR
TACHOMETER GENERATOR
INDUCTION MANIFOLD (TWO EACH SIDE)
KI-GASS PRIMER CONNECTIONS
THERMOSTAT HOUSING (ONE EACH SIDE)
RADIATOR OVERFLOW TANK (ONE EACH SIDE)
REAR CARBURETTORS
INDUCTION MANIFOLD BALANCE PIPE
(ONE EACH SIDE)
DISTRIBUTORS AND DISTRIBUTOR TEST BUTTON
EXHAUST OUTLET PIPE (TWO EACH SIDE)
FRONT CARBURETTORS
SCREENED IGNITION CABLES
AIR INLET PIPES (TWO EACH SIDE)
GENERATOR CRADLE
THROTTLE INTER-CONNECTING ROD
MAIN GENERATOR
RADIATOR FILLER (ONE EACH SIDE)
RADIATOR BY-PASS PIPE (ONE EACH SIDE)
BULKHEAD UPPER JUNCTION BOX

Fig. 21. Outline drawing of Fig. 20 with components lettered for identification.

for the distributor driving gears, governor bearings and timing chain. A spray is also provided from the top of the connecting rods to cool the underside of the piston crown.

Extending the whole length of the R.H. crankcase is a $\frac{5}{8}$ in. diameter drilled hole which forms the main oil duct. From this duct, oil is delivered to the main bearings *via* holes drilled diagonally through the crankcase end walls and intermediate partitions. The camshaft bearings are fed with oil delivered under pressure through drilled holes which connect up with the oil grooves in the main bearings. In each half of the crankcase there is also a $\frac{5}{8}$ in. diameter gallery, whereby oil is distributed under reduced pressure to the tappets.

Lubrication of the timing chain is by means of oil jets from each camshaft front bearing, through slots in the thrust plate. From these slots, oil is projected to the inner side of the chain sprocket, and thence by centrifugal action to the timing chain by a series of holes drilled through the sprocket rim. The bearing for the chain tensioner sprocket is lubricated independently, the hollow spindle being fed direct from one of the camshaft bearings.

Two gear-type pumps are used, one of which is a pressure pump and the other a scavenge pump. The pressure pump is driven, in tandem with one of the ignition distributors, by spiral gears from the R.H. camshaft. The scavenge pump is driven

ENGINE AND CLUTCH

in tandem with the second ignition distributor by spiral gears from the L.H. camshaft. Both pressure and scavenge pumps are bolted directly to the underside of the crankcase. A pressure relief valve is incorporated in the pressure pump. This valve is of the spring-loaded plunger type and it operates at a pressure of approximately 50 lbs. per sq. in. A gauze strainer is fitted to the suction pipe of the pressure pump. To strain the oil before it reaches the scavenge pump, a gauze strainer is fitted along the full length of the top face of the scavenge sump. If this gauze strainer becomes choked with sludge, oil can still pass to the scavenge pump through a hole in the strainer. This hole is protected by a weir so that it will only come into use when the strainer is choked.

Two oil sumps are fitted; one is beneath the R.H. side of the crankcase, and the other is centrally located below the crankshaft to receive the oil draining from the engine. The R.H. sump consists of a cast iron reservoir, which holds approximately 7 gallons of oil and in which the pressure pump is submerged. It is not open to the interior of the engine except by a $\frac{1}{2}$ in. dia. vent hole in the oil pump drive tunnel. The centre sump is an iron casting with a deep well forward of the centre of the engine in which the scavenge pump suction pipe is located. The scavenge pump is mounted under the crankcase alongside the centre sump. This ensures effective scavenging when the engine is inclined at any angle up to 30°.

Oil Circulation

Submerged in the right-hand sump, the pressure pump delivers oil to the main duct in the crankcase from which it is distributed round the engine. After circulating through the engine, the oil drains into the central sump, from which it is continuously removed by the scavenge pump.

The scavenge pump delivers the oil to coolers, which are incorporated in the rear of each radiator block. As air is mixed with the oil, the mixture is then delivered to a de-aerator. After the air is extracted by this device, the oil returns to the right-hand sump by gravity.

The de-aerator is a cylindrical container, housing a detachable strainer made from brass perforated sheet. A breather pipe connects the de-aerator to the right-hand rear tappet cover and thence to the crankcase and right-hand rear carburettor air intake. A dipstick incorporated in the centre of the de-aerator for the purpose of checking the oil level is accessible on removing the oil filler cap. The oil filler cap is on top of the de-aerator. NOTE.—The de-aerator cap can be removed with tool TP.5650 (special spanner for final drive coupling bolts).

The oil is filtered by two AC filters of the detachable element type. These are mounted on the bulkhead behind the engine, and are fed (on the by-pass principle) from the pipe to the main crankcase oil duct. The return pipes from the filters are led to the rear ends of the two oil ducts which supply the tappets.

In addition to the pressure relief valve in the pressure pump, a relief valve is provided at the point where the main oil pipe enters each oil cooler. These valves are of the spring-loaded plunger type and their purpose is to allow the oil partially to by-pass the coolers when cold, or if any restriction in the coolers becomes excessive. As the oil temperature rises, the pressure difference drops, the relief valve closes and the whole of the oil delivered by the pump then passes through the coolers.

The distributor drive gears are fed by pipes connected to holes from two of the crankshaft bearings, and the governor is lubricated by an intermittent feed from the rear camshaft bearing. The tachometer generator bearings are splash lubricated.

A drain plug is located on the R.H. side of the R.H. sump. The drain plug for the central sump is located at the front of the well.

VEHICLE HISTORY AND SPECIFICATION

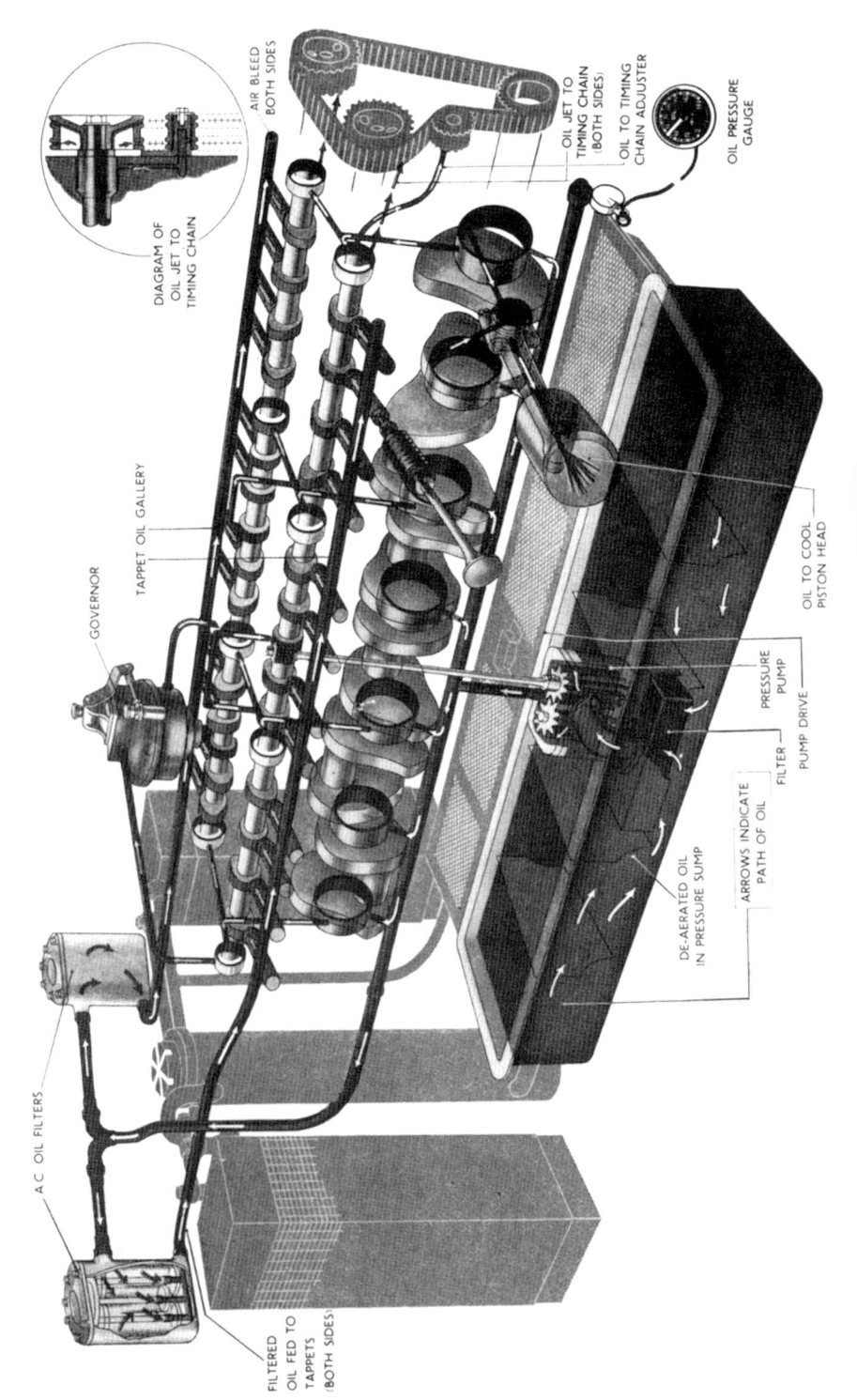

Fig. 22. Perspective diagram of engine lubrication—PRESSURE system.

ENGINE AND CLUTCH

Carburettors and Induction Manifolds

Four Solex horizontal type carburettors are fitted, each mounted on a separate induction manifold which serves three cylinders. Although the manifolding is thus divided into four separate units, the front and rear manifolds on each side are connected by large balance pipes. The induction manifolds and balance pipes are of cast iron, and the whole induction system, including the carburettor and controls, is readily accessible.

The 46 F.N.H.E. type Solex is a non-spillable, dust-proof carburettor for heavy duty engines, and is provided with a Solex membrane pump and economy device.

Composition of Carburettor

The carburettor is rendered non-spillable by mounting the main jet assembly in the centre of a single free float in a circular float chamber, which is below the choke tube barrel. (See Fig. 25.)

The constant level is maintained by a special forked toggle arm which operates near its hinged end upon a normal inverted needle valve. (See Fig. 26.)

The dust-proofing arrangement is shown in Fig. 25. All the air entering the carburettor by the main intake at the extreme left of the diagram has, of course, passed already through a filter, and the main and auxiliary jet air bleeds (Y) and (Z) therefore, which get their supply *via* the channel at (X), are similarly provided with dustless air.

The main and idling fuel supply can also be seen in Fig 25.

The petrol is metered and passed to the spraying assembly first *via* the main jet (C), mounted in its carrier (D). From there it rises into the slow running guide (E), which acts as a locating member for the tube (F) and also as a support for the float guide (G) which is a press fit thereon.

Into the top of (E) dips the lower end of the thin tube (F), a suitable clearance being provided for the fuel to by-pass this junction into the upper member (G). Here the petrol for slow running is drawn up into (F) through the calibration in the upper end.

At the top, it turns to the right into a channel, where it is emulsified by the air bleed (Z), and thence passes downwards, round a circular duct, and arrives at the volume screw (W) which controls the amount of the idling mixture. Turning the volume screw in a clockwise direction decreases the amount of mixture. Anti-clockwise rotation, therefore, increases the amount of mixture.

The small hole shown immediately on the atmospheric side of the closed throttle edge is called " the by-pass." It acts as an air bleed with an almost closed throttle, thus preventing an over-rich idling mixture, and permits a larger volume of mixture as the throttle opens

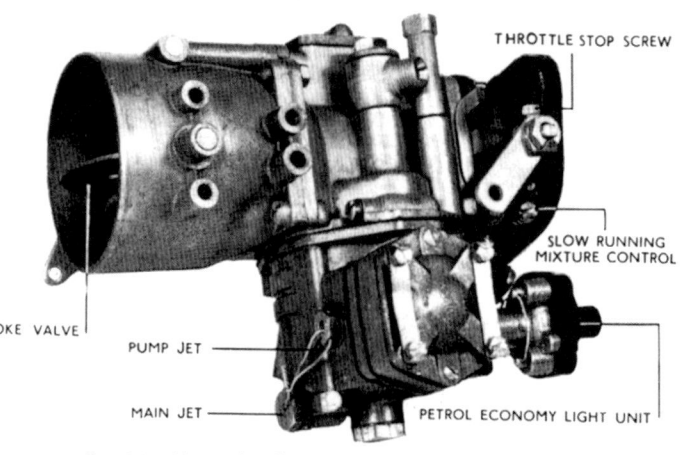

Fig. 24. View of carburettor removed from engine.

ENGINE AND CLUTCH

and passes across the by-pass. This bridges the lean mixture gap which would otherwise occur on the pilot/main jet transfer.

Turning to the main supply, the emulsion tube (H) makes an inner annulus with the slow running tube (F), and an outer annulus with the float guide (G), and is supported from the member (Y), above. The holes in (Y) supply a metered quantity of air down the inner annulus, at the bottom of which it meets the rising fuel.

This air passing outwards through the six emulsion holes meets and breaks up the rising fuel in the outer annulus, and the resulting mixture enters the choke tube through the float guide (G). It will be noticed that the float guide has a step-down portion at the top, with the step-down towards the engine. Here the metered fuel is caught up and atomised in the main air stream.

Carburettor Starting Arrangement

A choke is fitted for easy starting from cold. To prevent over-choking, however, the choke valve is mounted out of centre of the air intake. When the shutter (J) is rotated in an anti-clockwise direction by the lever (K) to the closed position, there is a considerably greater area above than below the spindle, and any excess vacuum created on starting will tend to force the choke valve open.

Advantage is taken of this by providing a spring-controlled arc of movement, so that above a certain pull the shutter will re-open by this amount regardless of the closing effort of the hand controlled lever (K), and thus prevent the engine from being over-choked.

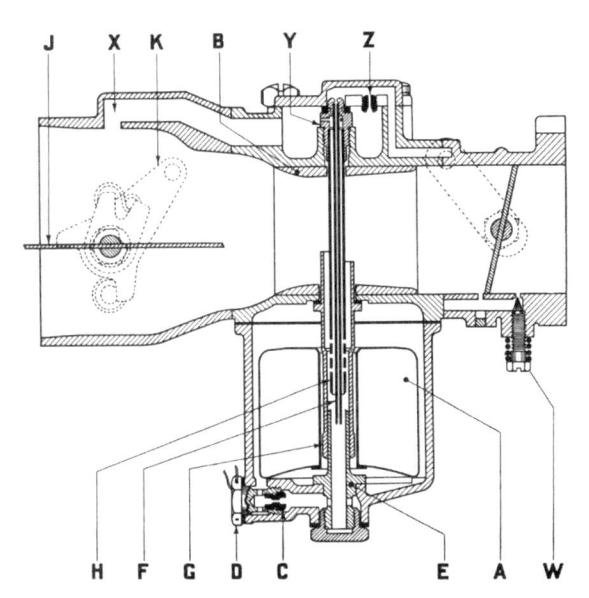

Fig. 25. Longitudinal section of carburettor.

(A) Float. (B) Choke tube. (C) Main jet. (D) Main jet carrier. (E) Slow running guide. (F) Slow running tube. (G) Float guide. (H) Emulsion tube. (J) Choke valve. (K) Choke valve lever. (W) Slow running mixture control. (X) Main air bleed. (Y) Main air bleed. (Z) Auxiliary jet air bleed.

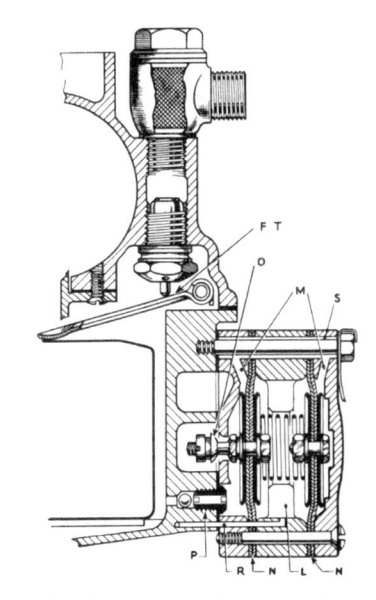

Fig. 26. Section of carburettor showing economising device.

(L) Vacuum section of pump chamber. (M) Petrol section of pump chamber. (N) Diaphragms. (O) Delivery valve. (P) Inlet valve. (R) Air passage. (S) Annular transfer passage. (FT) Float lever.

ENGINE AND CLUTCH

Carburettor Pump and Economising Device

Reference to Figs. 26 and 27 will show the construction and operation of these features. The pump chamber, it will be seen from Fig. 26, is divided into three compartments by the two diaphragms (N), these being the vacuum compartment of the pump (L), and the two petrol compartments (M). To the inner diaphragm is attached the economy valve (O).

When the throttle is shut, a strong suction is applied in the compartment (L), *via* a duct (R), which communicates with the throttle barrel. This draws the diaphragms (N) inwards and towards each other, shuts the valve (O) and draws petrol into the compartments (M), through the non-return valve (P).

When the throttle is suddenly opened, the vacuum in (L) is instantly relieved, the spring forces the diaphragms (N) outwards and away from each other, and the petrol in the compartments (M) is ejected, *via* the pump jet into the base of the main spraying assembly, where it gives a temporary enrichment of the mixture strength, thus assisting acceleration.

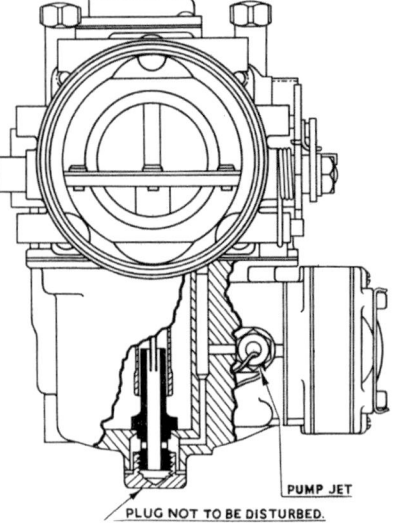

Fig. 27. Part-sectioned diagram of carburettor showing position of pump jet.

The economising action takes place as follows. When the throttle is wide open, or nearly so, the suction in (L) is low, the diaphragms (N) are kept in the outward position by the spring, and the valve (O) is open. In this condition, which indicates that power rather than economy is required, a supply of fuel is available *via* the non-return valve (P), the compartments (M), and the pump jet, to the base of the main spraying assembly (Fig. 27). Thus, the main and pump jets together supply the petrol for full throttle operation.

Under conditions where the throttle is partially closed, suction is conveyed to the compartment (L), the diaphragms (N) are drawn inwards, and the valve (O) is therefore closed. The supply of petrol to the pump jet is then cut off, and consequently the mixture strength at part throttle loads, where economy rather than maximum power is called for, is reduced.

The setting for the carburettor is as follows :—

Choke Tube	37 m/m.	Pilot Jet	75
Main Jet	165	Pilot Jet Air Bleed	200
Speed Jet	105	Pump Economy Device	Double Diaphragms
Correction Holes	3 × 115		
Pump Spring	2 Kilo	Pump Diaphragm Travel	1.7 m/m.
		Needle Valve	2.5 m/m.

Air Filtration

Two two-stage heavy duty air cleaners are fitted. These are located one in each rear corner of the fighting compartment and are connected to the four carburettors by four long intake pipes which pass over the top of the engine.

Air Cleaners

For engine air intake filtration, an AC two-stage air cleaner is used which has been designed to clean the air thoroughly under extremely dusty operating conditions, the

ENGINE AND CLUTCH

air stream being made to pass first through a centrifugal cleaning chamber and then through a large oil bath cleaner.

The path of the air is shown by the arrows on the illustration, Fig. 28. The air is drawn in through the entry louvres around the outer casing, passing through the vanes into the cleaning chamber. The louvres and vanes are formed to give a centrifugal action so throwing out the heavier dust particles which drop down and collect in the dust container. This is of the canvas bag type and is easily removed for emptying.

The air stream then passes through a second cleaning chamber, this being of the normal oil bath type. The air, impinging on the oil, splashes oil on to the wire mesh elements, the two bottom elements becoming thoroughly oil washed under normal operating conditions. In passing through these elements the remaining very fine particles of dust are trapped on the oily surface by impingement, and carried back with the oil into the oil pan, where they settle to the bottom. The dust-free air finally passes through a third wire mesh element to remove any remaining traces of oil before entering the carburettor inlet pipes. As the amount of silt in the oil pan increases so the volume of oil displaced from the oil pan into the compensating chamber increases. By means of this compensating chamber, the oil in the cleaner is maintained at a constant level. (See Fig. 28.)

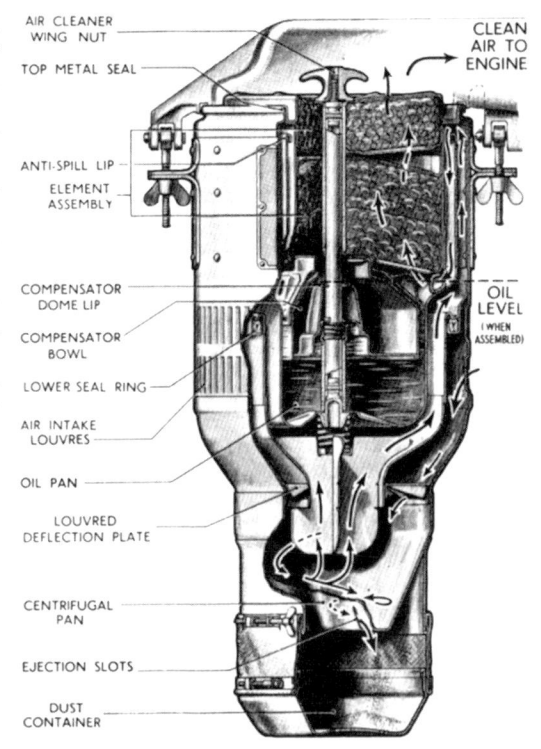

Fig. 28. Cut-away view of AC two-stage air cleaner.

Carburettor Controls

The throttle spindles of the four carburettors are interconnected by a system of rods and levers, which in turn is coupled to the governor. Coupled to the governor-controlled system, but arranged to function independently of it up to the governed maximum speed, is a hydraulic system operated by the accelerator pedal. The hydraulic system comprises a pedal-operated transmitting cylinder, connected by a pipe line to a receiving cylinder unit which is located adjacent to the governor.

The four carburettor choke valves are operated by a single hand control located in the driving compartment.

For method of cleaning carburettors, see Operation A.19 on page 145.

For method of overhauling carburettors, see Operation B.10 on page 165.

Priming

" Ki-gass " priming equipment is fitted to facilitate starting. This has a hand-operated pump with pipe connections, so that petrol can be delivered as a fine spray into each induction manifold.

CHURCHILL TANK

ENGINE AND CLUTCH

Governor and Drive

The governor is of the centrifugal type, driven at half crankshaft speed from the L.H. camshaft, and is attached to the top of the crankcase by a flange and two bolts. Plain bearings are used for the governor shaft, and these are pressure lubricated through an external feed pipe connected to the No. 4 bearing of the R.H. camshaft.

Crankcase Ventilation

A breather pipe is attached to the R.H. front top of the timing cover and connected to one of the carburettor air intake pipes, thus drawing deleterious gases from the crankcase. Another breather pipe is connected from the top of the crankcase (near the governor) to the R.H. rear carburettor air intake pipe.

A flame arrester is included in each breather pipe assembly. The rear pipe also includes an oil trap.

Exhaust System

Four cast-iron exhaust manifolds are fitted, each serving one group of three cylin-

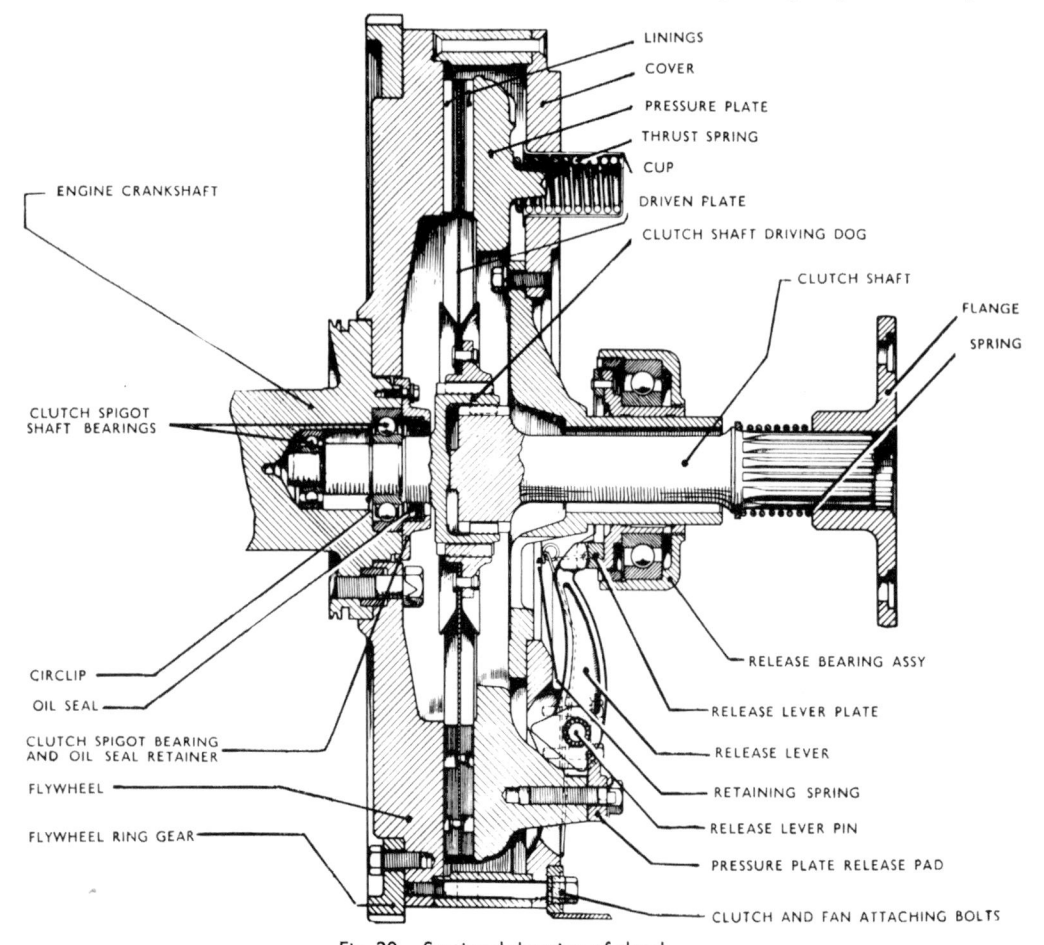

Fig. 29. Sectional drawing of clutch.

ENGINE AND CLUTCH

ders. Each pair of manifolds is connected by pipes to a single silencer, mounted across the rear of the vehicle.

Tachometer Generator and Drive

The generator unit for the Smith tachometer is driven at crankshaft speed by an 18-tooth spiral gear machined on the R.H. camshaft. This gear meshes with a 9-tooth pinion which is pinned to the generator driving shaft, and the shaft runs in two ball bearings. Formed with a spigot and flange, the housing for the driving shaft bearings is attached to the top of the crankcase by three setscrews, these setscrews also passing through the flange of the pedestal bracket of the tachometer generator. The pedestal bracket is spigoted into the bore of the bearing housing.

The Clutch

The clutch is a single dry plate unit with a nominal disc diameter of 18 in. and follows closely the usual Borg & Beck clutch design. The assembly is bolted to the flywheel, with the flywheel forming one friction face of the clutch.

Pressure on the driven plate is exerted by 24 helical springs located in cups and disposed around the clutch cover in two staggered rows. For purposes of disengagement this spring pressure is removed from the driven plate through six toggle levers pivoted on the cover and lifting the pressure plate.

The clutch release pressure is exerted upon the toggles by the hydraulic air assisted mechanism through the medium of a ball thrust bearing.

The clutch cover itself is composed of composite steel forgings, to which is affixed at its centre the cast throw-out bearing sleeve.

The driven plate is mounted on an intermediate spigot shaft carried in two ball bearings within the crankshaft. The clutch shaft is driven through internal teeth formed in the bore of the enlarged rear end of the spigot engaging with similar teeth formed upon the outer end of the clutch shaft. This feature permits small degrees of misalignment of the clutch shaft relative to the crankshaft.

For method of adjusting clutch pedal clearance, see Operation A.6 on page 132.

For method of removing clutch, see Operation B.9 on page 165.

TRANSMISSION

GEARBOX
TYPE H41
(Four-Speed Box complete with Steering Mechanism)

GENERAL DATA

Gear Ratios. (Gearbox Input to Final Drive Sprocket)	1st Speed	120.2 to 1
	2nd Speed	42.32 to 1
	3rd Speed	23.75 to 1
	4th Speed	15.02 to 1
	Reverse	168.5 to 1
Turning Radii in each Gear	1st Speed	8.88 ft.
	2nd Speed	25.2 ft.
	3rd Speed	44.9 ft.
	4th Speed	71.0 ft.
	Reverse	6.33 ft.
Speed in each Gear at 2,200 r.p.m. Engine Speed	1st Speed	1.59 m.p.h.
	2nd Speed	4.51 m.p.h.
	3rd Speed	8.03 m.p.h.
	4th Speed	12.70 m.p.h.
	Reverse	1.13 m.p.h.
Gear Case		In two halves. Split horizontally
Bearing Location		Held by separate bearing caps
Drive from Input Coupling to Primary Shaft		Through bevel pinion direct to primary shaft
Gear Engagement		Dog-clutch engagement throughout
Selector Rods		Enclosed
Position of Air Compressor		On top of gearbox
Drive to Air Compressor		Gear-driven from gearbox
Oil Level Indication		Dipstick
Oil in Gearbox—		
To Fill a Dry Box		3 gallons
To Refill after Draining		$2\frac{1}{2}$ gallons

DESCRIPTION

From the clutch, the drive is taken to the gearbox through a shaft and a " Layrub " coupling bolted to the input flange of the gearbox.

VEHICLE HISTORY AND SPECIFICATION

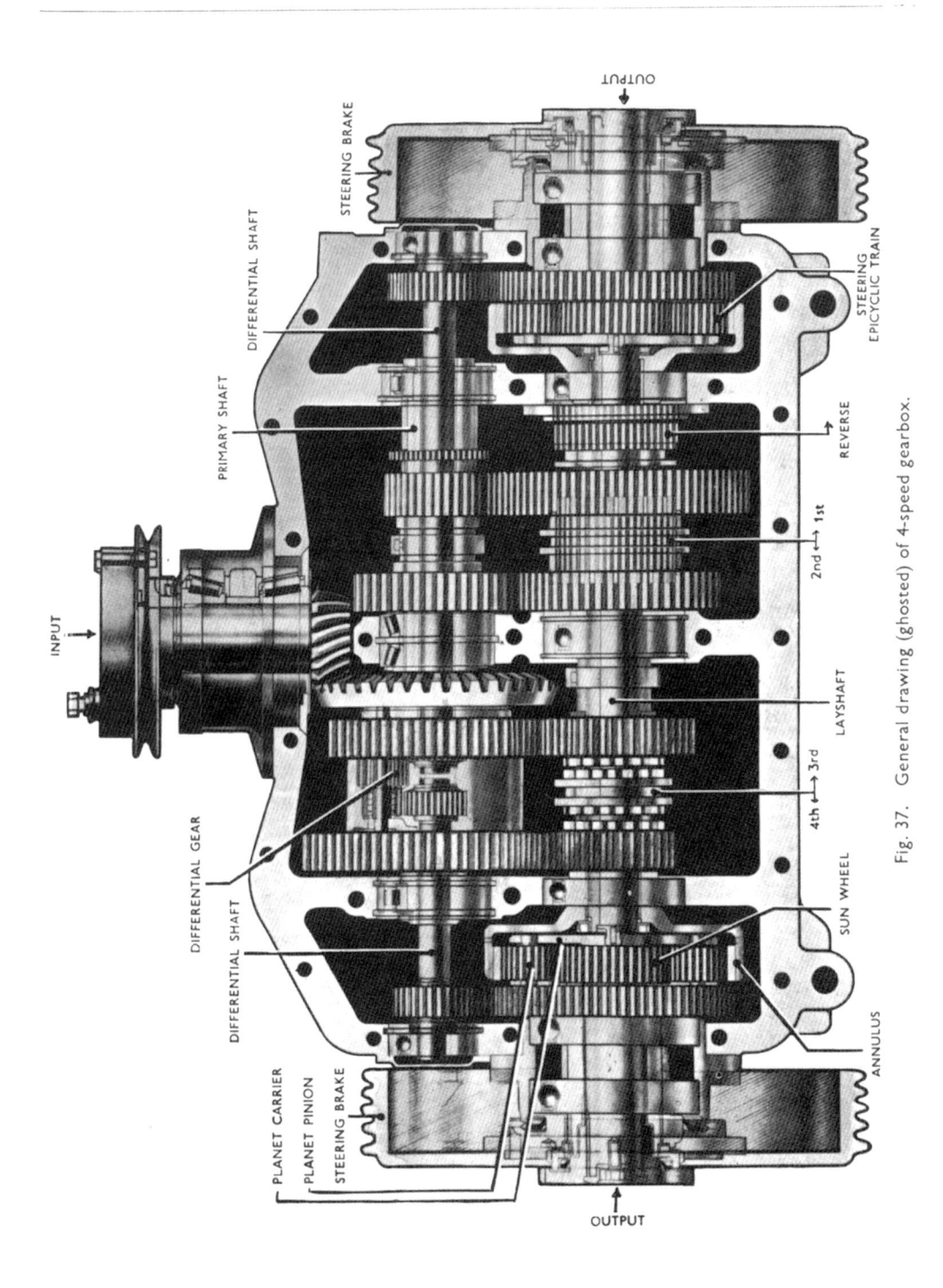

TRANSMISSION

Fig. 37. General drawing (ghosted) of 4-speed gearbox.

TRANSMISSION

Fig. 38. General view of gearbox compartment.

TRANSMISSION

Fig. 39. View of 4-speed gearbox (top cover removed).

The gearbox assembly incorporates, with the change speed gears, the steering mechanism which is of the controlled differential type so arranged that a fixed turning radius is obtained, this radius depending on the change speed gear engaged.

In this system, use is made of epicyclic gear trains in conjunction with a differential gear, so that by application of either of the two steering brakes, the output shafts of the differential are "controlled," thus causing the speed of one track to be increased and the other reduced. The locking of the steering drum gives a definite ratio difference between the two output shafts, giving what is known as a "geared" turn. Power loss is therefore avoided. The ratio difference of the output shafts varies for each gear, the turning radius being greatest in top and smallest in bottom gear.

The input shaft of the gearbox—to which the clutch shaft is connected—rotates in a clockwise direction. The two output shafts are at right-angles to the input shaft and are connected one to each final drive unit. Some universal movement is provided between the box and final drive by a composite muff coupling. Rotation of the output shafts is backwards when the vehicle is running in a forward direction.

The steering brakes mounted at each end of the gearbox are of the two leading shoe type.

A gear-type pump is used to circulate oil through the hollow primary shaft and layshaft to lubricate by pressure the needle-roller bearings and steel-backed white metal bushes and steering epicyclics. The remainder of the parts are lubricated by splash.

TRANSMISSION

To ensure that clean oil is circulated through the gearbox, a gauze type filter is fitted to the suction side of the oil pump.

Principle of Operation

Fig. 40 is a diagrammatic layout of the box.

The input bevel drives the primary shaft (A) through the usual crown wheel and pinion. Mounted rigidly to the primary shaft are the four drive gears for first, second, third and fourth speeds. These gears drive their corresponding gears on the layshaft (B), the gears running freely on needle roller bearings.

Integral with the primary shaft and its gears is a spur-type differential gear complete with the normal type of half-shafts to transmit power to the epicyclic gear trains at each end of the box. This is marked (C) in Fig. 40.

The gears on the layshaft run on needle roller bearings and are in constant mesh with the corresponding gears on the primary shaft. Each of the layshaft gears can be coupled to the layshaft by dog clutches, operated by rods from the change speed gate in the driver's compartment. At each end of the box is an epicyclic gear, consisting of a sun wheel which meshes with planet pinions running on pins in the planet pin

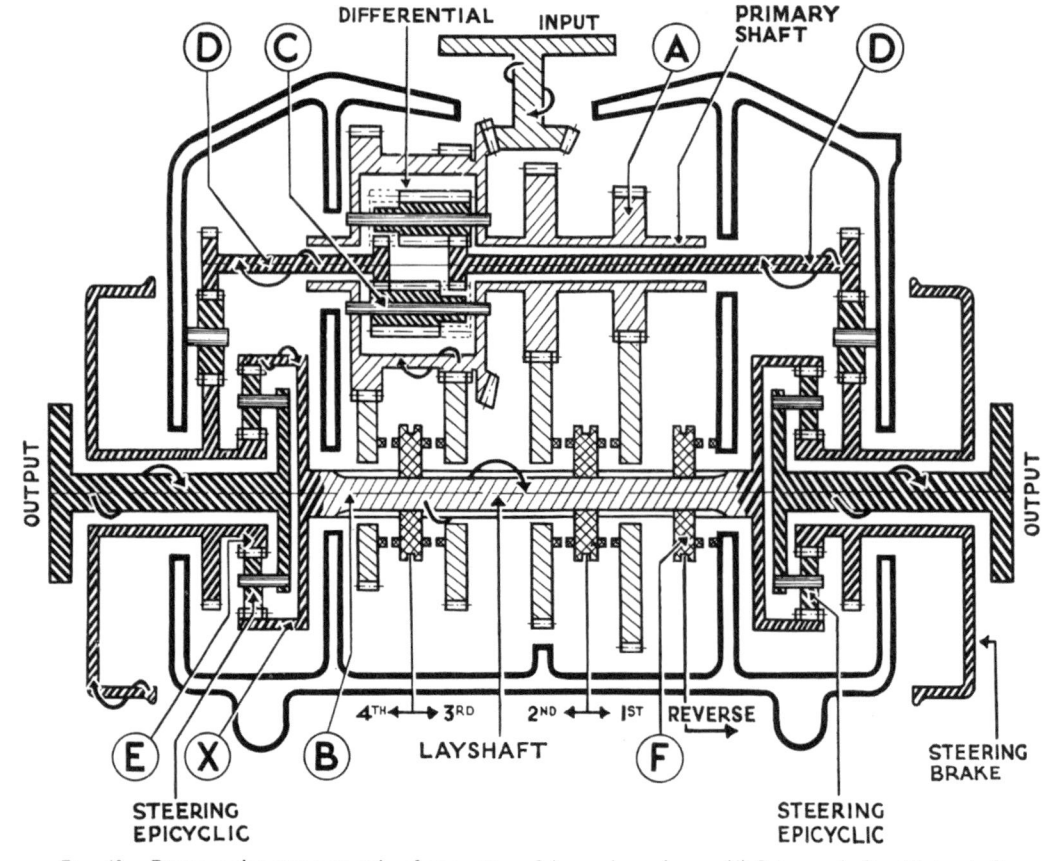

Fig. 40. Diagram showing principle of operation of 4-speed gearbox. (A) *Primary shaft.* (B) *Layshaft.* (C) *Differential gear.* (D) *Differential shaft.* (E) *Sun wheel.* (F) *Reverse gear dog clutch.* (X) *Epicyclic annulus.*

TRANSMISSION

Fig. 41. View of steering epicyclic train.

carrier. These pinions mesh also with an internally-toothed ring gear called the annulus. Mounted as a fixed part of the sun wheel is a gear to receive the drive from a differential half-shaft. At the outer end of the sun wheel shaft a steering brake drum is mounted, and the whole assembly runs on two ball bearings located in the brake anchor bracket. An idler gear between the differential half-shaft and the gear on the sun wheel shaft completes the train. It will be seen from Fig. 40 that the planet pin carrier is an integral part of the output shaft.

The above describes the parts of one epicyclic gear, and it is clear from Fig. 40 that the two assemblies are alike. Also, it will be seen that the annulus of each is fixed to the layshaft and that the layshaft and two annuli become an integral part.

Due to the idler gear, the sun wheel (E) rotates in the opposite direction to that of the epicyclic annulus (X). The final drive is taken from the planet pin carrier of the epicyclic steering gear, and the numbers of teeth in this gear are such that the output coupling rotates in the same direction as the layshaft, but at a slower speed. This reduction in speed is due to the fact that the sun wheel is rotating in the opposite direction to the annulus, and the greater the difference between these two speeds the slower the speed of the output shaft relative to the annulus. Also, if the sun wheel is held stationary, the speed of the output shaft increases. Therefore, a reduction in gear ratio is obtained through the change gears on the primary and layshaft, and a further reduction is obtained through the steering epicyclic gears.

Thus, for a given engine speed, the sun wheels rotate at a constant speed whereas the speed of the annulus is governed by the change gear selected. To obtain reverse, the reverse dog clutch (F) locks the layshaft to the casing, and as the steering annulus is then stationary, the output shaft rotates in the same direction as the epicyclic sun wheel—i.e. the reverse direction to that when in the forward gears.

Steering

Steering in the Forward Gears.—When steering, one steering brake drum is locked. Assuming that the right-hand brake drum is locked, the epicyclic sun wheel and the right-hand differential shaft are therefore held stationary. Thus the output coupling

63

TRANSMISSION

on that side must speed up for a constant engine speed. Due to one differential shaft being held stationary, the other differential shaft speeds up to twice the speed. This in turn speeds up the sun wheel in the left-hand steering epicyclic and slows down the output shaft on the left-hand side.

It will be seen, therefore, that if the right-hand drum is locked, the right-hand track speeds up and the left-hand track slows down, giving a turn to the left. In other words, to steer left the right-hand drum is locked, and *vice versa*.

The ratio between the speeds of the two tracks when steering is determined by the change gear engaged. This is obvious when it is borne in mind that for a given engine speed the sun wheels remain at constant speed but the annulus speed is dependent on the gear engaged. The effect of this is to give four turning radii in the forward direction plus a pivot turn in neutral.

Steering in Reverse.—When reverse gear is engaged, the steering annuli (X in Fig. 40) are held stationary. If now the right-hand drum is locked, both the sun wheel and the steering epicyclic annulus on that side are locked; the output coupling is also locked and the right-hand track remains stationary. Due to the locking of the right-hand side differential shaft, the left-hand differential shaft speeds up, and due to the left-hand annulus also being locked, the left-hand output coupling and the track rotate in the reverse direction. Therefore, when the right-hand steering brake is locked in reverse the tail of the vehicle swings round to the right.

Steering in Neutral.—It is possible to obtain a pivot turn in neutral. With the gear lever in neutral, the locking of the right-hand drum causes the right-hand track to move forwards and the left-hand track backwards, thus giving a pivot turn to the left. *Therefore, the steering controls should not be operated when the engine is running, even though the gear may be in neutral, unless a definite turn is required.*

(*The procedure for changing the gearbox unit is detailed in Operation B.20 on page* 178.)

FINAL DRIVE UNIT

GENERAL DATA

Location	One each side at rear of the vehicle
Weight of Unit	1100 lbs.
Oil Capacity	$1\frac{3}{4}$ gallons
Number of Teeth on Sprocket	23

DESCRIPTION

The final drive unit converts the rotary motion of the engine into the straight line motion of the track. There are two units, one fitted to each side of the vehicle at the rear. Each drives one track, and both final drive units are identical in detail.

The unit consists of a rotating casing running on ball bearings carried by a stationary member known as the planet carrier. It is provided with two sprockets to transmit the drive to the track.

VEHICLE HISTORY AND SPECIFICATION

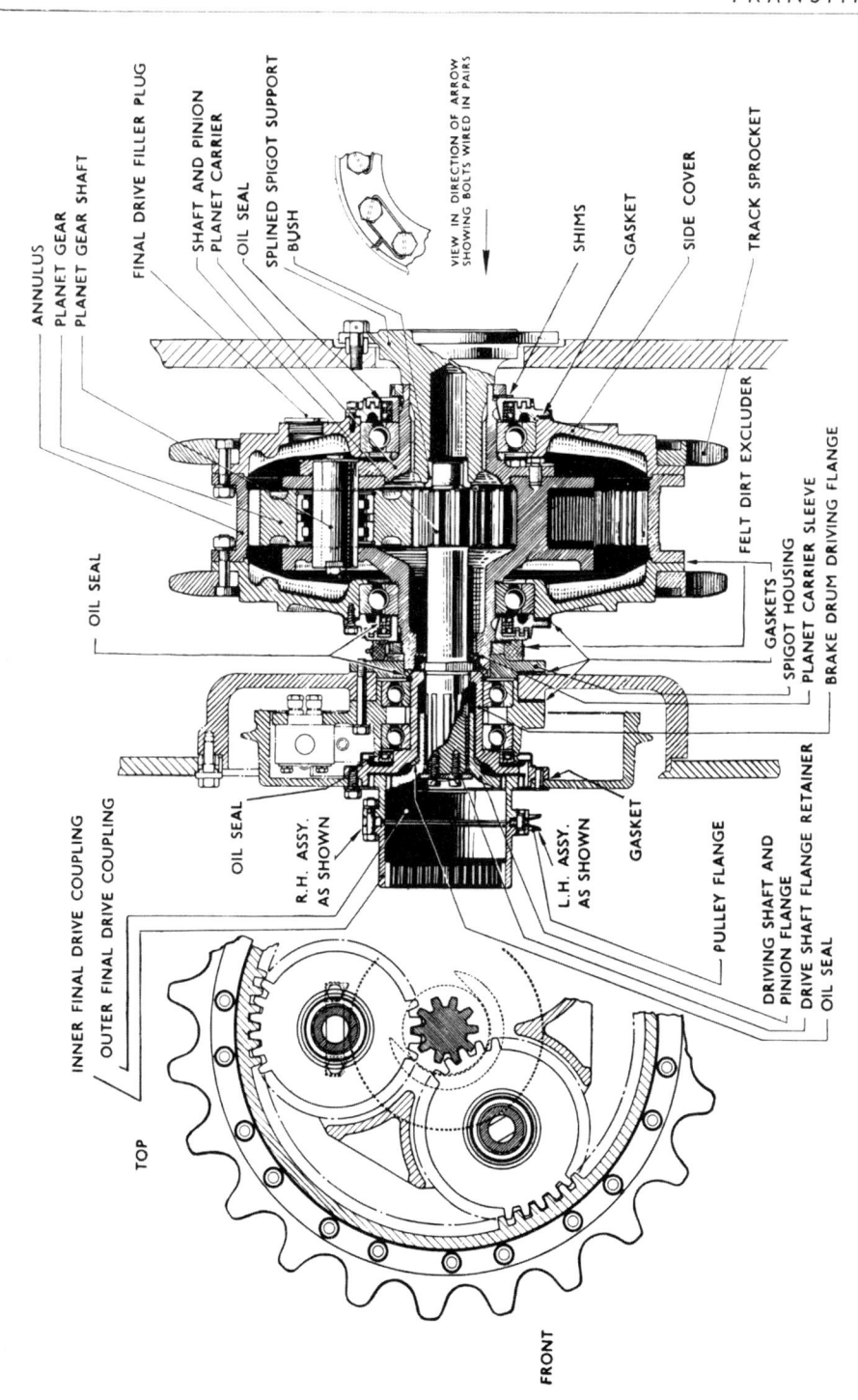

TRANSMISSION

Fig. 42. Sectioned drawing of final drive unit.

CHURCHILL TANK

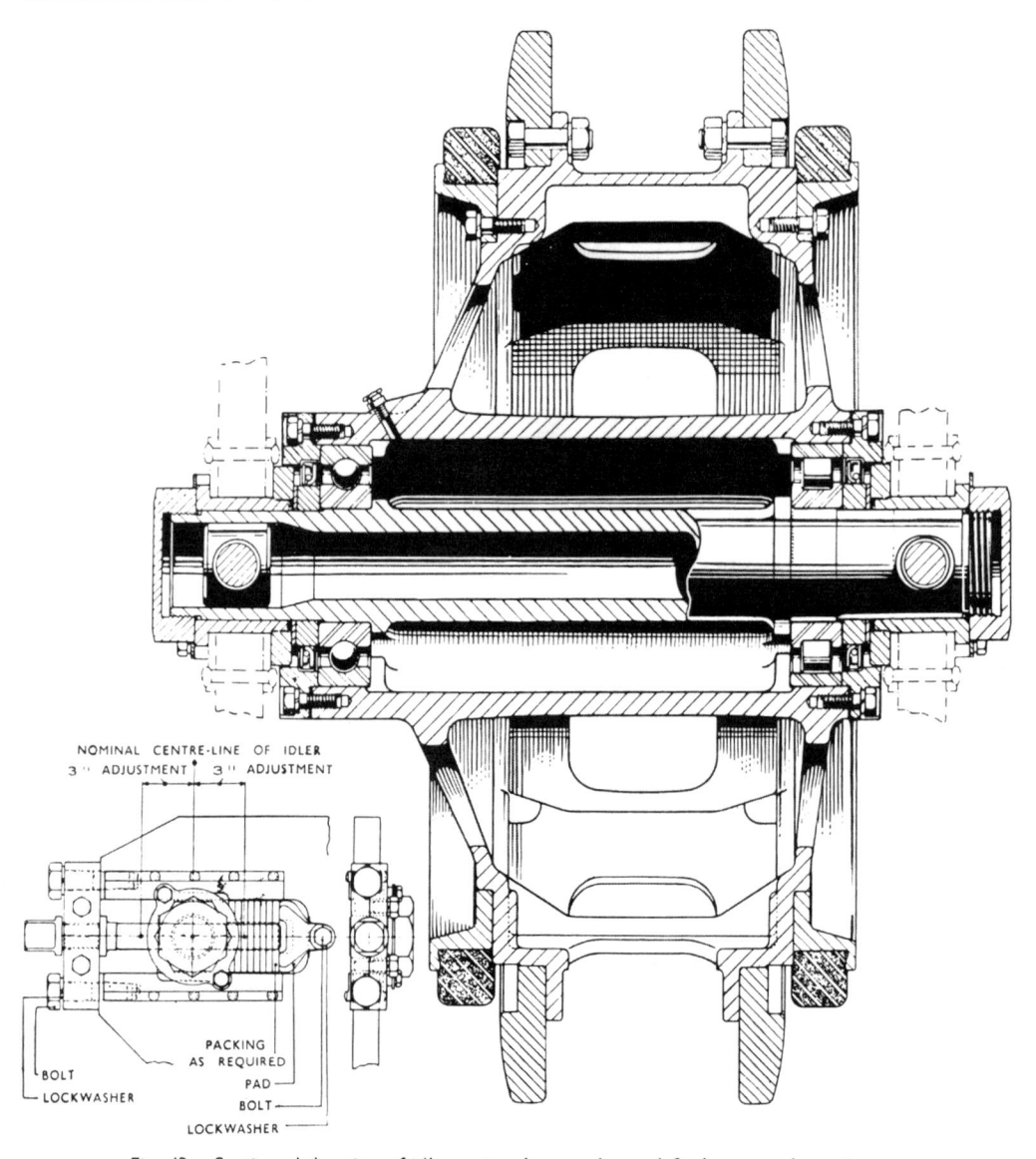

TRANSMISSION

Fig. 43. Sectioned drawing of idler unit.   Inset at lower left shows track tensioner.

    The rotating casing has a toothed ring on its inner circumference engaging with three planet gears carried on the stationary planet carrier. These, in turn, mesh with a central shaft driven from the gearbox.

    Rotation of the shaft produces rotation of the final drive casing, through the planet gear, but in the opposite direction and at a reduced speed.

    (*The procedure for changing a final drive unit is detailed in Operation B.5 on page* 162.)
    (*For replacement of sprocket rings, see Operation B.6 on page* 163.)

TRANSMISSION

IDLER UNIT

GENERAL DATA

Location	**One each side at front of the vehicle**
Weight of Unit	**674 lbs.**
Number of Teeth on Sprocket	**23**

DESCRIPTION

An idler unit is fitted at each side of the front end of the vehicle. It consists of a rotating drum mounted on ball and roller bearings. It is provided with two rubber tyres to carry the track, and two sprockets serve to keep the track in correct alignment.

The complete assembly is on blocks arranged to slide in horns, and is provided with screws for movement backwards and forwards for the necessary track adjustment. The two units are identical.

(The procedure for changing an idler unit is detailed in Operation B.4 on page 161.*)*

(For replacement of sprocket rings and rubber tyres, see Operations B.6 and B.7 on pages 163 *and* 164.*)*

TRACKS AND SUSPENSION

GENERAL DATA

TRACKS

Rail Centres	...	11⅛ in.
Pitch of Link	Manganese Steel Track	7.96 in.
Number of Links	Manganese Steel Track	72
Weight of one Link	Manganese Steel Track	48 lbs.

SUSPENSION

Number of Bogies	22
Weight of Bogies	336 lbs.
Weight of Twin Bogies, Nos. 2 and 3	814 lbs.
Number of Springs (Load)	2 (One on No. 11)
Number of Springs (Bumper)	1 (Not on No. 11)
Number of Springs (Retainer)	1 (,, ,, ,, ,,)
Diameter of Wheels (running diameter)	10 in. (except No. 11)
Diameter of Axle	2¾ in.
Axle Bearings	White metal lined
Diameter of Fulcrum Shaft	2 in.
Fulcrum Shaft Bearings	Bronze bushes
Lubrication	Pressure oil gun by nipple

DESCRIPTION

The track, in conjunction with the bogie units, has to meet the following conditions :—

Driving, reversing, steering and climbing.

Float on a 14 lbs. per sq. in. ground pressure when fully laden.

A speed of 12.7 m.p.h. without wearing out too quickly (a figure of 2,000 miles is anticipated).

And it must be capable of crushing moderately large stones and keeping out barbed wire.

Tracks

The tracks are of manganese steel and are of the end lobe drive type. They are composed of steel shoes, connected together by pins. Rubber tyres are fitted to the idler units to carry the tracks. On the final drive units the tracks are carried by the sprockets.

The track pins are designed to run dry and therefore need no lubrication.

Each track pin is located in its link by a stainless steel retainer welded to each side of the link, covering approximately half the hole.

TRACKS AND SUSPENSION

To enable a temporary track repair to be made when welding equipment is not available, a special stepped service pin is available. This service pin is grooved so that when the track is adjusted, the inner bosses of the links engage in the grooves, and no retainers are required. As soon as possible, however, a service pin must be replaced by a standard pin and held in place by new welded retainers.

The track is carried over the top of the vehicle on skid rails. These consist of " L " shaped steel runners, and are continuous along the tops of the panniers. Guide flanges keep the track in alignment.

For method of adjusting track tension, see Operation A.7, page 133.

For method of replacing track link or pin, see Operation A.24, page 149.

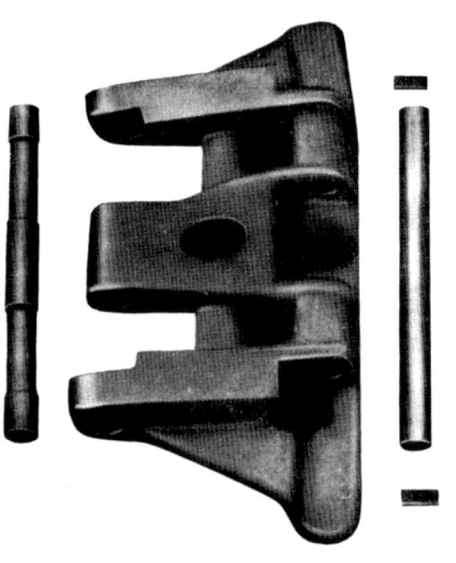

Fig. 44. Track link and pin. Service pin shown on left.

Suspension

The vehicle is equipped with twenty-two bogies, eleven each side, of which six each side (numbers three to eight) are allowed the full spring deflection of 3 in. and 2 in. rebound.

Number one bogie has a curtailed rebound and functions only when the tank is nosing or climbing.

Numbers two, nine and ten also have varying degrees of curtailed rebound and number eleven unit, which functions chiefly as a track guide, is unsprung, and therefore has no deflection.

Each suspension unit consists of the bogie support bracket, the bogie frame, the bogie axle and wheels and the necessary springs and spring locations.

With the exception of Nos. 2 and 3, each suspension unit is independent and is separately bolted to the pannier floor. Units Nos. 2 and 3 have a combined support bracket, the complete assembly being bolted to the pannier floor.

The bogie support bracket, made up of welded plates, is provided with a large boss to carry the bogie frame. At its approximate centre the bogie frame is hinged to the bogie support bracket by the fulcrum shaft, one end of the bogie frame carrying the axle and wheels and the other end forming the lug for the rebound stop. The fulcrum shaft runs in bronze bearings and the axle shaft in white metal bearings. Both are provided with pressure nipples for oil gun lubrication. On the upper side of the axle shaft boss of the bogie frame a hard steel knife edge is fitted, and the springs are located in suitable pads between the knife edge and the top of the bogie support brackets.

The knife edge keeps spring buckling down to a minimum, as the springs are perfectly free to take up their own axial alignment.

Slight buckling is unavoidable owing to the working radius of the wheels, but the springs have been positioned to give a straight line at maximum bump ; thus no buckling stress is added to the spring at maximum stress.

Four springs are fitted to each bogie, except No. 11. The outer two carry the

TRACKS AND SUSPENSION

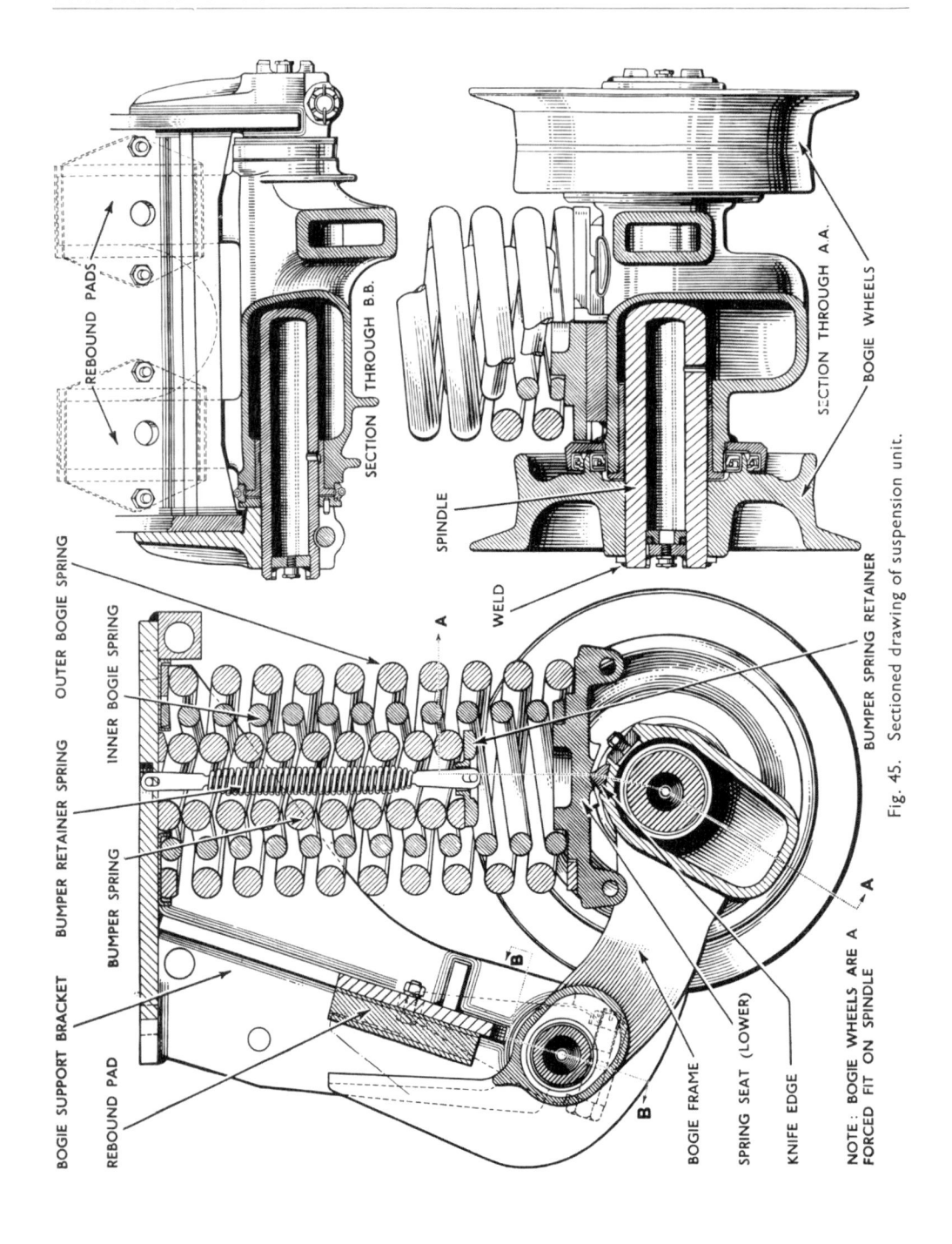

Fig. 45. Sectioned drawing of suspension unit.

TRACKS AND SUSPENSION

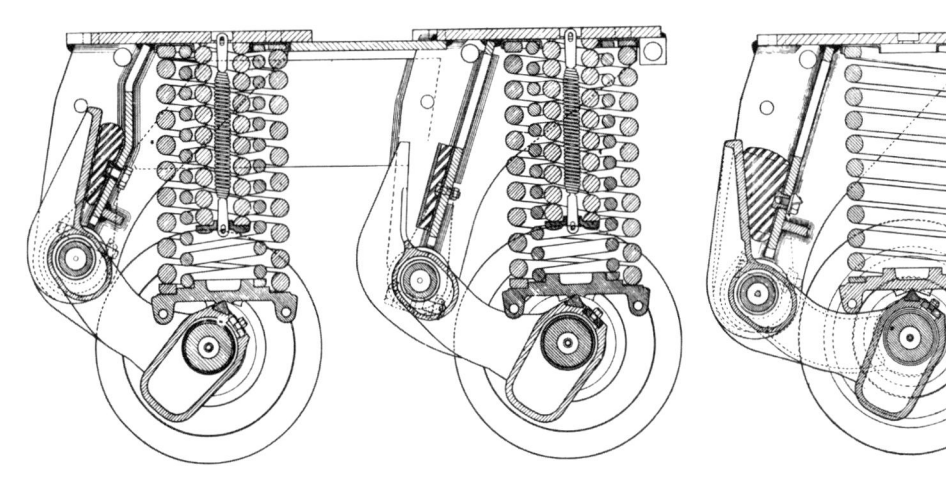

Fig. 46. Longitudinal section of Nos. 2 and 3 coupled suspension units.

Fig. 47. Transverse section of No. 11 suspension unit.

load, the next inner spring controls the " bump through " load, and the small inner coil is provided to hold the bumper spring in position. On No. 11 the two inner springs are omitted and only one load spring is used.

The bumper spring operates only for the last $\frac{3}{4}$ in. of " bump through."

Axle and Wheels

The wheels are a press fit on the axle, and rotate as a unit in white metal bearings in the bogie frame. The axle is hollow and acts as an oil reservoir. It is replenished by means of a pressure oil gun through a suitable nipple at the end of the axle. A nipple is fitted to both ends of the axle, to make the units interchangeable for both sides of the vehicle. The nipples are housed in recesses at the ends of the axle.

A nipple in the centre of the bogie frame (directly under the knife edge) is provided for pressure release, and is designed to blow off at 15-25 lbs. per sq. in. It also shows when the oil system is full. *This nipple is not for lubrication.*

When lubricating the axles, oil should be forced through the nipples until it escapes from the pressure vent.

The fulcrum shaft is clamped in the bogie support bracket, and the bogie frame, mounted on bronze bushes, pivots in it. This shaft, like the wheel axle, is hollow, and has oil nipples at each end. When it is lubricated, oil should be forced in until it exudes at each side of the bogie support bracket.

Suitable oil seals are fitted close to the bushes at each end of both the axle shaft and the fulcrum shaft. These seals are designed not only to keep oil in the bearings, but also to keep dirt out.

The operation of changing bogie units or springs has been made as easy as possible in the design.

For method of replacing suspension assembly, see Operation B.2, page 157.

For method of replacing suspension spring, see Operation B.3, page 160.

BRAKES

GENERAL DATA

Diameter of Brake Drums	20 in.
Width of Linings	3½ in.
Area of Steering Brakes	123 sq. in.
Area of Stopping Brakes	123 sq. in.
Weight of Brake Assembly (with Brake Drum)	188 lbs. each
Weight of Brake Drum only	94 lbs. each
Brake Lining—Make	Mintex
Type	N.M.T.

DESCRIPTION

The brakes are used for steering and stopping, and there are two assemblies for each purpose.

Both sets of brakes are Lockheed Hydraulic and each brake assembly consists of two shoes which, together with their operating gear, are mounted on a back-plate. Each brake shoe is carried by spring pads on a rocking beam and can be lifted off without dismantling any other part once the respective brake drum is removed. The brake shoes are interchangeable throughout the two brake systems, but as the *steering brake assemblies* vary from the *stopping brake assemblies*, the *assemblies* are not interchangeable.

The steering brakes are of the two leading shoe type, and have a powerful self-servo effect to increase the braking power. As the brake drums always rotate in the same direction, the self-servo action of the shoes operates correspondingly in one direction.

The stopping brakes are similar in most respects to the steering brakes, but as they must be equally effective in going forward or in reversing, the self-servo action is operative in both directions. The operating cylinders and the rocking beams differ, therefore, from those on the stopping brakes, and must not be interchanged.

There are two brake shoes in each brake drum, each shoe being carried on a rocking lever. Between both ends of the rocking levers a Lockheed hydraulic cylinder is mounted, the two cylinders being connected in series to ensure synchronized operation.

When the brake is applied the leading end of each rocking beam is pushed towards the brake drum, thus applying the brakes.

The drums are of special alloy cast iron, and are dimensionally the same both for the steering brakes and the stopping brakes. The steering brake drums, however are ribbed for cooling, while the stopping brakes are plain.

BRAKES

Brake Operating Gear

All the brakes are operated by hydraulic pressure. The stopping brakes are operated by the right-hand foot pedal in the driving compartment; also by a hand lever, so that the brakes can be locked on. The handbrake must not be relied on for parking the machine for long periods on sloping ground. It is operated hydraulically and the fluid pressure will not be maintained indefinitely. *When it is necessary to park on sloping ground, first speed should be engaged.*

The steering brakes are controlled by the steering handle-bar, a separate master cylinder operating the left-hand or the right-hand steering brake. Air pressure servos are provided to help in applying the steering brakes.

Suitable piping transmits the pressure from the foot pedal or the steering handle-bar to the brake cylinders.

Location of Adjusters

Adjustment is effected by means of wedges, controlled by adjusting screws, between the shoes and rocking bars. Access to the adjusters is provided through removable plugs in the sides of the brake drums.

Servicing Points

Once the drums are detached, all the shoes can be removed without tools, simply by pulling them off the rocking beams. When replacing the shoes it is advisable to slacken off the adjusters completely to facilitate fitting the drums, and to prevent the wedge moving about while it is being entered into its slot.

The feed pipes to the stopping brakes are a fairly close fit between the outside of the drum and the inside of the final drive support casting. If they are properly fitted, this small clearance will not cause trouble, but the pipes should be inspected carefully after fitting to ensure that they do not rub. Care must also be taken when removing brake drums not to let them fall or rest on the feed pipes.

Fig. 48. View of main brake unit showing removable plugs over brake adjusters.

Fig. 49. View of steering brake unit with drum removed showing brake adjusters.

BRAKES

The wearing surfaces of all brakes must be kept *scrupulously clean*. Even contact between the linings and oily or greasy hands should be avoided. As a safeguard, some form of protective covering of the liners should always be used until the brake drums are ready to be fitted.

Incidentally, it is important to bear in mind that oil on brake linings, in addition to reducing braking efficiency, is certain to cause " spragging." One result of this is that the brakes may be reluctant to release, and although such a condition is not of great moment in stopping brakes, it is certainly undesirable in brakes used for steering. If the steering brakes do not release instantly when the steering control is operated, the vehicle will continue to steer.

A slight film of oil on the surface of the linings can usually be removed by washing with carbon tetra-chloride. This practice is not recommended, however, because the oil may penetrate deeply into the linings and the only cure then is to fit new linings.

For method of adjusting steering brakes, see Operation A.15, page 141.
For method of adjusting main brakes, see Operation A.16, page 142.
For method of changing steering brakes, see Operation B.15, page 169.
For method of changing main brakes, see Operation B.16, page 172.
For method of bleeding hydraulic controls, see Operation A.22, page 147.

THE TURRET

GENERAL DATA

Control	1. Power by Electricity 2. Hand operation
Diameter of Turret Head Ball Race (Centre of Track)	$58\frac{1}{4}$ in.
Construction	117 steel balls in bronze cage (made in 13 sections)
Diameter of balls	$1\frac{1}{4}$ in.

TURRET HEAD

Construction	Composite. The centre section is cast, and the roof and floor are of plate welded to the centre section
Material	Bullet-proof steel
Power Operation	Electric
Hand Operation	Through reduction gear

TURRET ROTARY PLATFORM

Suspension	By tubes from head at three points. Located below centre of platform by rollers
Material	Plymax. (Multi-ply wood faced each side with sheet metal)
Thickness	$\frac{5}{8}$ in.

DESCRIPTION

The three essentials of a tank turret are:—

(1) To provide a gun mounting.
(2) To provide unobstructed visibility for the commander.
(3) To provide an armour covering for the three occupants of the turret.

General Description

The turret consists of a bullet-proof structure, the centre portion being cast and the roof and floor being of plate welded to the centre section, to which is suspended a platform capable of rotating with the turret head.

The guns and telescope are mounted on a co-axial mounting in the turret. In the roof of the turret a cupola is provided which is rotatable by hand independently of the turret.

The whole is mounted on the hull so that it is rotatable through 360° and is suspended on a ball race located just below the turret head.

The stationary race is mounted on the hull plates and the moving race is bolted to the turret casting.

ENGINE AND CLUTCH

The turret can be controlled electrically so long as the engine is running, or it can be manipulated by hand when the engine is stopped.

The electricity required to operate the turret, and for the electrical gear inside the turret, is passed from the hull to the rotatable turret through a series of slip rings. This series of slip rings is called the base junction. It is located below the turret platform, and is described on page 93.

The Turret

The head of the turret is provided with a ball race track to match up with a race track mounted on the top of the hull. A series of steel balls in the track completes the bearing and enables the turret to turn easily.

Six nipples are provided on the inner ring for lubrication of the ball track. These points should be lubricated with C.600, but excessive lubrication should be avoided.

The turret platform is made of "Plymax." It is $\frac{5}{8}$ in. thick and consists of plywood, covered on both sides with sheet metal. It is three-point suspended on tubular members from the turret head, but is insulated from the turret head by rubber bushes.

Below the platform, the base junction is fitted on the hull floor, and the platform is centred on this housing by a locating ring containing three rollers with spherical faces. The rubber bushes at the top end of the platform suspension members are intended to give sufficient flexibility to ensure that the platform will rotate freely on its three rollers even if there is slight eccentricity between the turret ball race and the junction housing.

A sheet metal inspection cover on the platform floor contains a spring-loaded dowel peg, which engages a slot in the top of the electrical slip-ring gear in order to rotate it. Another sheet metal inspection cover is provided on the platform floor beneath the commander's pedestal. It is retained in position by three screws and is provided to scavenge anything which may be dropped under the platform floor.

The turret is provided with a cupola for the use of the commander, and this cupola is rotatable by hand independently of the turret. It is mounted on three ball races and is fitted with two periscopes. Two other periscopes are provided in the turret, one each for the gunner and loader. A large hatch, closed by steel doors, is provided in the roof, and a similar hatch is provided in the cupola.

Turret Seats

A pedestal type seat, adjustable for height is provided for the gunner. Fold-up seats are provided for the commander and the wireless operator.

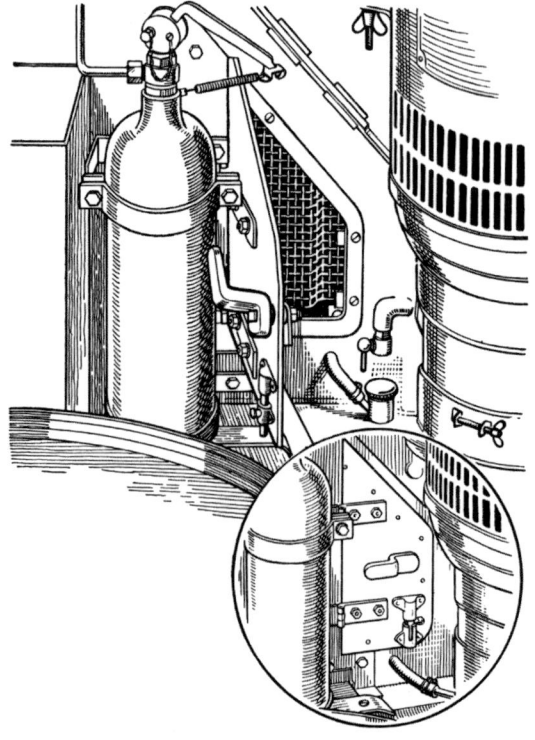

Fig. 58. Bulkhead ventilator door and retaining catch.

VEHICLE HISTORY AND SPECIFICATION

ENGINE AND CLUTCH

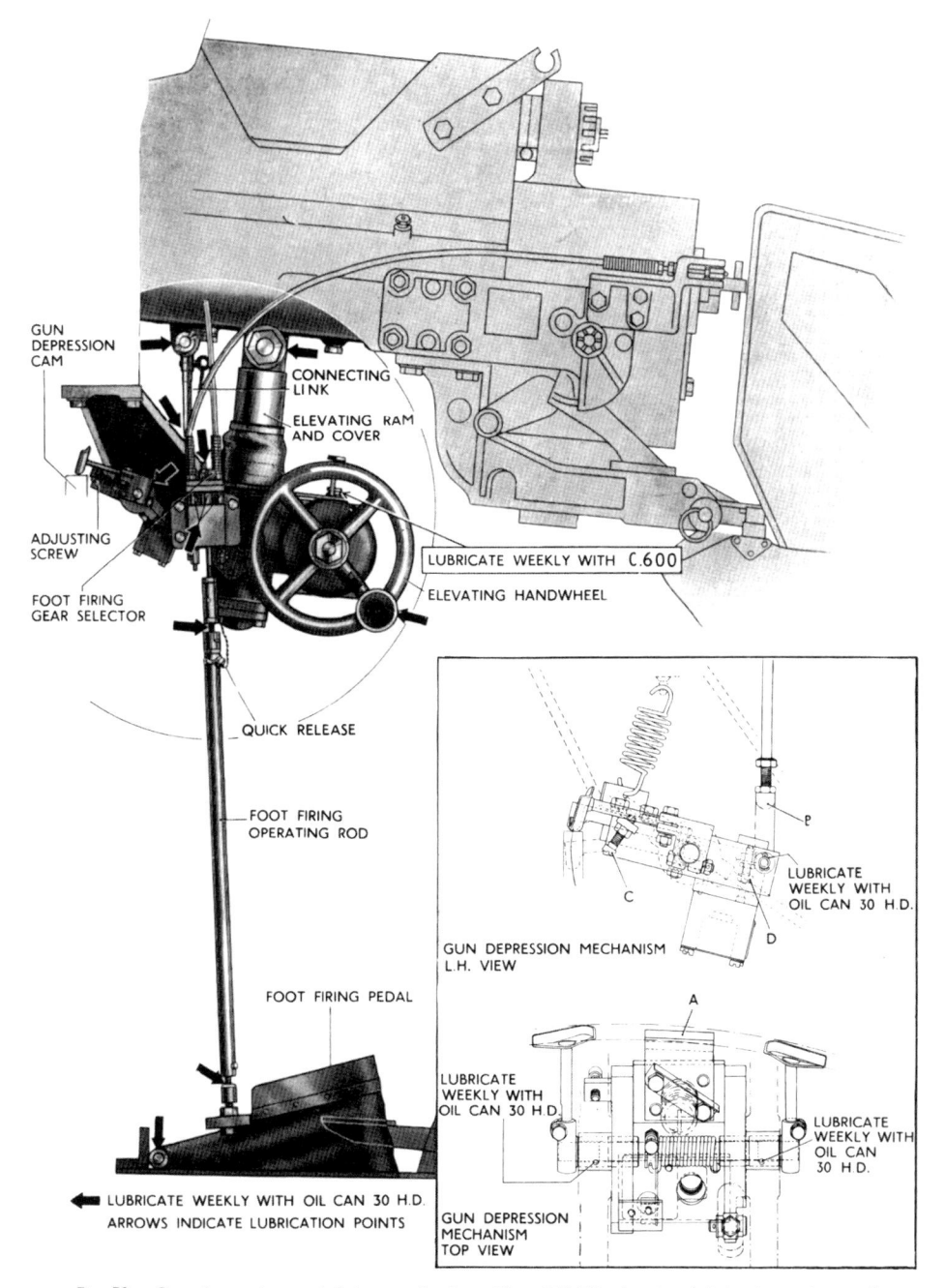

Fig. 59. Gun depression and firing mechanism, Churchill VII, showing lubrication points and adjustment details.
(Note : Churchill VIII is not fitted with gun depression mechanism. Other details shown above apply to both models).

TURRET

Extra Ventilation when Firing

To clear fumes rapidly from the turret, a ventilator is fitted in the bulkhead between the fighting and engine compartments. It consists of a wire mesh covered opening through the bulkhead, closed with a steel door and locked by a handle.

When the guns are being fired, the door should be opened and secured in the open position by the retainer provided for the purpose.

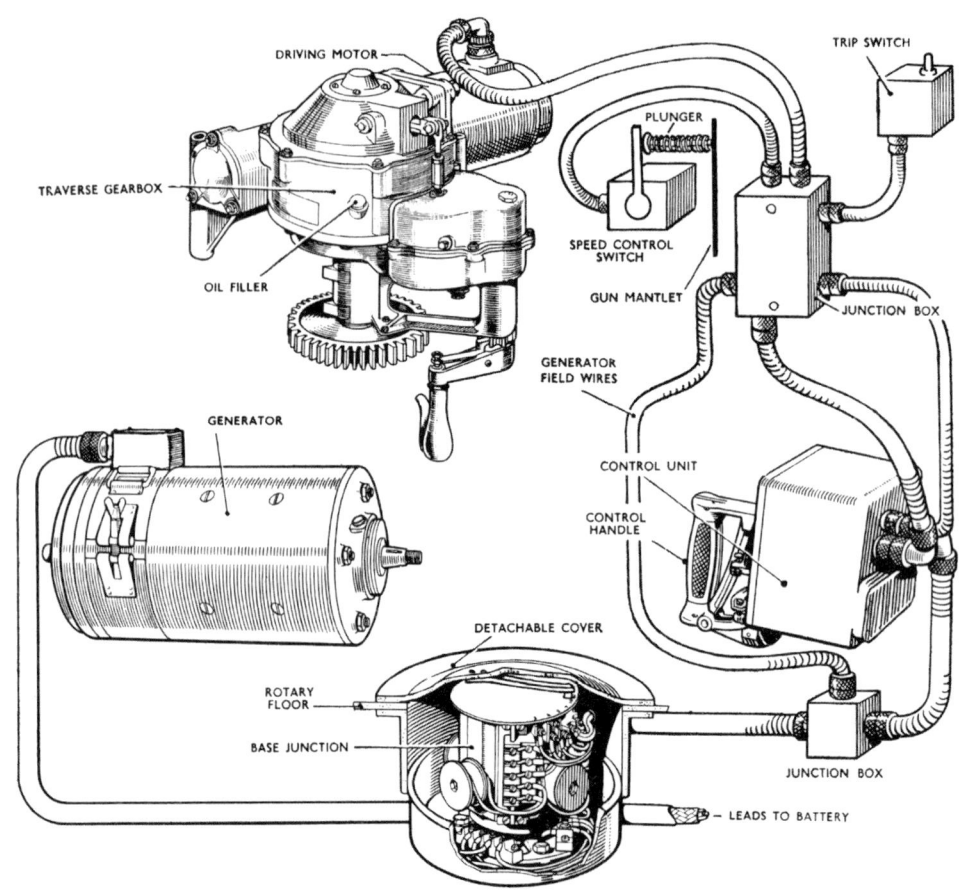

Fig. 60. Layout of turret operating mechanism.
(The speed control switch and trip switch are not fitted to Churchill VIII.)

An electrically-driven fan is fitted to the turret roof, close to the Besa machine-gun, with an armour-protected vent through the roof.

The Armament

Churchill VII. A 75 mm. gun and a Besa gun and telescope are fitted in a co-axial mounting. The elevation of the guns is mechanically limited as necessary.

Beneath the race, and in the fore and aft direction on the tank, are fitted two gun depression cams. These cams limit the depression of the guns so that it is impossible to fire on the extreme fore and aft ends of the vehicle.

TURRET

Broadside, a greater gun depression is possible because the vehicle is narrower in this section and the cams are therefore designed to limit this depression as necessary.

The cams are "stepped" and are so arranged that a skid rides over them when the gun approaches an obstruction and in doing so trips a switch which cuts off the power traverse. A limited amount of hand traverse is possible beyond this point, the amount being restricted by a stop which follows up the skid and butts against the cam. When the stop is reached the gun must be elevated for further traverse.

A lever type switch is mounted on the lower splash plate to cut down the speed of turret rotation when the gun is depressed. This avoids a violent "crash-through" on to the solid stop when the skid-operated switch is opened.

Churchill VIII. A 95 mm. howitzer and a Besa gun and telescope are fitted in a co-axial mounting. The gun depression has a fixed limitation and does not require a a special control gear such as is fitted to Churchill VII.

Operation of the Turret. (*see* Fig. 60.)

An electric motor bolted to the movable turret is geared to a fixed toothed ring on the hull roof. The motor is operated by a special controller located on the turret side near the gunner's left-hand. A separate generator, driven from the clutch shaft, provides power for the turret motor. When the engine is stopped, the turret can be rotated by hand gear built in to the traverse gearbox. The hand control is automatically out of action when released.

The electric controller is arranged to give variable speed of rotation, either to the right or the left, and the turret can be swung to very fine limits. The control handle has a trigger lever which is depressed when the handle is grasped, thereby switching on power to the driving motor. Rotation of the handle to the right or left swings the turret, and the greater the movement of the handle to left or right, the faster the turret

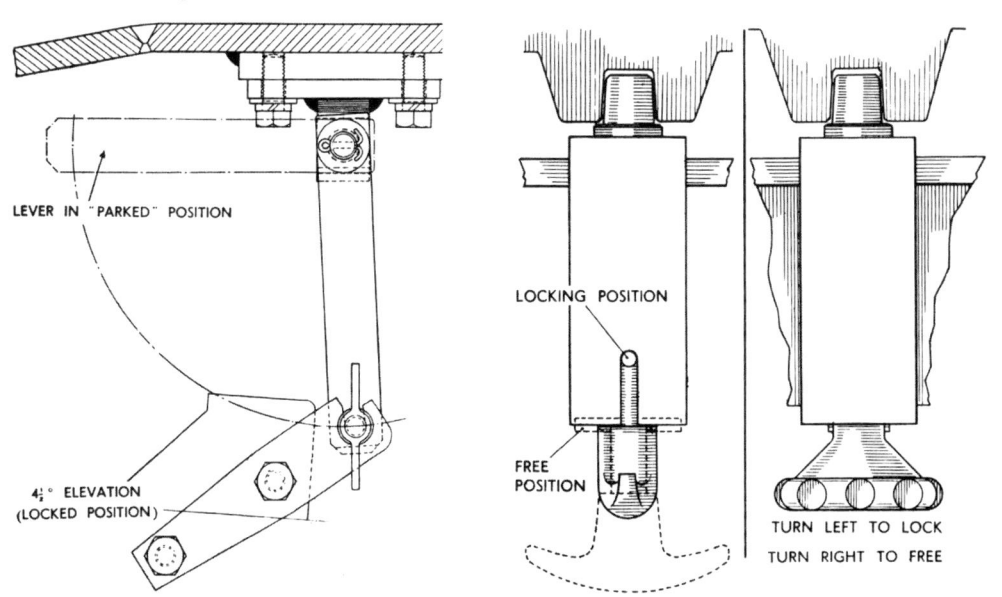

Fig. 61. (Left). Lock fitted to prevent gun mounting movement when travelling. (Right). Lock fitted to prevent turret movement when travelling.

TURRET

swings. When the guns are on the target, the handle is returned to the central position. *Providing the trigger lever on the power traverse handle is kept depressed the braking effect of the driving motor will give a quick stop to the turret.* The trigger lever on the power traverse can be released, however, at the same time as the handle is centred, but the impetus of the turret swing will probably carry the guns past the target.

A turret lock is provided to prevent fidgeting of the turret when travelling. The lock is operated by a spring-loaded handle located on the rear depression cam, *and must be released before attempting to traverse the turret.*

To take all loads off the gun elevating mechanism, a lock is also provided against movement of the gun mounting when the vehicle is travelling and the guns are not being used. This is suspended from the turret roof and consists of a swinging link pivoted at its top end and secured to a bracket on the gun cradle by a wing nut. When not required the link can be folded up parallel to the roof and retained in this position by a spring-loaded catch.

The Wireless Equipment

The wireless set is housed in the turret, and intercommunication between the crew is provided by a telephone installation. This radio and communications equipment is described on page 106.

Stowage

It will be noticed that some stowage fixtures are attached to the turret platform. These bolt on to tapped retaining plates which are secured to the underside of the floor. The purpose is to simplify the removal of any fixtures after the turret assembly is in the tank, and there are no nuts or loose pieces to drop off under the platform.

For method of changing turret traverse gear see Operation B.8 on page 164.

For method of setting gun depression stop adjustments see Operation B.21 on page 179.

TURRET

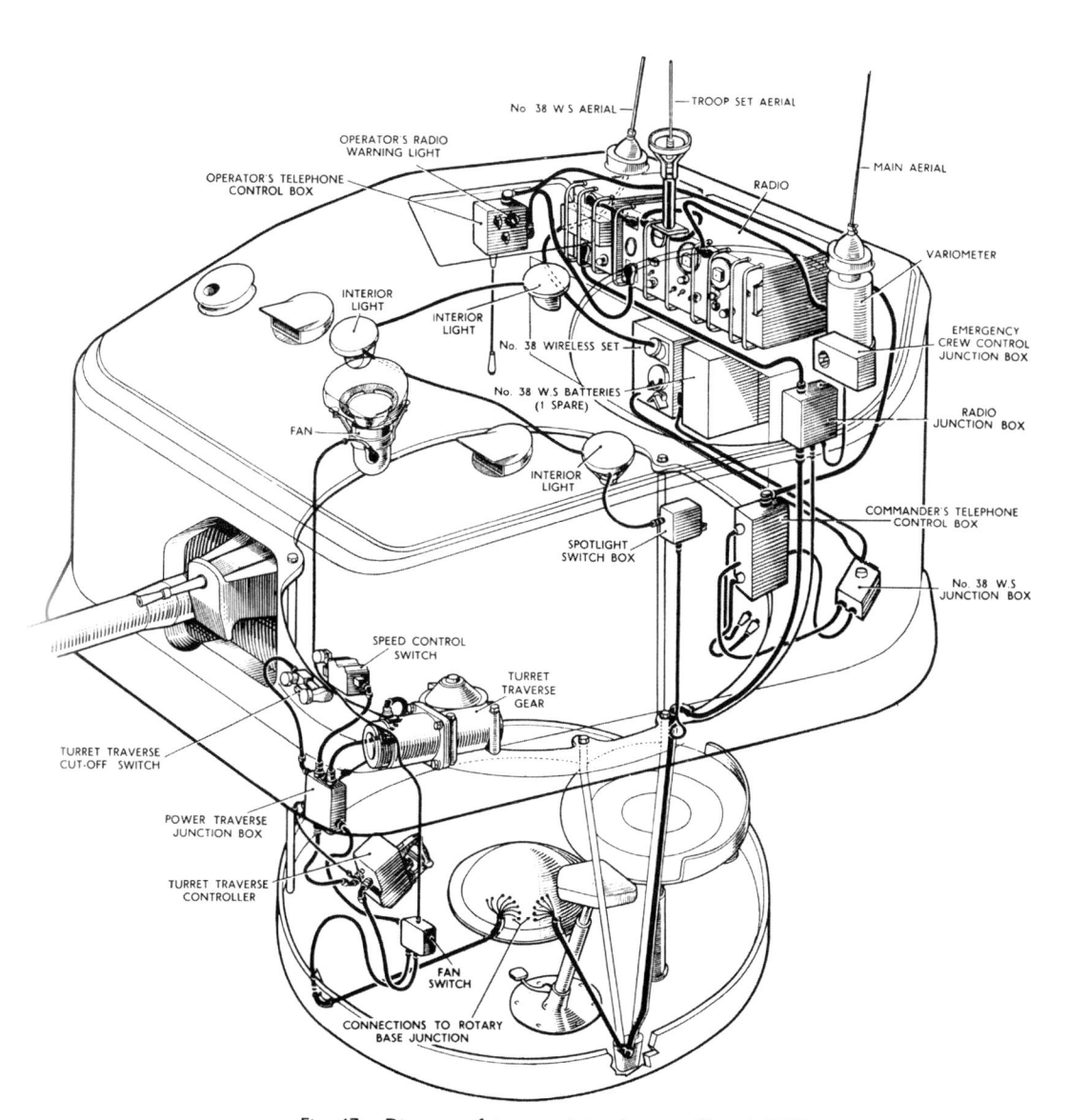

Fig. 67. Diagram of turret wiring layout—Churchill VII.

CHURCHILL TANK

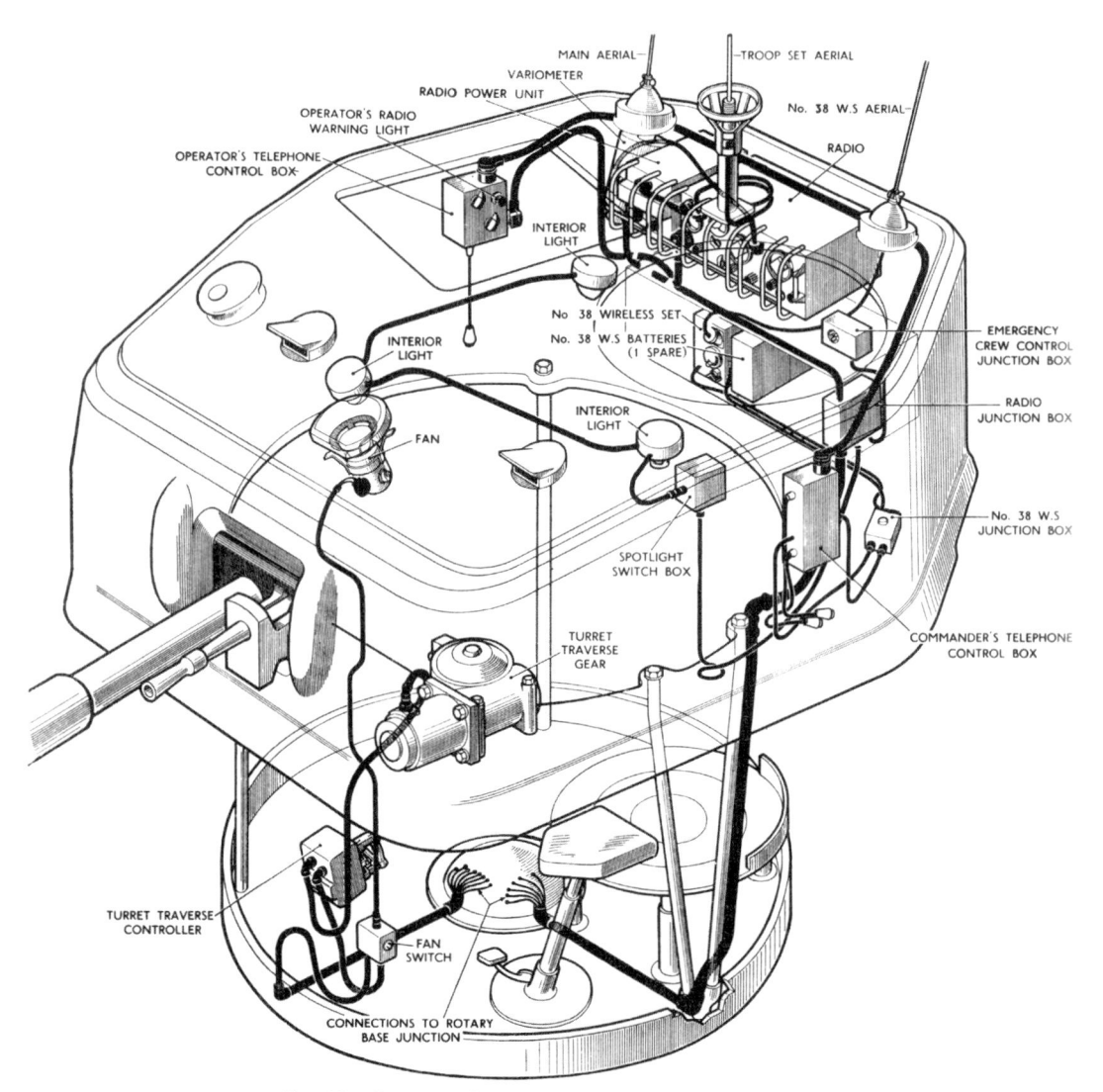

Fig. 68. Diagram of turret wiring layout—Churchill VIII.

CHURCHILL VII AND VIII INSTRUCTION BOOK

ARMAMENT SECTION

Covering

ORDNANCE, Q.F., 75mm. MARK V and VA

AND 7·92mm. BESA M.G.

Fitted to

CHURCHILL VII

AND

ORDNANCE, Q.F., 95mm. TANK HOW. MARK I

AND 7·92mm. BESA M.G.

Fitted to

CHURCHILL VIII

ARMAMENT

75 MM. MARK V OR VA AND 7.92 BESA M.G.
fitted to
CHURCHILL VII

95 MM. HOW. MARK I AND 7.92 BESA M.G.
fitted to
CHURCHILL VIII

The principal armament mounted in the Churchill VII is the Ordnance, Q.F., 75 mm., Mk. V or VA, which is mounted co-axially with a Besa Machine Gun in the turret.

The principal armament mounted in the Churchill VIII is the Ordnance, Q.F., 95 mm. Tank Howitzer, Mark I, which is also mounted co-axially with a Besa Machine Gun in the turret.

Each vehicle also carries a Besa Machine Gun mounted forward in the vehicle in a compartment to the left of the driving compartment, and a 2-inch Bomb-thrower mounted in the roof of the turret to the right of the co-axial mounting.

ORDNANCE, Q.F., 75 MM., MARKS V AND VA

The 75 mm. Marks V and VA guns fire fixed ammunition and are designed for use in tanks as replacement guns for the Ordnance, Q.F. 6-pr. 7-cwt., Marks III and V. The barrel is externally similar to that of the Ordnance Q.F., 6-pr. 7-cwt., Mk. V.

Firing is by percussion, and obturation is effected in the usual Q.F. manner by the radial expansion of the cartridge case in the tapered chamber of the barrel when the gun is fired.

It may be noted that, with the exception of the extractor levers and the firing pin of the striker, the majority of the parts comprising the breech mechanism are identical and, therefore, interchangeable, with similarly named and numbered components of the Ordnance, Q.F. 6-pr., 7-cwt., Marks III and V.

Alternative designs of various parts are introduced from time to time and incorporated in the equipment, usually to simplify manufacture and thus hasten production. Parts of guns in the service may therefore be found to differ in some particulars from those about to be described, but these differences do not usually affect the functioning of the weapon, although they may occasionally concern the user when dismantling or reassembling. Whenever possible, particulars of alternative designs have been given.

Except where stated to be otherwise, terms such as left, right, front, rear, upper and lower describe the position on the assembled gun of the various parts when viewed from the breech end with the gun in the firing position.

PARTICULARS

Diameter, bore	2.953 ins.
Distance to centre of gravity from breech end—	
Barrel	32.15 ins.
Barrel with breech mechanism and muzzle brake	32.6 ins.
Gauge, striker protusion	No. 40 (0.148 ins. to 0.158 ins.)

75mm. GUN

Length—
    Barrel, without muzzle brake ... 107.8 ins.
    Rear face of breech to muzzle brake extremities ... 118.576 ins.

Weights (estimated)—
    Barrel ... 3 cwts, 3 qrs. 2 lbs.
    Breech ring ... 1 cwt. 1 qr. 21 lbs.
    Barrel with breech ring and muzzle brake—
        with breech mechanism ... 6 cwts. 0 qrs. 20 lbs.
        without breech mechanism ... 5 cwts. 1 qr. 16 lbs.

OPERATION

To Load

Open the breech by grasping the breech mechanism lever by the handle portion so as to release the retaining catch lever and pulling the lever downwards to the rear. *Return the breech mechanism lever to the "breech closed" position as soon as the breech is fully opened.* Insert the round, pushing it into the chamber with a sharp movement. The breech will automatically close.

To Fire

Ensure that the selector of the firing gear is set to fire the 75 mm. gun ; press the pedal of the remote firing control gear.

To Unload

Open the breech slowly, using the breech mechanism lever. Extract the round carefully, preventing it falling from the breech opening with the free hand. Replace the round in the ammunition rack. Take the pressure of the actuating spring with the breech mechanism lever, release the extractors using some suitable implement to keep the hand clear of the breech opening and allow the breech block to rise slowly under control of the breech mechanism lever. Ease the firing mechanism by pressing the firing lever on the gun with one hand while controlling the cocking handle with the other.

STRIPPING AND ASSEMBLING

Stripping and assembling is to be done with care and without violence. No unnecessary force is to be employed and every precaution is to be taken to avoid damage. Only those spanners and other implements that are provided with the equipment are to be used, and only for the purpose for which they are designed. When it is necessary to use a hammer, a piece of wood or soft metal should be interposed to transmit the blow.

TO DISMANTLE THE BREECH MECHANISM

Breech Block

With the breech closed, striker cocked and safety-catch at SAFE.

Pull back retaining catch plunger, revolve striker case clockwise for one-sixth of a revolution and remove it. (The breech block can also be removed with the striker case in position.)

Remove keep pin and slotted nut from actuating shaft. Support breech block and withdraw shaft towards left until the breech mechanism lever and rack pinion can be removed. Still supporting the block, complete the withdrawal of shaft and then lower block a little, push up and remove extractor levers and lower block clear of breech ring. Remove the striker cocking link actuating pin, arm of crank and striker cocking link from the breech block.

75mm. GUN

Striker Case

With the striker case removed from the breech block, striker cocked and safety-catch at SAFE.

STRIKER.—Turn safety-catch to FIRE. Grasping cocking handle in one hand and case in the other, press toe of trigger sear inwards to uncock and ease main spring. Remove keep pin and unscrew cocking handle whilst controlling expansion of main spring. Withdraw striker spindle with main spring from case and remove cocking sleeve. Remove firing pin retaining staple. Insert No. 18 drift through hole in rear of spindle head to eject firing pin.

SAFETY CATCH.—Remove keep pin from retaining pin and withdraw latter. Pull catch out to rear. Remove keep pin from the spindle portion of catch and withdraw plunger and spring.

TRIGGER SEAR.—Withdraw sear and spring from left of case. Remove keep pin and withdraw spring seat from right.

ROLLERS.—Remove keep pins from roller axis pins and withdraw axis pins and rollers. (*These are not to be removed as a matter of routine.*)

RETAINING CATCH PLUNGER.—Remove keep pin and head, then withdraw plunger and spring from front of case.

Breech Mechanism Lever (*Not to be removed as a matter of routine*)

Drive out axis pin. Remove retaining catch lever, plunger and spring.

Firing Lever (*Not to be removed as a matter of routine*)

Remove firing lever support plate with its four securing screws from breech ring. Remove keep pin, slotted nut and firing lever from axis stud. To remove roller from firing lever withdraw the keep pin and axis pin and to remove the spring and plunger withdraw the keep pin and collar.

Spring Case (*Not to be removed as a matter of routine*)

With rack pinion removed from actuating shaft, unscrew two fixing screws and slide case downwards to remove it. To dismantle the spring case, remove check screw and unscrew cap. Withdraw bearing disc, spring and rack, from case.

Actuating Shaft Sleeve (*Not to be removed as a matter of routine*)

With the spring case removed, withdraw sleeve from right hand bushed bearing in breech ring.

TO ASSEMBLE THE BREECH MECHANISM

Actuating Shaft Sleeve (*If removed*)

With spring case removed from breech ring, ensure that left and right actuating shaft bushes are correctly assembled in breech ring. Insert sleeve into right-hand bushed bearing in breech ring.

Spring Case (*If removed*)

Place rack and breech block actuating spring in case, with teeth of rack facing aperture for rack pinion. Insert bearing disc in cap and screw cap on case, engaging only a few threads of the screw. Place case in position and secure with its two fixing screws.

Firing Lever (*If removed*)

Assemble the roller with its axis pin and keep pin, and the spring and plunger with its collar and keep pin, on the firing lever. Place the lever on axis stud with

75mm. GUN

roller towards left and secure with slotted nut and keep pin. Position lever on firing lever support plate and secure plate with its four screws.

Breech Mechanism Lever (*If removed*)

Assemble spring in plunger and insert both into hole near top of lever. Insert retaining catch lever in groove in lever with toe at bottom of slot and upper end bearing against head of plunger. Drive in axis pin.

Striker Case

RETAINING CATCH PLUNGER.—Insert plunger and spring from front of case. Attach head and secure with keep pin.

ROLLERS.—Place rollers in their recesses. Insert axis pins and secure with their keep pins, manipulating axis pins with screwdriver as necessary.

TRIGGER SEAR.—Insert spring seat in right of case and secure with keep pin. Insert sear spring and sear from left side of case, with toe of sear to front.

SAFETY CATCH.—Insert plunger with spring from front into arm of catch and secure with keep pins. Insert complete catch into striker case. Insert retaining pin from top of case and secure with keep pin.

STRIKER.—With safety catch at FIRE and whilst pressing sear inward assemble cocking sleeve with its upper arm in its recess in case. Assemble main spring around spindle and insert spindle into case from front, with slot for cocking-sleeve dowel pin on right. Push spindle rearward against pressure of main spring and through cocking sleeve, then screw on cocking handle, making certain that slot in spindle coincides with dowel in cocking sleeve, and secure with keep pin. Insert firing pin into head of spindle and secure with retaining staple, closed end of staple uppermost. Cock striker and turn safety-catch to SAFE.

Breech Block

Ensure that left actuating shaft bush is correctly assembled in breech ring. Insert striker cocking link in its recess in block from rear. Connect arm of crank to striker cocking link with the actuating pin. Insert block a short distance into breech ring from underneath, place in position the two extractor levers with their hooks pointing inwards towards each other and raise block to closed position. Put striker cocking link flush with rear face of breech block, align arm of crank and extractor levers and insert actuating shaft from left. Place breech mechanism lever and rack pinion in position push home the actuating shaft and secure with its nut and keep pin.

With striker cocked and safety-catch at SAFE and uppermost, insert striker case into breech block and turn counter—clockwise until retaining catch plunger engages in its recess. Place safety-catch at FIRE and ease striker.

Screw home cap on spring case until sufficient compression is obtained on breech block actuating spring to close the breech without undue slamming. When correct compression is obtained, insert check screw in spring case to lock the cap.

TO DISMANTLE AND ASSEMBLE MUZZLE RECOIL BRAKE

Remember that the threads on the brake and securing nut and the corresponding threads on the barrel are left-handed.

To dismantle

Straighten those portions of the washer which have been stabbed into the recess in the brake and the two recesses in the securing nut. Unscrew nut to ease it from washer, using a tommy. Then unscrew brake, slip off washer and unscrew nut to remove from barrel.

75mm. GUN

To assemble

Coat threads in brake and securing nut and corresponding threads on barrel with graphited grease.

Assemble nut, washer and brake on barrel. The brake must be screwed fully home, then adjusted so that one of the two axis lines that are cut on its external surface at the rear end coincides with the axis line situated on the top surface of the barrel, immediately behind the muzzle threads. (The muzzle brake will then be as depicted in Fig. 1 with the ports horizontal.) The nut must then be tightly screwed against the washer and brake, the washer afterwards being firmly stabbed into a recess in the brake, and the two recesses in the nut.

TO GAUGE PROTRUSION OF THE STRIKER

The breech block must be removed from the gun. The No. 40 striker protrusion gauge is then applied to the face of the firing-hole bush, with the striker in the fired position. The minimum clearance should foul the firing pin and the maximum should clear it. If either test fails the firing pin must be exchanged.

CARE AND PRESERVATION

The bore of the gun and the muzzle recoil brake are to be cleaned and oiled daily and must be free from rust. The breech is to be open when the bore is being cleaned.

Before firing is commenced the bore is to be visually inspected to ensure that it is clear and clean, and, when circumstances permit, it should also be wiped dry.

Fouling in the bore attracts moisture and hastens the formation of rust. Especial care must be taken to clean out the bore thoroughly after firing ammunition with H.H., F.N.H., F.N.H./P., N.N./S., N.Q. and N./F.Q. propellant charges as they may cause a blue deposit to form in the bore. Fouling must be removed without unnecessary delay and advantage should be taken of lulls during firing for this purpose.

The bore is to be thoroughly washed out and allowed to drain immediately firing has ceased. Fresh hot water should be used whenever available. When the bore is very dirty it may be cleansed with paraffin but the use of soda, in any form, is forbidden. After cleaning, the bore will be dried and, when cool, will be well oiled, the oil being applied with a piece of cloth tied around the piasaba brush. When cleaning has been completed the bore and the chamber are to be inspected, preferably by an officer, and any defects found are to be reported immediately.

If a flaw or a crack in the gun is observed at any time, the gun must be placed out of action to await examination by the E.M.E.

When not actually in use the gun will be depressed to prevent rain or moisture lodging in the bore and the gun will be protected by means of the breech and muzzle covers.

When the accumulation of sand in the bore is a possible contingency and it is necessary that the gun should remain loaded ready for instant action, an improvised sand-proof cover of paper or light cotton fabric will be secured over the muzzle by a length of elastic or string. When circumstances demand the gun may be fired without removing this cover of paper or light cotton fabric.

Care must be taken to avoid damaging the clinometer plane which will be well oiled when the gun is in general use and coated with mineral jelly at other times.

The muzzle recoil brake is to be frequently inspected. Damage, or anything observed to be unusual, is to be reported immediately.

75mm. GUN

The breech mechanism is to be inspected and tested frequently to ensure that it works perfectly and is serviceable in every respect. Any fittings found to be cracked or flawed are to be exchanged immediately, and any burrs on the breech block, or the mortise in which it works, will be removed by an artificer.

The breech fittings will not be stripped more frequently than is necessary to ensure that they are serviceable, clean and lubricated, but, when guns have to be kept ready for action, the striker case will be stripped and cleaned daily, after which a thin film of the approved lubricant will be applied. The use of grease or other incorrect lubricant is forbidden for this purpose as they are likely to seriously diminish the force of blow of the striker and cause the gun to misfire.

More frequent cleaning of the chamber and firing mechanism is necessary when firing nitrocellulose propellants (N.H., F.N.H. and F.N.H./P.) so that any risk of an increased incidence of misfires may be avoided.

The firing-hole bush will only be removed for the purpose of replacement.

In order to prevent damage and reduce wear to a minimum the striker case will be removed from the breech block whenever it is intended to use the service breech mechanism for drill purposes.

Whenever the breech ring or muzzle recoil brake are removed from the gun, the external screw-threads at each end of the barrel and the corresponding threads inside the ring or brake are to be coated with graphited grease before they are re-assembled.

The muzzle brake will be dismantled occasionally and any fouling in the screw-threads of the brake and barrel will be removed to prevent seizure.

All spare parts are to be tested for interchangeability as soon as practicable after they have been received.

LUBRICATION

In order that the gun may operate, and be manipulated, with normal ease and celerity it is generally necessary that the various lubricants employed should be thinned as the temperature falls. The following table indicates the several stages, throughout the range of likely temperatures, where dilution or a change of lubricant will probably be necessary. The table will only be used as a guide. The temperature at which dilution actually becomes necessary, and the extent to which it should be done, must be determined as the result of experience in the field.

The type of kerosene to be used as a diluent is known as burning kerosene, and the proportion should not normally exceed 25 per cent. of the whole. The exact proportion to be used varies with the temperature, and will increase as the temperature falls.

The temperatures quoted are those of the air surrounding the equipment and, due to the effects of radiation or conduction, they will not necessarily coincide with those of the mechanism or part to be lubricated.

Fresh lubricant is not to be applied to an accessible surface until all the old lubricant has been removed. When necessary, kerosene burning oil may be used for that purpose. When oiling has been completed the mechanism is to be operated to ensure the even distribution of the lubricant. Over-lubrication is to be avoided and any surplus is to be at once wiped off to avoid an accumulation of dust or grit that inevitably collects on any oil surface.

All lubricators are to be kept bright. They must be kept free from dirt, and any that become lost or damaged are to be replaced at the first opportunity.

AMMUNITION, 75-mm. GUN

The ammunition for this equipment is obtained from the U.S.A. and is used with the American N2 and M3 75-mm. tank guns.

The ammunition is issued in the form of fixed complete rounds, the word " fixed " signifying that the cartridge case, which contains the propellant charge and primer, is crimped rigidly to the projectile. Each round contains all the ammunition components required for the service of the gun and is loaded as a unit.

The standard types of ammunition most likely to be found with this equipment are given in the tables on pages 21 and 22.

GROUPING

An ammunition lot number is stamped or otherwise marked on each complete round, on all packing containers and on the accompanying ammunition data card. All the rounds in any one lot of ammunition are so assembled as to consist of :—

(a) Projectiles of one lot number (one type and one weight zone).

(b) Fuzes, where applicable, of one lot number.

(c) Primers of one lot number.

(d) Propellant of one lot number.

An ammunition data card is placed in each package of ammunition. When necessary, firing instructions are printed on the reverse of the card.

PACKING

Complete rounds are packed in individual, moisture resistant, fibre containers and then in a wooden packing case or bundle.

PAINTING

All projectiles are painted to prevent rust and, by means of colour, to provide a ready means of identification of type. The colours used are as follows :—

Armour-piercing and
Semi-armour piercing :—

When inert except for tracer ...	Black—markings in white.
With high explosive filling ...	Yellow—markings in black.
High explosive	Yellow—markings in black.
Chemical	Grey—one green band denotes non-persistent gas ; two green bands, persistent gas ; one yellow band, smoke. Markings on the projectile are in the same colour as the band.
Practice	Blue—markings in white. (Projectiles may be inert or may contain a live fuze with a spotting charge of black powder.)
Dummy or drill (inert)	Black—markings in white.

75mm. AMMUNITION

AMMUNITION
Statement of Ammunition

Complete round	Case	Primer	Charge	Projectile	Fuze	Adapter and/or booster	Length inch	Weight lb.	Remarks
SERVICE AMMUNITION Shell, fixed, H.E. M 48, normal charge, w/fuze P.D. H 48, 75-mm. gun.	M 18	M 22	1.13 lb. F.N.H. powder	Shell, H.E. M 48	P.D., M 48	Booster M 20	26.6 (max.)	18.70	Issued fuzed
Shell, fixed, H.E. M 48, normal charge w/fuze T. and SQ., M 54, 75-mm. gun	M 18	M 22	1.13 lb. F.N.H. powder	Shell, H.E. M 48	T.SQ., M 54	Booster M 20	26.6 (max.)	18.70	Issued fuzed
Shot, fixed, A.P.C. M 61, supercharge, with tracer, 75-mm. gun.	M 18	M 31	2 lb. F.N.H. powder	Shot, A.P.C. M 61	—	—	26.28 (max.)	19.36	Fitted with tracer composition
Shot, fixed, A.P. M 72, supercharge, with tracer, 75-mm. gun.	M 18	M 31	1.9 lb. F.N.H. powder	Shot, A.P., M 72	—	—	20.81 (max.)	18.8	Fitted with tracer composition
PRACTICE AMMUNITION Shell, fixed, practice, sand loaded, Mark I, 75-mm. gun (with inert P.D.F., Mk.IV).	M 18	M 22	1.35 lb.	Target practice	P.D., IV, inert fuze	Adapter, Mk. III	—	11.85	Issued fuzed

91

75mm. AMMUNITION

PROJECTILES

Nature	Driving band	Length (without fuze) (inches)	Diameter (inches) Body	Diameter (inches) Band	Weight (lb.) Shell	Weight (lb.) Bursting charge w/o booster	Weight (lb.) Booster nature and weight	Total weight (lb.) filled w/o booster and fuze	Fuze, nature and weight	Remarks
Shell H.E., 75-mm. M 48	Gilding metal	11.291	2.945	3.011 (max.)	10.97	1.49 T.N.T. or 1.36 Amatol and 0.11 T.N.T. booster surround or 1.52 Trimonite	M. 20 0.73	12.46 T.N.T., 12.44 Amatol, 12.51 Trimonite	P.D. M. 48 1.41 lb. or T.SQ. M 54 1.42 lb. (approx.)	—
Shot, A.P.C., 75-mm. M 61 (with tracer)	Gilding metal	13.22 (including wind shield)	At shoulder, 2.945	3.011 (max.)	14.39 (approx.)	—	—	14.4 (approx.)	—	Contains 49 grains of red tracer composition and 20 grains of igniter composition (approx.)
Shot, A.P., 75-mm. M 72 (with tracer)	Gilding metal	9.17 (max.)	At shoulder, 2.945	3.011 (max.)	13.93	—	—	13.94	—	Contains 49 grains of red tracer composition and 20 grains of igniter composition (approx.)

75mm. AMMUNITION

MARKINGS

To facilitate identification, the following will be found on each round of ammunition:

Projectile
- (a) Calibre and type of weapon in which used.
- (b) Filling (T.N.T., W.P., smoke, etc.).
- (c) Mark or model of projectile.
- (d) Weight zone marking when required.
- (e) Lot number. This appears below the rotating band and is obscured by the cartridge case when the round is assembled.

Cartridge case

Stencilled on the Body of the Case, as applicable :—

REDUCED CHARGE—Between two black bands to denote reduced charge; or NORMAL below one black band to denote normal charge; or SUPER to denote supercharge. There is no marking on the body of the cartridge case of the shot, fixed, A.P., M 61, or shot, fixed, A.P., M 72.

On Base of Case :—
- (a) Ammunition lot number and initials of loader.
- (b) Mark or model of projectile.
- (c) NORMAL—Below one diametrical stripe to denote normal charge; or REDUCED and two diametrical stripes at right-angles to denote reduced charge; or SUPER to denote supercharge (whichever is applicable).
- (d) Calibre and model of cartridge case.
- (e) Cartridge case lot number, initials of cartridge case manufacturer and year of manufacture.

    Items (d) and (e) are stamped in the metal.

Fuze (stamped on body) :—
- (a) Type and model of fuze.
- (b) Manufacturer's initials.
- (c) Year of manufacture.
- (d) Lot number.

Percussion Primer—Stamping on Base :—
- (a) Initials of loader.
- (b) Loader's lot number.
- (c) Year of loading.
- (d) M22A3, or as applicable.

WEIGHT ZONE MARKING

M 48 H.E. Shell

Zone	Filled shell and fuze well cup		Mark
	Over	Up to and including	
	lb.	lb.	
L	11·8	12·1	L
1	12·1	12·4	×
2	12·4	12·7	× ×
3	12·7	13·0	× × ×

75mm. AMMUNITION

DESCRIPTION
CARTRIDGE CASE

The case, which contains the propellant charge, tapers slightly towards the mouth. The base has a central hole prepared to receive the primer and is flanged to facilitate extraction.

PRIMER

The primers used with this equipment are a push fit into a central hole through the base of the cartridge case. They are of the percussion type.

The M22A3 percussion primer (Fig. 11) contains about 65 grains of American army black powder. When the firing gear is operated, the point of the firing pin strikes the firing plug with sufficient force to drive it forward and crush the cap against the anvil, thus igniting the cap composition. The resulting flash passes through the holes in the anvil and body of the primer head to ignite the powder which, in turn, ignites the propellant charge.

The M22A2 percussion primer differs from the M22A3 in that the latter has a firing plug with a boss, increasing the over-all height of the plug to 0.229 inches.

The M22A1 percussion primer differs from the M22A2 in that the former has 75 grains of black powder and the latter 65 grains.

The M31 percussion primer differs principally from the M22A1 percussion primer in having 150 grains of American army black powder.

PROPELLANT CHARGE

The propellant charge is made up of F.N.H. powder, which is loaded loose into the cartridge case.

PROJECTILES

General.—The projectiles are classified as high explosive shell and armour piercing or semi-armour piercing shot. They are fitted with a rotating (driving) band which is pressed into a knurled groove near the base. Below the band is a circumferential cannelure into which the mouth of the cartridge case is crimped.

Projectiles are grouped into weight zones in order that the appropriate ballistic correction may be applied, the particular weight zone of each individual projectile

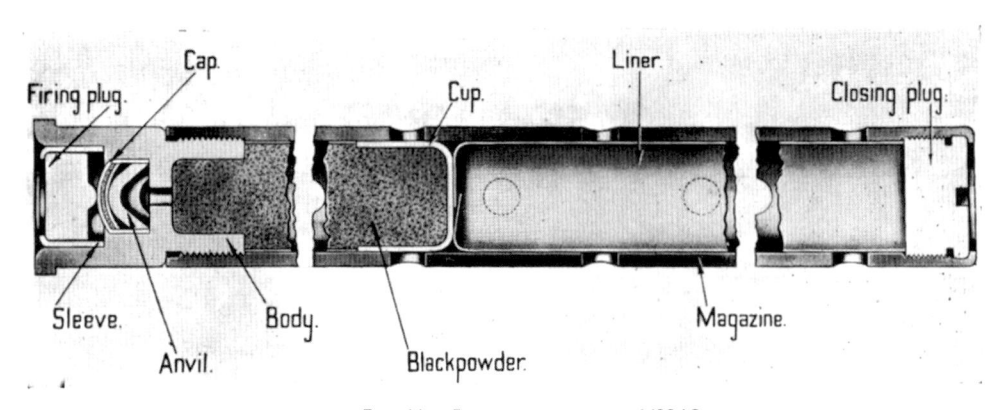

Fig. 11. Percussion primer, M22A3.

75mm. AMMUNITION

being indicated on it by means of one or more crosses or the letter L, depending on the weight of the projectile. A weight zone lighter than one cross is indicated by L. LL indicates a weight zone lighter than L. Two crosses indicate normal weight. Armour piercing projectiles without an explosive filling are machined to correct weight when manufactured.

THE M48 H.E. SHELL (Fig. 12) has a head radius of about 4 calibres and is streamlined at the rear end. A steel circular base cover is welded to the base to prevent the gases from the propellant charge gaining access to the explosive charge in the shell through possible defects in the metal of the base.

The shell may be filled with 1.49 lb. of T.N.T., or 1.36 lb. of 50/50 amatol, or 1.52 lb. of trimonite. Shell filled with 50/50 amatol have a booster surround of T.N.T., weighing about 0.11 lb., placed on top of the amatol. A fuze well cup, of moulded bakelite, is fitted in the booster cavity of shell filled with trimonite.

The M20 booster and M48 or M54 fuze are used with this shell.

THE M61 A.P.C. SHOT (Fig. 13) consists of a body with an armour-piercing cap and a windshield (ballistic cap) covering the cap. When fitted with a windshield the head radius is about 4 calibres.

The base is closed with a screw-threaded base plug which is recessed from the rear face, the recess being filled with a charge of red tracer composition, followed with igniter composition and closed with a celluloid cup.

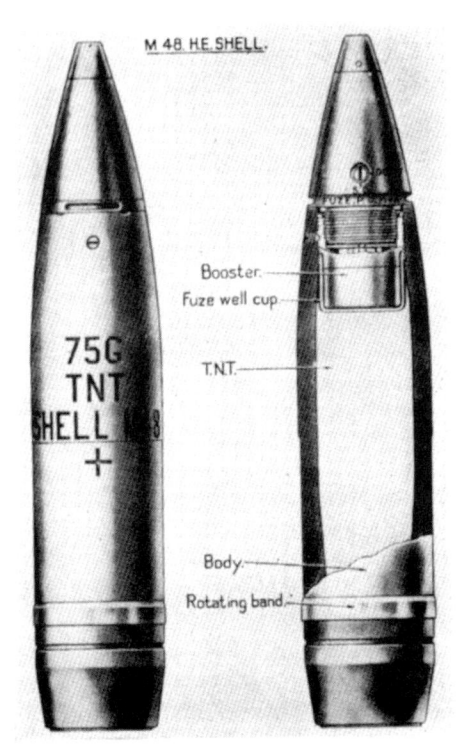

Fig. 12. Shell, H.E., M48.

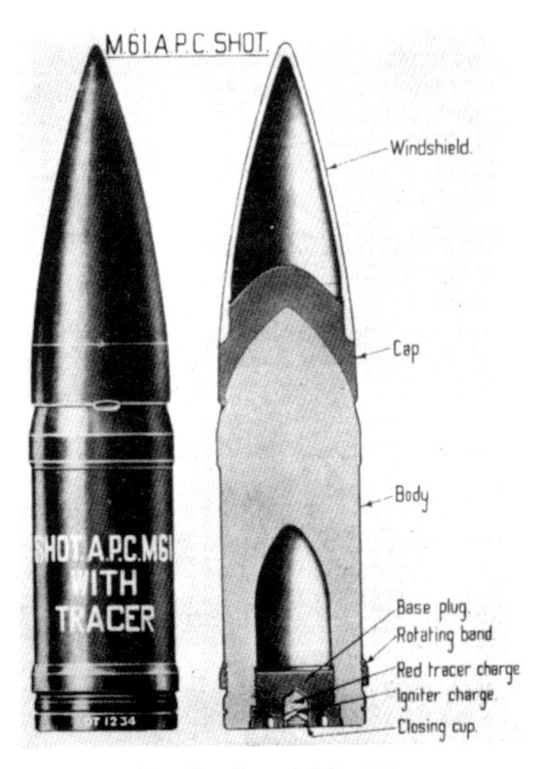

Fig. 13. Shot, A.P.C., M61.

75mm. AMMUNITION

The M 72 A.P. shot is solid except for a small tracer cavity in the base. It has an ogival head of approximately 2 c.r.h. and is streamlined at the rear end. The tracer cavity is filled with a charge of tracer composition, followed by igniter composition, and closed with a celluloid closing cup.

BOOSTERS

General.—A booster consists essentially of an explosive contained in a case which is located between the bursting charge of a high explosive shell and its fuze. The booster, which is initiated by the fuze, ensures the complete detonation of the bursting charge.

The M20 booster (Fig. 14) is threaded externally to screw into the head of the M 48 H.E. shell and internally to receive the fuze.

Action

On firing.—The lock pin sets back against its spring, clear of the centrifugal pin.

During flight.—Due to centrifugal force the centrifugal pin moves outwards, compressing its spring and permitting the rotor to move around its pivot until it strikes the rotor stop pin and brings its detonator coincident with the flash channel of the fuze. When in this position, a rotor lock pin, which is housed in a hole in the periphery of the rotor, moves outwards under a centrifugal force into a recess in the body to lock the rotor.

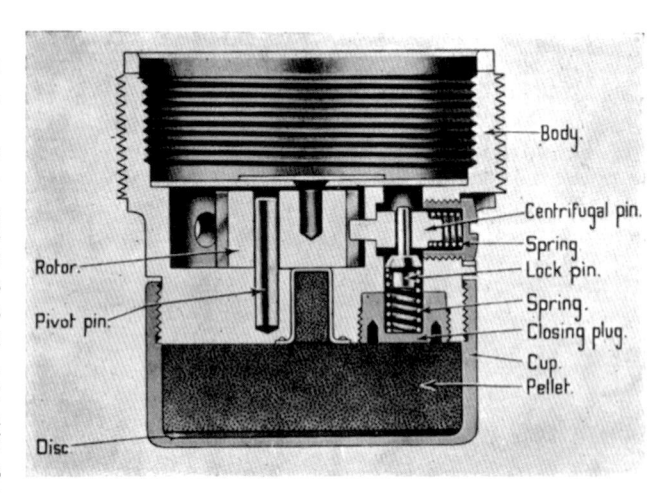

Fig. 14. Booster, M20.

As the shell decelerates a rotor lock pin lock, which is housed in a hole in the rotor, moves forward by creep action and engages in rear of the rotor lock pin to obstruct the latter and thereby prevent it moving inward.

On impact.—The fuze initiates successively the rotor detonator, the pellet in the booster body and the booster charge, the latter detonating the bursting charge in the shell.

The M20A1 booster is similar to the M20, differing only in having a larger diameter flash hole.

FUZES

The M48 point detonating fuze (Fig. 15) is a combination type that can be used to give either direct action or graze action with delay.

A slotted setting sleeve is inserted into a hole near the base of the fuze and on the exterior near the sleeve are two lines, one parallel to the longer axis of the fuze, the other at right angles thereto. The line parallel to the longer axis is marked S.Q. (denoting superquick), the other DELAY. To give direct action it is set to S.Q., and to give delay on impact or graze, it is set to DELAY.

75mm. AMMUNITION

The fuze is issued with the sleeve set to S.Q., and when delay action is required it is necessary to turn the setting sleeve, with a screwdriver or similar implement, until the slot is in prolongation with the line marked DELAY. The setting may be made at any time prior to loading, even in the dark, by noting the direction of the slot in the sleeve.

The setting sleeve is so designed that when set to S.Q. the spring cup is in direct contact with the interrupter, but when set to DELAY one of the legs of the setting sleeve obstructs the eccentrically located interrupter, thus preventing the latter from moving outwards.

The delay action will operate if a fuze set to S.Q. fails to function as intended, but when the fuze is set to DELAY the superquick action is always stopped at the interrupter.

To prepare for firing

Turn the setting sleeve so that the slot is in prolongation with the lines marked S.Q. or DELAY, whichever is required.

Action of fuze

ON FIRING.—On acceleration the interrupter is unable to fly outwards due to set-back and the inclination of its channel. The plunger support sets back and engages the centrifugal plunger pins and thus prevents the primer in the plunger body making contact with the delay firing pin.

DURING FLIGHT.—When acceleration ceases, the interrupter, under centrifugal force, flies outwards against the spring cup, compressing its spring, and thereby unmasks the central channel in the body of the fuze.

When set at DELAY

ON IMPACT.—The firing pin in the head of the fuze is forced inwards, crushing the support, until the point of the firing pin penetrates the detonator, thereby initiating a detonating wave that passes directly to the detonator of the booster.

If for any reason the superquick action fails to function, the delay element will operate as described hereafter.

When set at S.Q.

DURING FLIGHT.—When acceleration ceases the centrifugal pins fly outwards compressing their springs, but the plunger head and plunger body are still held apart by means of the spring that surrounds the plunger support.

ON IMPACT.—Immediately the progress of the shell is retarded the plunger body moves forward, overcoming the spring and carrying the primer on to the delay firing pin, thus firing the primer. The flash from the primer passes around the baffle, igniting in turn the delay, the relay and the detonator in the booster.

THE M54 TIME AND SUPERQUICK FUZE (Fig. 16) combines the characteristics of an igniferous time fuze with those of a direct action, percussion fuze. It contains a safety wire (safety pin) which must be withdrawn before the round is loaded into the gun.

The time rings, graduated for 25 seconds, are generally similar to those of other igniferous time fuzes.

The fuze is issued with the time ring set at S, denoting safe, and when time action is desired it is set to the required time of burning, which must be greater than 0.4 seconds, by means of a fuze setter. An internal device in the fuze prevents the time action from functioning should the fuze inadvertently be set for a time less than 0.4 seconds.

75mm. AMMUNITION

The device consists of a safety disc which in those circumstances masks the ignition end of the powder train in the graduated time train ring and prevents the flash reaching the powder pellet in the body.

The percussion portion of the fuze is always operative, once the gun has been fired, and if a fuze set to a given time fails to function as desired the percussion portion will do so on impact. When percussion action is required the time ring must be set at S, or for some time of burning greater than the expected time of flight.

If a fuze is prepared for firing and not used the safety wire must be replaced in the fuze before the round is returned to its container.

To prepare for firing

TIME ACTION.—Set the fuze at the graduation ordered. Withdraw the safety wire before loading.

DIRECT ACTION.—Ensure that the fuze is set at S. Withdraw the safety wire before loading.

Time action of fuze

ON FIRING.—The plunger sets back, shearing the shear pins and bending the primer striker against the primer. The resultant flash ignites in turn the powder pellet and powder train in the upper time train ring.

DURING FLIGHT.—The power train in the upper time train ring burns round until, after an interval of time determined by the setting, it ignites the powder pellet in the graduated time train ring. The pellet transmits the flame to the powder train of this ring. In due course this powder train burns and communicates the flame to the powder pellet in the body, and the flash from this pellet reaches the magazine and passes thence to the detonator of the booster.

Percussion action of fuze

ON FIRING.—On acceleration the interrupter is unable to fly outwards due to set-back and the inclination of its channel.

DURING FLIGHT.—When acceleration ceases, the interrupter, under centrifugal force, flies outwards against its spring, thereby unmasking the central channel in the body of the fuze.

ON IMPACT.—The firing pin is forced inwards, crushing the support, until the point of the firing-pin penetrates the detonator, thereby initiating a detonating wave that passes directly to the detonator of the booster.

ORDNANCE, Q.F., 95-mm. TANK HOWITZER, MARK I.

The howitzer fires fixed ammunition and is designed for use in tanks. Firing is by percussion and obturation effected in the usual Q.F. manner by expansion of the cartridge case in the tapered chamber of the barrel, when the howitzer is fired.

With the exception of the breech block, firing lever and extractor levers, the majority of the parts comprising the breech mechanism are interchangeable with similarly named and numbered components of the Ord. Q.F. 25-pr., Mark II.

Alternative designs of various parts are introduced in the equipment, usually to simplify manufacture and thus hasten production. Parts of howitzers in the service may therefore be found to differ in some particulars from those described, but the differences do not usually affect the functioning of the weapon, although they may affect dismantling or assembling. Where possible, particulars of alternative designs are given.

Except where otherwise stated, terms such as left, right, front, rear, upper and lower describe the position on the assembled howitzer of the various parts when viewed from the breech end.

PARTICULARS

Gauges used—
    Clearance firing-hole bush to cartridge ... ... No. 36
    Striker protrusion ... ... No. 16
Protrusion of striker ... ... 0.11 to 0.09 in.
Length—
    Barrel ... ... 80.47 in.
    Howitzer with breech mechanism and counterweight ... ... 85.52 in.
Weight—
    Barrel ... ... 3 cwt. 2 qrs. 6 lb.
    Body with counterweight
        With breech mechanism ... ... 7 cwt. 2 qrs. 27 lb.
        Without breech mechanism ... ... 6 cwt. 3 qrs. 14 lb.
    Counterweight ... ... 1 cwt. 1 qr. 12 lb.
Shipping dimensions ... ... 7 ft. 5¼ in. × 1 ft. 7 in. × 1 ft. 2 in. = 13.75 c. ft.

OPERATION

To load

Open the breech by grasping the breech mechanism lever by the handle portion so as to release the retaining catch lever and pulling the lever downwards to the rear. Insert the round, pushing it into the chamber with a sharp movement. The breech block will be raised sufficiently to retain the cartridge in the chamber. Close the breech by returning the breech mechanism lever until it is held by the retaining catch.

To fire

Ensure that the selector of the firing gear is set to fire the howitzer; press the pedal of the firing gear.

To unload

Open the breech slowly using the breech mechanism lever. Extract the round carefully, preventing it falling from the breech with the free hand. Replace the round in the ammunition rack. Take the pressure of the buffer spring with the breech mechanism lever, release the extractors and close the breech by returning the breech

95mm. HOWITZER

mechanism lever until it is held by the retaining catch. Ease the fixing mechanism by pressing the firing lever on the howitzer with one hand whilst controlling the cocking handle with the other.

STRIPPING AND ASSEMBLING

This is to be done with care and without violence; no unnecessary force is to be employed and every precaution is to be taken to avoid damage. Only spanners and other implements provided with the equipment are to be used and only for the purpose for which they are designed. When it is necessary to use a hammer, a piece of wood or soft metal is to be interposed to transmit the blow. The firing-hole bush will not be removed except for replacement purposes.

TO DISMANTLE THE BREECH MECHANISM

Breech block

With the breech closed, the mechanism cocked and the safety catch at SAFE:—

(a) Pull back the retaining catch plunger, revolve the striker case clockwise for one-sixth of a revolution and remove it. (The breech block can also be removed with the striker case in position).

(b) Withdraw the split pin, turn the locking screw clockwise to the full extent, slide the bracket downward and remove complete the breech block buffer. When necessary withdraw the split pin, remove the plunger nut, plunger and spring of the buffer.

(c) Support the breech block and pull the breech mechanism lever rearward until the block is clear of the breech ring.

Intermediate cocking lever

With the breech block removed from the howitzer:—

(a) Remove the split pin from the axis pin and withdraw the latter.

(b) Remove the lever.

Breech mechanism lever

(a) Withdraw the split pin, remove the nut from the actuating shaft and withdraw the lever from the shaft.

(b) Withdraw the keep pin from the collar of the retaining catch. Remove the catch and the actuating lever.

(c) Remove the retaining screw and withdraw the plunger and spring.

Actuating shaft

With the breech block removed from the breech ring and the breech mechanism lever from the shaft:—

(a) Support the extractor levers and crank and drive the shaft out of the breech ring, using a No. 27 drift when necessary and taking care to avoid damaging the screw-threads.

(b) Remove the extractor levers and crank.

(c) Withdraw the sleeve from the bushed hole in the right side of the breech ring.

Striker case

With the striker case removed from the breech block, the mechanism cocked and the safety catch at "SAFE":—

(a) COCKING LEVER—Remove the retaining screw, withdraw the axis pin and lever.

95mm. HOWITZER

(b) STRIKER—Turn the safety catch to " FIRE." Grasping the cocking handle in one hand and the case in the other, press the toe of the sear inward to uncock. Remove the split pin and unscrew the cocking handle whilst controlling the expansion of the main spring. Remove the cocking sleeve and withdraw the striker spindle with the main spring from the case. Remove the firing pin retaining staple. Insert a number 18 drift into the recess in the rear of the spindle head to eject the firing pin.

(c) SAFETY CATCH—Remove the retaining screw and pull the catch out to the rear. Withdraw the split pin from the plunger spindle to remove the plunger and spring.

(d) TRIGGER SEAR—Withdraw the sear and spring from left side of the case. Remove the split pin and withdraw the spring seat from the right.

(e) ROLLERS—These are secured by stabbing the metal of the case into the screwdriver slots and are not to be removed as a matter of routine.
In case of necessity they are to be removed and replaced by a gun fitter.

(f) RETAINING CATCH PLUNGER—Remove the split pin and head. Withdraw the plunger and spring from the front of the case.

Firing lever
(a) Remove the split pin and slotted nut
(b) Remove the lever from the axis stud.

TO ASSEMBLE THE BREECH MECHANISM

Firing lever
(a) Place the lever on the axis stud with straight edge of the long arm to the left.
(b) Replace the slotted nut and split pin.

Striker case

(a) RETAINING CATCH PLUNGER—Insert the plunger with the spring from the front of the case. Attach the head and secure with a split pin.

(b) TRIGGER SEAR—Insert the spring seat in the right side of the case and secure with a split pin. Insert the spring and sear from the left side of the case with the toe of the sear to the front.

(c) SAFETY CATCH—Insert the plunger with the spring from the front into the arm of the catch and secure with a split pin through the plunger spindle. Insert the complete catch into the striker case and secure with the retaining screw. Manipulate the sear whilst turning the catch to SAFE.

(d) STRIKER—Assemble the main spring around the spindle and push the latter into the case from the front against the pressure of the spring. See that the spindle is correctly positioned to receive the cocking sleeve and place the latter on the end of the spindle. Turn the safety catch to FIRE. Enter the arm of the cocking sleeve into the recess in the striker case, press the toe of the sear inward and push the sleeve home to engage the arm of the sleeve in the slot of the sear. Screw on the cocking handle and secure with a split pin. Insert the firing pin into the head of the striker spindle and secure with the retaining staple, closed end of the staple uppermost. Cock the striker, turn the safety catch to " SAFE."

(e) COCKING LEVER—Place the boss of the lever between the lugs with the thinner end of the lever uppermost within the slot through the striker spindle, rounded surfaces of the lever to rear. Insert the axis pin and secure with the retaining screw.

95mm. HOWITZER

Actuating shaft
With the breech block removed from the breech ring and the breech mechanism lever removed from the shaft :—
- (a) Insert the shaft into the left bushed bearing in the breech ring and assemble the left extractor lever, crank, and right extractor lever on the shaft, from inside the breech ring, in that order.
- (b) Insert the sleeve into the bushed bearing in the right side of the breech ring and push the shaft fully home.

Breech mechanism lever
- (a) Insert the plunger with the spring and secure with the retaining screw.
- (b) Insert the actuating lever into the recess in the handle with the rounded corner uppermost and outside the recess.
- (c) Secure the actuating lever in the recess by passing the spindle of the catch through the hole in the breach mechanism lever and square hole in actuating lever ; the arm of the catch to be in the recess in the inner surface of the breech mechanism lever and pointing rearward.
- (d) Place the collar around the end of the spindle and secure with a split pin.
- (e) Place the complete lever on the actuating shaft, both lever and crank in closed position, and secure with the nut and keep pin.

Intermediate cocking lever
- (a) Insert the boss of the lever between the lugs of the bracket on the rear of the breech block with the roller arm in the slot through the breech block, the roller to the left ready to enter the cam groove in the right face of the crank.

Breech block
- (a) Pull the breech mechanism lever rearward, past the fully open position, and with the extractor levers vertical, enter the block from underneath into the guides through the breech ring.
- (b) Manipulate the breech mechanism lever until the crank enters the slot in the breech block.
- (c) Lift the breech block and carry the breech mechanism lever forward until the weight is taken by the lever. Close the breech by continuing the forward movement of the lever until the retaining catch engages the stop stud on the breech ring. The roller on the intermediate cocking lever will enter the groove in the crank as the breech is closed.
- (d) Insert the plunger and spring in the bracket of the breech block buffer and secure with the nut and split pin.
- (e) Ensure that the head of locking screw is flush with the side of the breech ring. Insert the bracket into the recess and slide forward until the locking screw is visible.
- (f) Turn the locking screw anti-clockwise until the split pin can be inserted through the bracket and the circumferential groove in the locking screw.
- (g) With the mechanism cocked and the safety catch at " SAFE " and uppermost insert the striker case into the breech block and turn anti-clockwise until the retaining catch is engaged in the recess. Put the safety catch to FIRE and ease the striker main spring.

95mm. HOWITZER

MUZZLE COUNTERWEIGHT (*See Fig.* 17, *page* 37)

Frequent removal and replacement of the counterweight is to be avoided.

To dismantle, remove securing screw with spring washer and turn counterweight clockwise, as viewed from the front (left hand thread).

When replacing, ascertain that the tapped hole in the counterweight correctly registers with the hole in the barrel before inserting and securing screw with the spring washer in position.

JAMMED MECHANISM

If the breech is opened fully with the striker case removed from the breech block the roller on the intermediate cocking lever may leave the cam groove in the crank and thus jam the mechanism. This may be remedied by the combined manipulation of the breech mechanism lever and intermediate cocking lever.

TO GAUGE PROTRUSION OF STRIKER

With the breech block containing the striker case removed from the gun, and the striker in the fired position, apply the No. 16 protrusion gauge to face of the firing-hole bush. The minimum clearance should foul the firing pin and the maximum should clear it.

If either test fails the firing pin must be exchanged.

CARE AND PRESERVATION

The bore of the howitzer is to be cleaned and oiled daily and must be kept free from rust. The breech is to be open when the bore is being cleaned.

Before firing is commenced the bore is to be visually inspected to ensure that it is clear and clean, and, when circumstances permit, it should also be wiped dry.

Fouling in the bore attracts moisture and hastens the formation of rust. It must be removed without unnecessary delay and advantage should be taken of lulls during firing for this purpose.

The bore is to be thoroughly washed out and allowed to drain immediately firing has ceased. Fresh hot water should be used whenever it is available. When the bore is very dirty it may be cleaned with paraffin but the use of soda, in any form, is forbidden. After cleaning, the bore will be dried and, when cool, will be well oiled, the oil being applied with a piece of cloth tied around the piasaba brush. When cleaning has been completed the bore and chamber are to be inspected, preferably by an officer, and any defects found are to be reported immediately.

If a flaw or a crack in the howitzer is observed at any time, the howitzer must be placed out of action to await examination by the E.M.E.

When not actually in use the howitzer will be depressed to prevent moisture gaining access to the bore and the howitzer will be protected by means of the breech and muzzle covers.

When accumulation of sand in the bore is a possible contingency and it is necessary that the howitzer should remain loaded ready for instant action, an improvised sand-proof cover, of paper or light cotton fabric, will be secured over the muzzle by a length of elastic or string. When circumstances demand, the howitzer may be fired without removing this cover of paper or light cotton fabric.

Care must be taken to avoid damaging the clinometer plane which will be kept oiled when the howitzer is in general use and coated with mineral jelly at other times.

95mm. HOWITZER

The breech mechanism is to be inspected and tested frequently to ensure that it works perfectly and is serviceable in every respect. Any fittings found to be cracked or flawed are to be replaced immediately and any burrs on the breech block, or the mortice in which it works, will be removed by a gun fitter.

The breech fittings will not be stripped more frequently than necessary to ensure that they are serviceable, clean and lubricated, but, when the howitzer has to be kept ready for action, the striker case will be stripped and cleaned daily, after which a thin film of approved lubricant will be applied. The use of grease or other incorrect lubricant is forbidden for this purpose as they are likely to seriously diminish the force of blow of the striker and cause the howitzer to misfire.

In order to prevent damage and reduce wear to a minimum the striker case will be removed from the breech block whenever it is intended to use the service breech mechanism for drill purposes.

Whenever the muzzle counterweight is removed from the howitzer the external screw-threads at the end of the barrel and the corresponding threads inside the counterweight are to be coated with graphited grease before they are reassembled.

LUBRICATION

In order that the howitzer may operate, and be manipulated, with normal ease and celerity, it is generally necessary that the various lubricants employed should be thinned as the temperature falls. The following table indicates the several stages, throughout the range of likely temperatures, where dilution or a change of lubricant, will probably be necessary. The table will only be used as a guide and the temperature at which dilution actually becomes necessary and the extent to which it should be done, must be determined as the result of experience in the field.

The type of kerosene to be used as a diluent is known as burning kerosene and the proportion should not normally exceed 25 per cent of the whole. The exact proportion to be used varies with the temperature, and will increase as the temperature falls.

The temperatures quoted are those of the air surrounding the equipment and, due to the effects of radiation or conduction, they will not necessarily coincide with the mechanism or part about to be lubricated.

Fresh lubricant is not to be applied until the old lubricant has been removed and, when necessary, kerosene burning oil may be used for that purpose. When oiling has been completed the mechanism is to be operated to ensure the even distribution of the lubricant. Over-lubrication is to be avoided and any surplus is to be at once wiped off to avoid an accumulation of dust or grit that will otherwise collect on the oiled surfaces.

Changes in lubricants will be ordered by Force Headquarters when considered necessary.

AMMUNITION 95 MM. TANK HOWITZER

PRIMER, PERCUSSION, Q.F. CARTRIDGES, No. 1, MARK II

THE PRIMER (Fig. 25) is fitted to the cartridges of all ammunition used with this equipment. It has a short magazine and contains the copper ball type of sealing device.

When the firing gear is operated the cap is struck by the point of the firing pin, so that the contained composition is pinched between the anvil and the interior of the cap and thus fired. The resulting flash passes through the fire holes in the anvil and plug to ignite the powder in the magazine, which in turn ignites the propellant charge. The soft copper ball is driven to the rear and the primer body is expanded radially so preventing the escape of gas through the fire channels and past the screw-threads that secure the primer in the cartridge case.

CARTRIDGE CASE

THE CARTRIDGE CASE (Fig. 26) of solid drawn brass, has the rear portion tapered towards the front to suit the contour of the howitzer chamber whilst the front portion is cylindrical to fit over the base of the projectile to which it is secured by identations engaging a cannelure and the front extremity being closed into a groove immediately in rear of the driving band of the projectile.

The base is bored centrally and screw-threaded to receive a No. 1 percussion primer whilst an external flange is formed to be engaged by the extractor levers of the breech mechanism to eject the case after firing.

The case contains the propellant charge held in position at the rear by the projecting primer and at the front by a paper sleeve.

PROPELLANT CHARGE

THE PROPELLANT CHARGE, for use with the H.E. projectile, consists of 12 oz. 4 dr. of W.M. 042 cordite.

The cordite is cut into lengths of nearly five inches and about one-third of the charge is formed into a bundle and tied at the centre with sewing silk. This forms the core. The remaining two-thirds is arranged circumjacent to the core and secured towards each end with sewing silk.

The core protrudes at the front and enters the paper sleeve whilst the recess at the rear accommodates the front end of the primer.

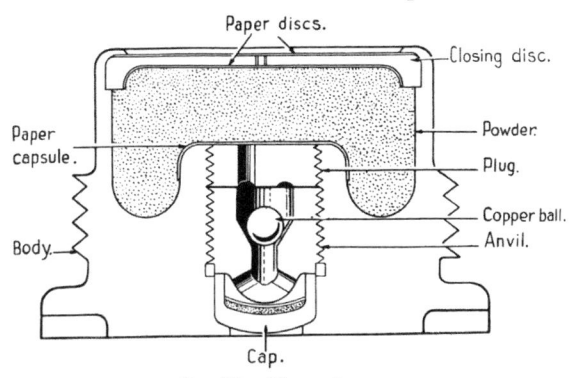

Fig. 25. The primer.

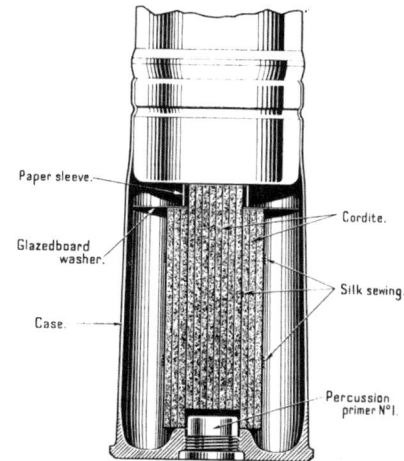

Fig. 26. Cartridge case.

95mm. AMMUNITION

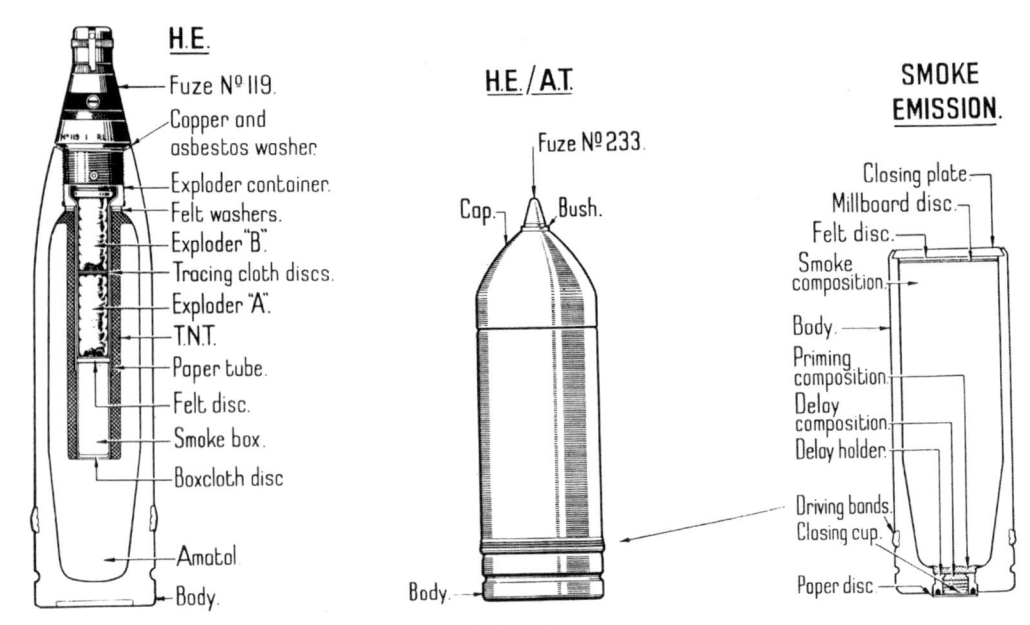

Fig. 27. Shell, H.E., H.E./A.T., and smoke emission.

The weight of charge and size of cordite for use with other projectiles can be obtained from the appropriate Range Table.

SHELL, Q.F., HIGH EXPLOSIVE, 95 MM. TANK AND S.P. HOWITZERS, MARK IA

THIS SHELL (Fig. 27) is filled with amatol and has a head that is curved to a radius of four calibres. It is fitted with a nose fuze and has a steel plate that is screwed or riveted into a recess prepared in the base.

The shell body is provided near the base with a driving band and below it is a cannelure to which the cartridge case is secured.

A boxcloth disc is inserted into the bottom of a cavity, lined with pure T.N.T. that is formed in the shell filling immediately below the screw-threaded fuze hole, and a smoke box, surmounted by a felt disc, is located immediately above it. From a little below the top of the smoke box the upper portion of the cavity in the T.N.T. is lined with a paper tube containing the closed lower end of an exploder container that is screwed into the nose end of the shell above one or more waxed felt washers. An A type exploder of C.E. or T.N.T. is inserted into the container followed by a B type exploder containing similar substance and the shell is completed by screwing home a No. 119B, Mark IV fuze.

SHELL, Q.F., H.E./A.T., 95 MM. TANK HOWITZER

THIS SHELL (Fig. 27) which is filled with 50/50 pentolite, has a nose fuze and an internal base tracer. The body is provided near the base with a driving band and below it is a cannelure to which the cartridge case is secured. The body is hollow and open at both ends, the upper portion being reduced in external diameter to accommodate a cap whilst a central hole through the base is prepared with a left hand screw-thread to take a No. 17 tracer (Fig. 28).

95mm. AMMUNITION

A bush, screw-threaded internally to take a No. 233 D.A. percussion fuze is secured in a central hole at the top of the cap.

SHELL, Q.F. SMOKE EMISSION, 95 MM. TANK HOWITZER MARK I

This shell (Fig. 27) which is filled with smoke composition, is flatheaded and is provided with a delay holder that screws into the base and serves as an igniter for the contents of the shell.

The body of the shell is provided near the base with a driving band, below which is a cannelure for securing the cartridge case. The body is hollow and open at both ends, the mouth being increased in internal diameter to receive a closing plate whilst a central hole through the base is prepared with a left-hand thread to take a delay holder.

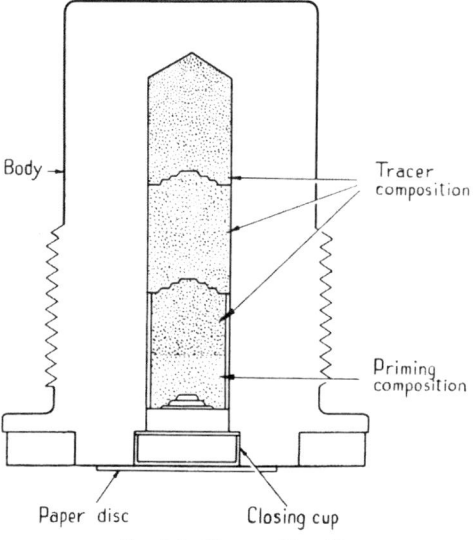

Fig. 28. Tracer, No. 17.

The upper surface of the smoke composition is covered with one or more millboard discs above which is a disc of felt and the closing plate. The plate has a bevelled upper corner and rests on the internal shoulder prepared near the mouth of the body where, after the joint has been made with cement, the lip of the body is pressed over the plate to secure it in position and seal the mouth of the shell.

The delay holder, which has two keyholes for fixing purposes, is filled with a delay composition consisting of two layers, each of a different priming composition, above a third layer of gunpowder, giving a delay of 5 seconds.

A celluloid closing cup is pressed into the delay holder, below the gunpowder, and secured there with cement. A layer of priming composition, in the base of the shell cavity, is interposed between the bottom of the smoke composition and the inner surface of the delay holder. Before the delay holder is screwed home the threads are coated with cement and after finally screwing home the base is covered with a disc of bakelised paper secured to it with cement.

FUZE, D.A. AND PERCUSSION, No. 119

This fuze (Fig. 29) is a combined direct action and graze fuze. It has two distinguishing bands around the body, one knurled and the other coloured black.

To prepare for firing

The steel cap has a label bearing the instruction " THE CAP SHOULD BE LEFT ON WHEN THE TARGET IS BEHIND COVER." It is not to be removed from the fuze until the shell, to which it is fitted, is prepared for firing. It may then be removed, or allowed to remain in position, the decisions depending upon the nature of the target about to be engaged.

The brass striker cover under the cap is NEVER to be removed and a label on it bears the warning " DO NOT REMOVE."

CHURCHILL TANK

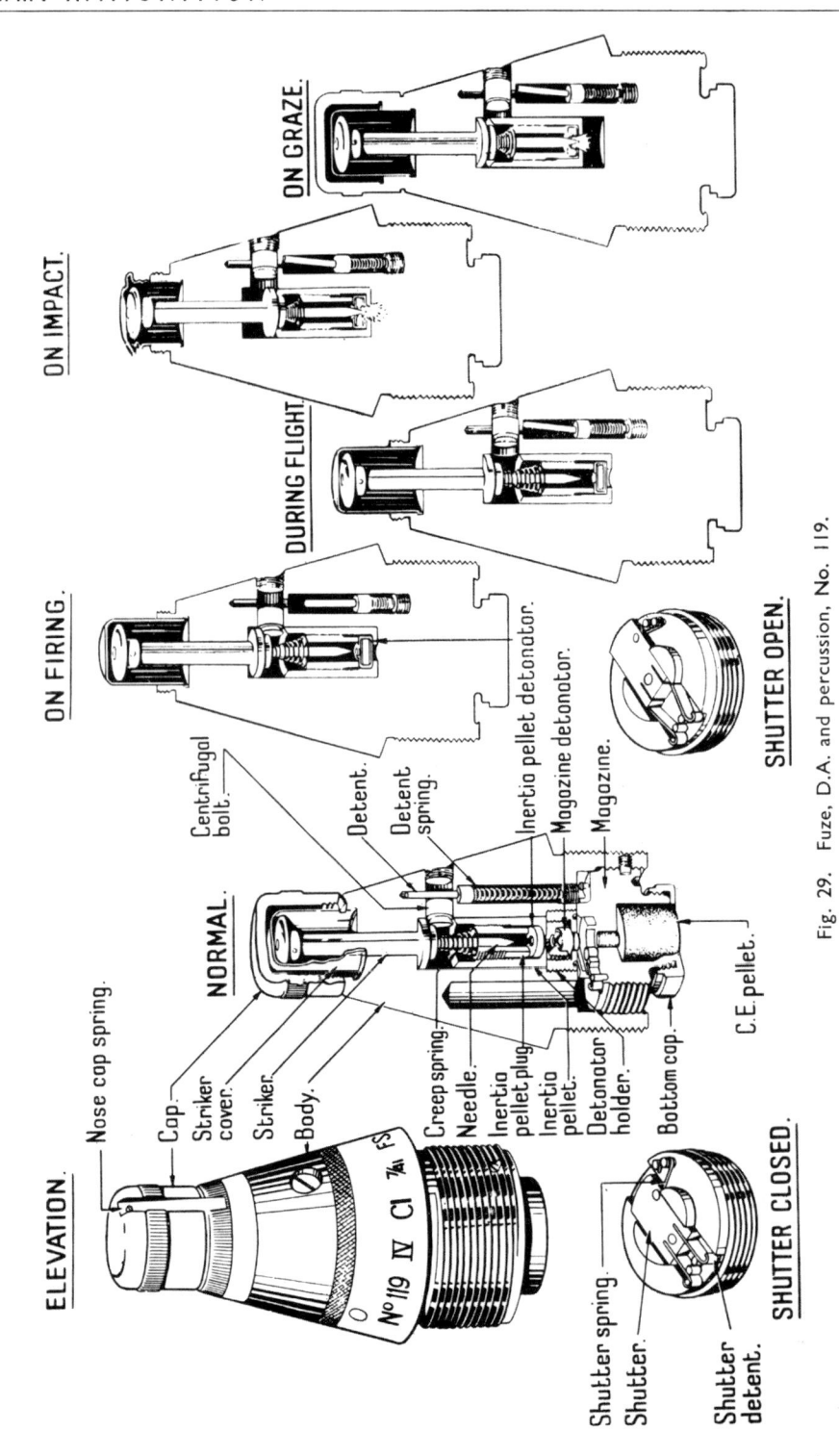

95mm. AMMUNITION

Fig. 29. Fuze, D.A. and percussion, No. 119.

95mm. AMMUNITION

Action of Fuze

On firing:—Due to the acceleration of the projectile the striker and detent set back, compressing the creep and detent springs respectively, until the shaped under-surface of a flange around the striker engages a similarly shaped portion of the centifugal bolt, thus preventing its movement, and the stem of the detent tilts under the shoulder in the detent bore. The shutter remains closed, due to friction caused by set-back, thus ensuring safety in the bore should either of the detonators function prematurely.

During flight:—When acceleration ceases the striker moves forward, helped by the creep spring, and centrifugal force now causes the shutter and the released centrifugal bolt to move outward, the former bringing a channel filled with stemmed C.E. into alignment with the detonators in the fuze. The shutter is retained in the open position by its detents. The inertia pellet now has a tendency to creep forward due to deceleration, but this tendency is resisted and checked by the creep spring.

On impact (cap off):—The fuze usually functions by direct action, the striker being driven inward and its point piercing the detonator in the inertia pellet. The resulting flash causes the magazine detonator to function and a detonating wave passes via the stemmed C.E. in the channels of the shutter and magazine, to the pellet in the latter and thence to the bursting charge in the shell.

If, due to the small angle of arrival or other causes, the striker is not driven in, the fuze will function by graze action. When this happens the inertia pellet with its detonator moves forward on to the point of the striker, immediately the projectile is retarded, and the detonator is fired. Except for the slight delay, that is inherent in fuzes functioned by graze action, all subsequent events are as previously described.

On impact (cap on):—Against light cover the striker is rendered inoperative by the presence of the cap and the fuze will function by graze action. Immediately the progress of the shell is retarded the inertia pellet travels forward carrying the detonator on to the striker point with the result already described.

FUZE, PERCUSSION, D.A., No. 233, MARK I

THIS FUZE (Fig. 30) is of the direct action, strikerless, detonating type. It is screwed into the bushed nose in the cap of the HE/AT shell where the plain portion of the fuze body, below the screw threads, is located in the central hole through the internal diaphragm of the cap.

The fuze body has an enlarged conical head, with a rounded tip, and the major circumference of the head is prepared with two flats to accept the key with which the fuze is assembled to the shell. A portion of the exterior, just below the flats, is prepared with screw-threads to suit the bush in the shell cap whilst a smaller portion at the bottom is reduced in diameter, the resulting shoulder being chamfered, and the bottom edge rounded.

The remaining length of fuze, beneath the head, is cylindrical and parallel.

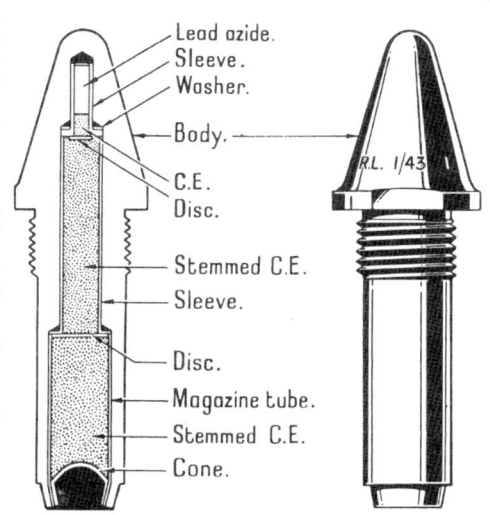

Fig. 30. Fuze, percussion, D.A., No. 233, Mk. I.

95mm. AMMUNITION

The body is hollowed internally, to three successively lesser diameters, commencing with the largest at the bottom. The part of least diameter, nearest the nose, contains a sleeve having an external flange around the bottom. The flange is accommodated in the middle chamber of the bore and a brass washer, semi-circular in section, is interposed between the flange and a shoulder in the body. This upper sleeve is filled with lead azide above a lower and thinner layer of exploding composition, both of which are pressed into the sleeve. The lead azide, which occupies approximately three-quarters of the available space, is topped with shellac varnish whilst at the bottom, the C.E. is covered with a paper disc.

A second similar but larger sleeve, filled with stemmed C.E., is contained in the larger chamber of the bore whilst the lowest and largest is filled with a magazine tube that is kept from contact with the flange of the sleeve above it by means of a metal disc.

The magazine tube is filled with three equal increments of stemmed C.E. and closed at the bottom with a cone which is secured in the interior of the tube with varnish, closed end uppermost.

The whole of the contents of the fuze is secured in position by a coning process which has the effect of still further reducing the diameter at the bottom of the fuze whilst forcing the contained sleeves and tube nearer the nose until the washer against the flange of the upper sleeve is pressed flat and the lip of the cone in the tube is brought flush with the base of the fuze.

When being transported the portion of the fuze below the head is contained in a paper tube which affords protection for the screw-threads.

Action

On impact with the target the lead azide in the upper sleeve is detonated by concussion and the resulting detonating wave proceeds via the C.E. in the sleeves and tube to the exploder system in the shell.

7.92 MM. BESA MACHINE GUNS
MARKS II, II*, III, III*

Reference numbers on figures used with the Besa gun are, for identification purposes, common to the Instruction Book for Armourers and drawing D.D.(E.) 2631.

The 7.92 mm. Besa Machine Gun used in A.F.V.'s is an air-cooled gas-operated weapon with buffered action, ammunition being supplied by a belt holding 225 rimless cartridges. The mark of the gun is stamped on the left side of the gun body.

The Mk. II gun is made as an A.F.V. weapon.

The Mk. II* gun is a transitional pattern between the Mk. II and Mk. III.

The Mk. III gun has a fixed high rate of fire.

The Mk. III* gun has fixed low rate of fire.

The 7.92 mm. Besa M.G. is intended for mounting in A.F.V.'s, has no ground mounting or sights, and aiming is carried out by means of a sighting telescope housed in the gun mounting.

The barrel cannot be changed unless the gun is removed from the A.F.V. mounting.

The gun can be fired dismounted provided the ejection opening is clear of the ground.

PARTICULARS

Approximate weight complete		48 lb. (varies according to mark).
Approximate weight of barrel		15 lb. (varies according to mark).
Overall length		3 ft. 7½ in.
Length of barrel with flash eliminator		2 ft. 5 in.

Rates of fire (rounds per minute)—

	High	Low	
Mark II	750/850	450/550	Without
Mark II*	750/850	450/550	Accelerator
Mark III	750/850	—Fixed accelerator	
Mark III*	—	600	No accelerator

OPERATION

To Load :—Grasp the pistol grip with the right hand with fingers clear of the trigger and pull back the trigger guard until the cocking catch lever can be pressed down with the thumb. Slide the trigger guard forward as far as it will go, then pull it back until retained by the cocking catch. The gun will then be cocked.

Pass the tag of the belt through the feed block from the right and pull to the left as far as it will go. The gun is then ready to fire. Tuck the end of the tag into the metal chute on the left side of the cartridge case deflector.

To Fire :—Ensure that the selector is set to M.G. fire and press the pedal of the foot firing gear.

Firing will continue until the pedal is released or the end of the belt reached. If the belt is expended, the gun must be cocked again before leading in a fresh belt.

To Unload :—With the gun cocked hold back the trigger guard, pull out the cover locking pin, raise the cover and hold it open by the ring suspended over the gun; remove the belt, see that the chamber is clear, lower the cover and engage the locking pin. Pull back the trigger guard, slightly depress the cocking catch lever and ease the working parts forward under control. With the trigger squeezed, pull the trigger guard back, release the trigger and draw the trigger guard right back until retained by the cocking catch.

CHURCHILL TANK

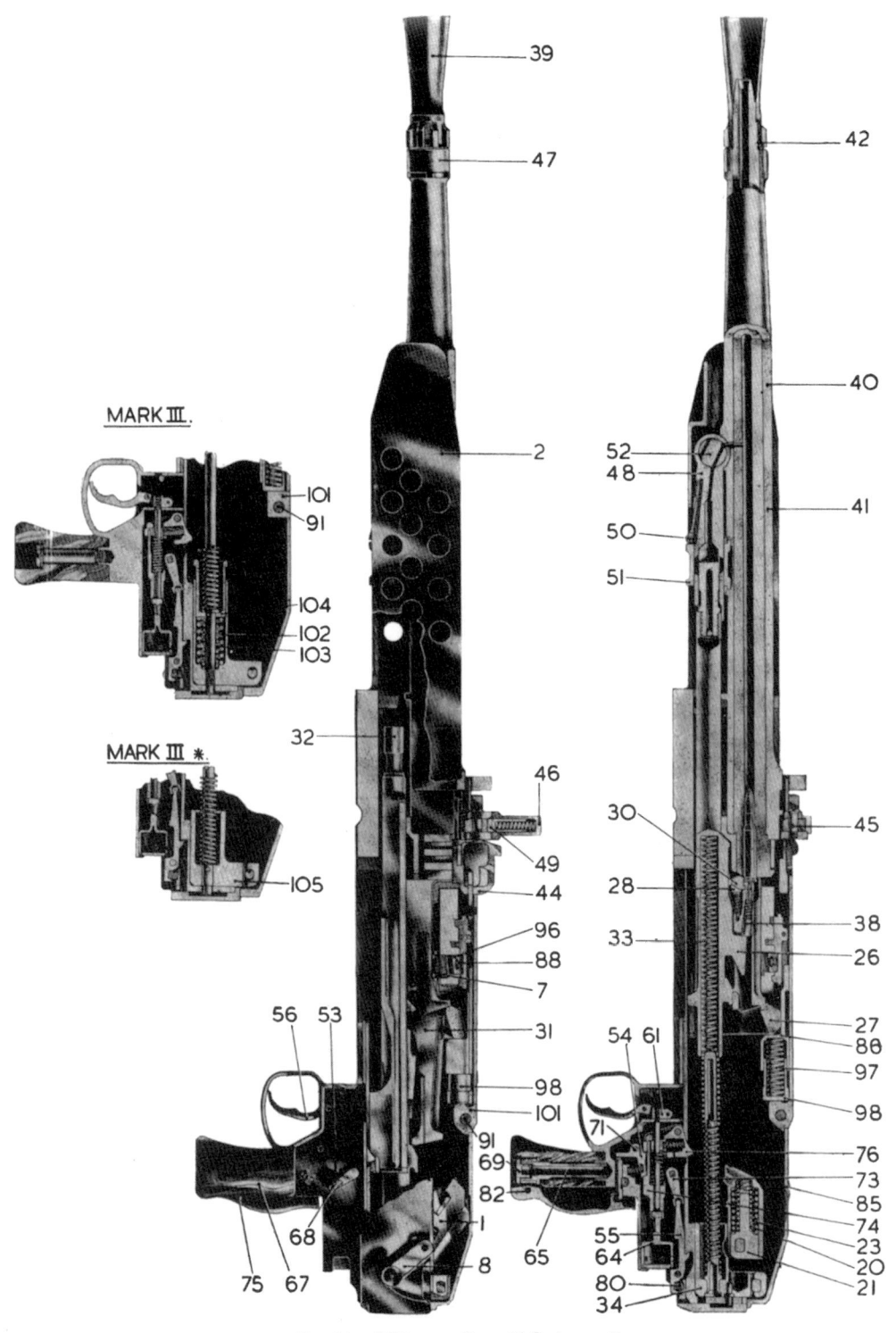

Fig. 31. **7.92** mm. Besa M.G. in section.

VEHICLE HISTORY AND SPECIFICATION

7.92mm. BESA M.G.

BARREL GROUP

BODY GROUP

PISTON & BREECH BLOCK GROUP

COVER GROUP

TRIGGER GUARD GROUP

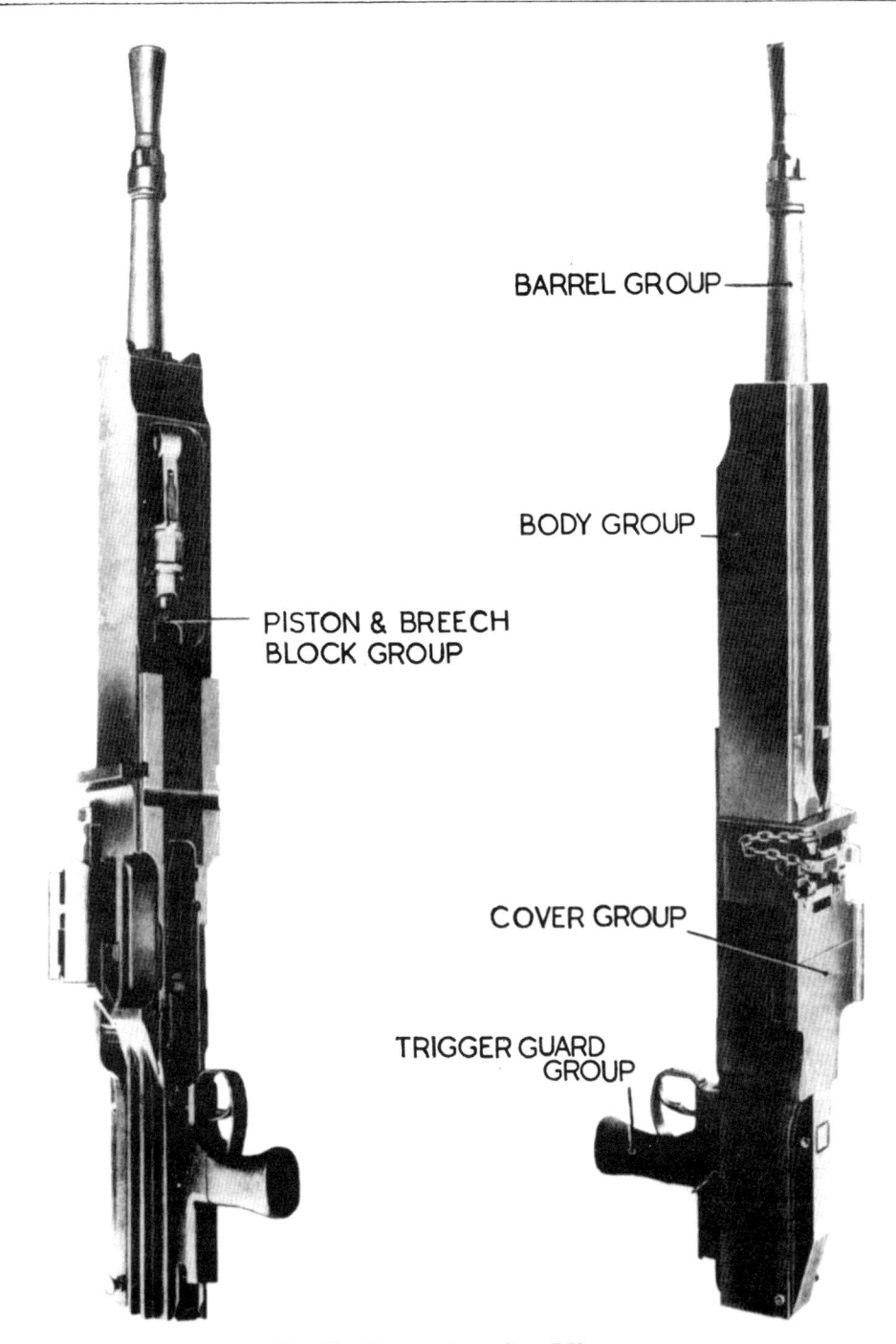

Fig. 32. Gun, machine, Besa 7.92 mm.

7.92mm. BESA M.G.

DESCRIPTION

7.92 MM. BESA MACHINE GUN

Main Parts, Mk. III*

The Besa 7.92 mm. machine gun, Mark III*, comprises the following main groups: Body (see Fig. 33), Piston and Breech Block (see Fig. 34), Barrel (see Fig. 35), Trigger Guard (see Fig. 36) and Cover (see Fig. 37).

A brief description of the main differences from guns of the preceding marks is given at the end of this description.

The Body

The body (Fig. 33 (2)) forms a protector and front support for the barrel (Fig. 35 (41)) and a housing for the breech mechanism. The base of the body is of dovetail cross-section to slide in the gun mounting, a transverse groove in the base receiving the recoil bolt to retain it. Immediately above the mounting base of the M.G. are a pair of trunnions for attachment of the cover plate (Fig. 37 (85)) which closes the top rear half of the body and protects the breech mechanism. A carrying handle (Fig. 35 (46)) is fitted into either of two recesses dependent upon the position it is desired to carry the gun, *i.e.* horizontally or vertically. A feed block (Fig. 34 (19)) is fitted in the right-hand side of the body and provides an entry for the cartridge belt which, after extraction of the cartridges during its passage through the M.G., leaves the body by way of a belt guide (Fig. 27 (5)). A slide on the underside of the body, which extends from the rear to the ejection opening, carries and guides the trigger guard (Fig. 36 (53)) during the cocking action which is effected by sliding the trigger guard to the front, and then back to its normal position at the rear.

The baffle plate (Fig. 33 (6)) slides into slots in the body in front of the carrying handle lugs and serves as a protection against splash.

Piston and Breech Block

The piston is formed in two parts, a piston stem (Fig. 34 (32)) and a piston extension (Fig. 34 (26)), the piston stem at its front being part cylindrical to fit a gas cylinder (Fig. 35 (48)) and threaded at its rear end to engage the piston extension. The piston extension at the rear half has a longitudinal passage for the reception of the return spring (Fig. 34 (33)), the front half of the extension being slotted for the passage of the empty cartridge cases. Longitudinal ribs are provided at each side of the piston extension to fit grooves in the barrel extension (Fig. 34 (27)) permitting the piston to slide to and fro during firing. The upper part of the piston extension towards the rear has a piston post which at the front strikes the firing pin (Fig. 34 (38)) and at the rear part constitutes an unlocking cam. The piston breech block (Fig. 34 (31)) fits the top of the piston extension in front of the piston post, a raised locking cam being formed at the rear top surface of the piston extension.

The breech block is of the rising and falling type, actuated by the cams on the piston extension, the movement of the breech block in the barrel extension being controlled by guide ribs. A central longitudinal hole in the breech block houses the firing pin and spring, the underside is recessed to receive the extractor (Fig. 34 (30)), extractor stay (Fig. 34 (28)) and spring, and the centre hollowed to accommodate the piston post. A rib on the top of the breech block feeds the cartridge from the belt into the breech chamber. A rear upper part of the breech block is formed with a lug which is raised into engagement with a locking shoulder on the barrel extension, and subsequently lowered by the locking and unlocking cams of the piston extension.

VEHICLE HISTORY AND SPECIFICATION

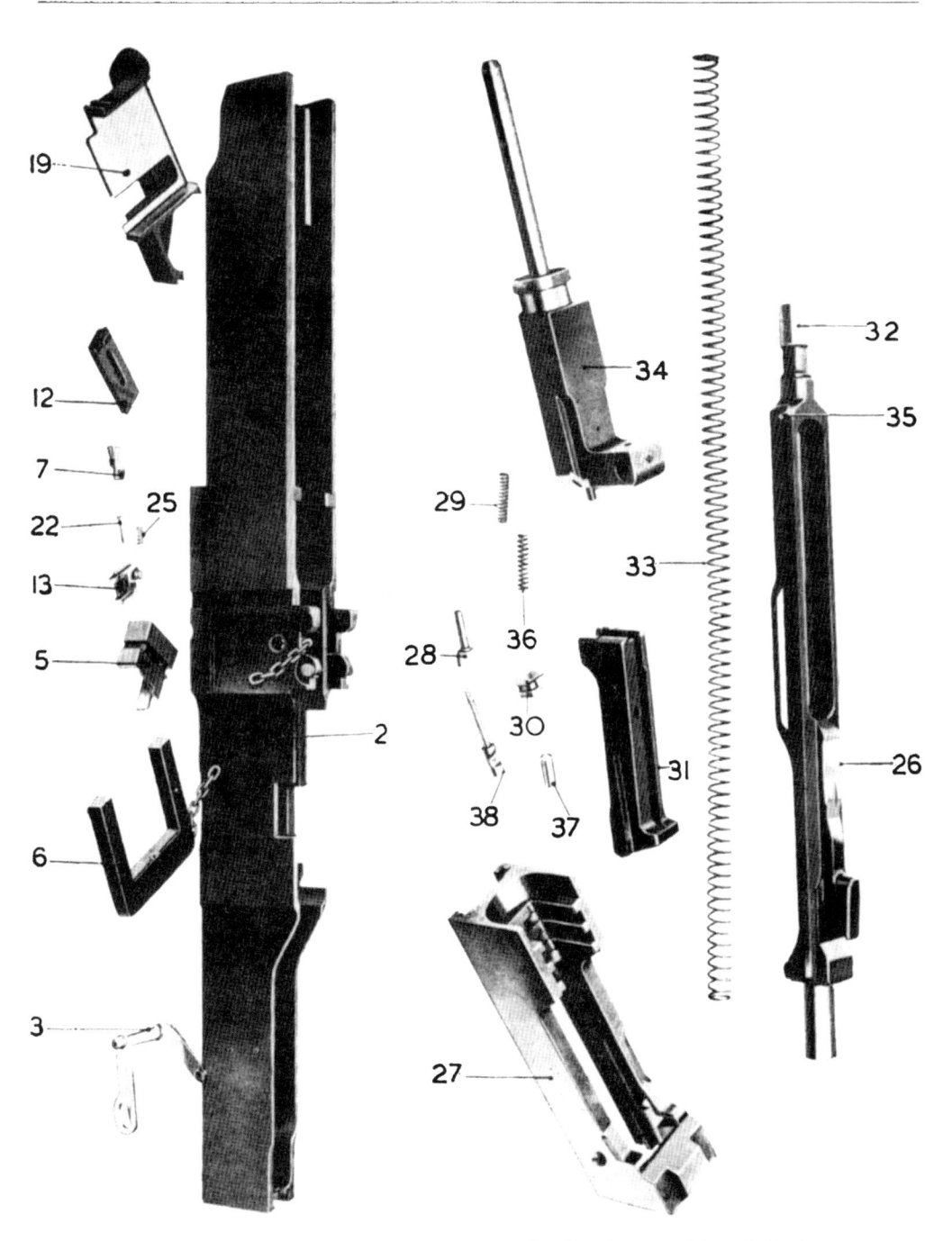

7.92mm. BESA M.G.

Fig. 33. Body group—Besa 7.92 mm. M.G.

Fig. 34. Piston and breech block group—Besa 7.92 mm. M.G.

115

7.92mm. BESA M.G.

THE RETURN SPRING (Fig. 34 (33)), housed within the piston extension, is guided by a return spring guide (Fig. 34 (34)) consisting of a block and rod. The block is slotted to engage locating ribs in the body. The cover locking pin extends through the block and the lower part of the block is recessed to receive the end of the return spring. The rod is secured to the block and extends through the centre of the spring to form a guide.

The Barrel

The breech end of the barrel (Fig. 35 (41)) has a series of tenons which engage slots in the barrel extension (Fig. 34 (27)) to lock the barrel. A steel barrel sleeve (Fig. 35 (40)) pressed over the barrel to absorb heat of firing, is fitted at the front with a flash eliminator (Fig. 35 (39)) and at the rear with a barrel retainer (Fig. 35 (44)) which locks with slots in the body. A carrying handle (Fig. 35 (46)) attached to the barrel retainer, is used for operating and locking the retainer and removing the barrel when hot. The barrel is supported at the front on guides in the body. The gas cylinder (Fig. 35 (48)), sleeve (Fig. 35 (51)) and the gas regulator (Fig. 35 (52)) are fitted to the underside of the barrel sleeve.

The barrel extension, which receives the breech end of the barrel, is slotted, full length, on the underside to provide a slide for the piston extension (Fig. 34 (26)) and the centre hollowed out to receive the breech block (Fig. 34 (31)) which is controlled in the forward movement, imparted by the piston post, by ribs which slide in channels in the barrel extension. Two internal studs give the breech block its initial rising movement. A bridge portion at the rear of the barrel extension forms the locking shoulder against which the breech block abuts when lifted by the piston extension.

The gas cylinder (Fig. 35 (48)) has a knuckle front end which fits a housing in the barrel sleeve and is recessed to receive the gas regulator (Fig. 35 (52)). The rear end of the gas cylinder is given a lead for the entry of the piston and is cut at an angle to deflect the escaping gases downwards. A port adjacent to the gas regulator directs gases from the barrel to the regulator, which then travel to the front of the cylinder to exert pressure on the piston to initiate the action of the gun. The gas cylinder is held in place by a gas cylinder sleeve (Fig. 35 (51)) which embraces the gas cylinder and fits a slot in the underside of the barrel sleeve.

The gas regulator (Fig. 35 (52)) is of cylindrical shape to fit the housing in the gas cylinder and is held in place by a lug and slot device. Ports of different sizes are drilled through the regulator and may be placed in corresponding positions to align with the gas port in the barrel.

Trigger Guard

The trigger guard body (Fig. 36 (53)) is carried in a slide on the underside of the body and is held by the cocking catch (Fig. 36 (55)). The trigger (Fig. 36 (56)), trigger shaft (Fig. 36 (64)), sear (Fig. 36 (76)), cocking catch and associated components, are housed within the trigger guard which may be removed complete as a unit after raising the trigger guard catch at the rear of the body. The thumbpiece (Fig. 36 (68)) of the cocking catch is on the left-hand side of the trigger guard. A pistol grip (Fig. 36 (67)) is bolted to the base of the guard.

The Cover

The cover (Fig. 37 (85)) closes the rear half of the body and protects the breech mechanism, two hooked projections at the front hinging on trunnions on the body. A locking pin (Fig. 37 (94)) holds the cover in place. A transverse channel is provided on the underside to accommodate the cartridge guide (Fig. 37 (89)), which has ribs to slide in slots in the sides of the channel. The front and rear recoil spring casings

7.92mm. BESA M.G.

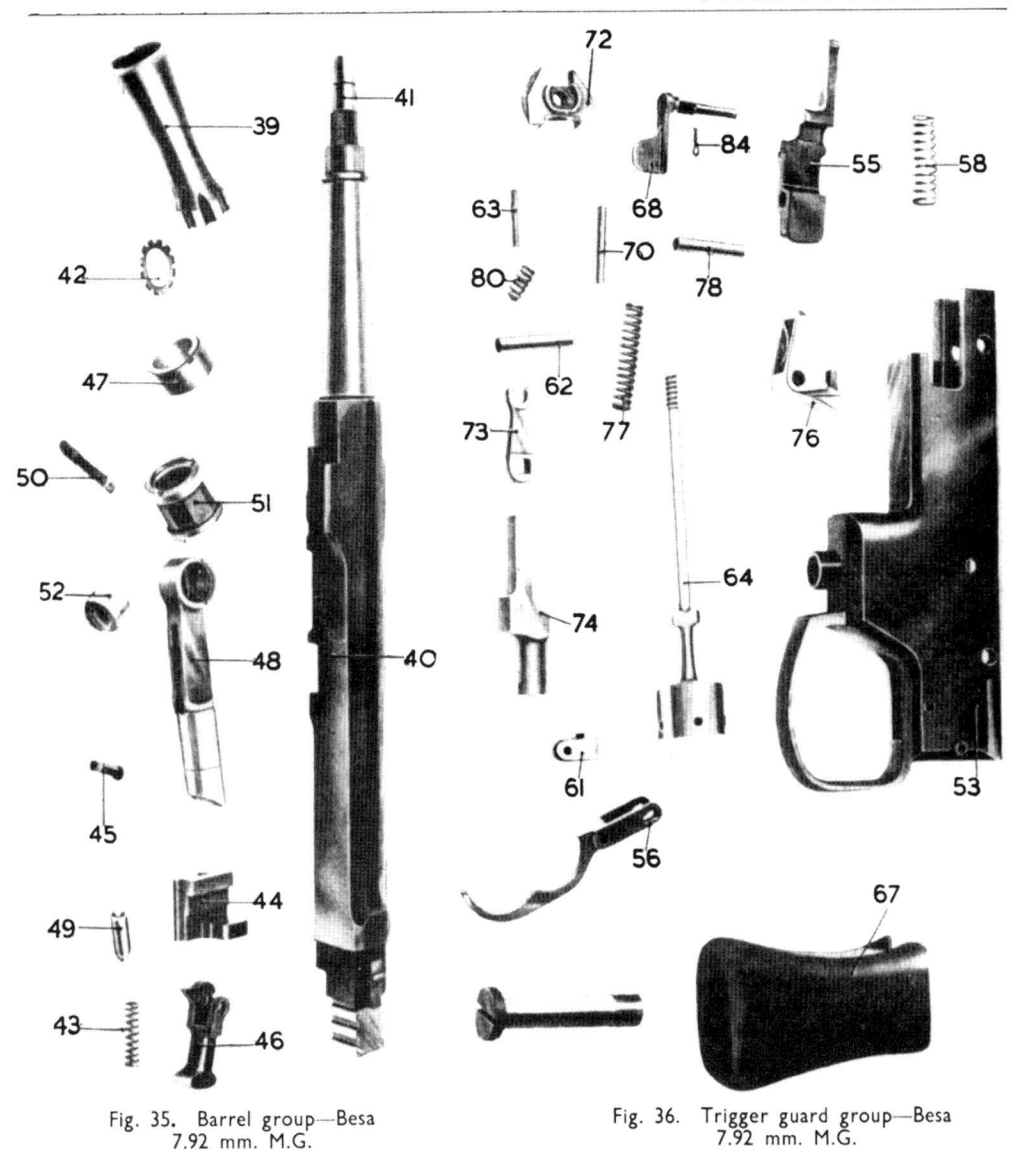

Fig. 35. Barrel group—Besa 7.92 mm. M.G.

Fig. 36. Trigger guard group—Besa 7.92 mm. M.G.

(Fig. 37 (86 and 98)) are also fitted on the underside of the cover, and a reaction block (Fig. 31 (101)) is secured by a pin to the cover to form a stop for the rear recoil spring casing (Fig. 37 (98)).

The cartridge guide co-operates with the feed block body (Fig. 33 (19)) to form the entry for the cartridge belt and for controlling the empty belt as it leaves the gun through the belt guide (Fig. 33 (5)).

The cartridges are guided into position by a pair of ramps on the underside of the cartridge guide, the retaining pawl (Fig. 37 (96)) and spring, being housed in a depression between the ramps.

117

7.92 mm. BESA M.G.

THE FEED BLOCK BODY (Fig. 33 (19)) is slotted to fit a gap in the right side of the body (Fig. 33 (2)), carries the feed slide (Fig. 33 (13)) and provides an upper bearing for the feed lever.

THE FEED LEVER (Fig. 33 (3)) has a vertical spindle which pivots in the body and the feed block. An arm is provided at each end of the spindle, the lower passing under the piston extension and engaging a camway on the underside by means of a stud, the upper arm having a slot to engage a stud on the feed slide.

THE RECOIL SPRING (Fig. 37 (97) is housed in the two tubular recoil spring casings, and reacts to return the parts to the forward position, after compression upon recoil of the barrel.

The foregoing description concerns the Mark III* Besa M.G.; the following description covers the main differences between the Mark III* and the preceding Marks, *i.e.* I. II, II* and III.

MK. I, MK. II, MK. II* AND MK. III

The Mk. I guns are converted from ground pattern guns for use in Armoured Fighting Vehicles. Mark II guns are manufactured as A.F.V. weapons. The difference between the Mk. I and the Mk. II series is manufacturing details. The Mk. II* is the transitional pattern between the Mk. II and the Mk. III, and all three Marks I, II and II*, embody accelerator mechanism. The Mks. I and II only, have a safety-catch.

The accelerator on the Mks. I, II and II* guns consists of a hollow casing (Figs. 31 and 38 (1)) which houses an inner (Fig. 31 (20)) and an outer (Fig. 31 (23)) accelerator spring. The casing is supported in the rear of the body by a crank arm (Fig. 31 (8)) and may be placed in or out of the path of the piston extension which strikes it at the end of its rearward travel, and as a result increases the rate of fire due to the additional reaction of the accelerator springs.

The safety-catch (Fig. 31 (54)) fitted to the Mk. I and Mk. II is embodied in the trigger guard and consists of a pivoted three-armed catch which engages the sear (Fig. 31 (76)), the sear tripper (Fig. 31 (74)) and a safety-catch rod which, in turn, is engaged by a safety-catch lever (Figs. 31

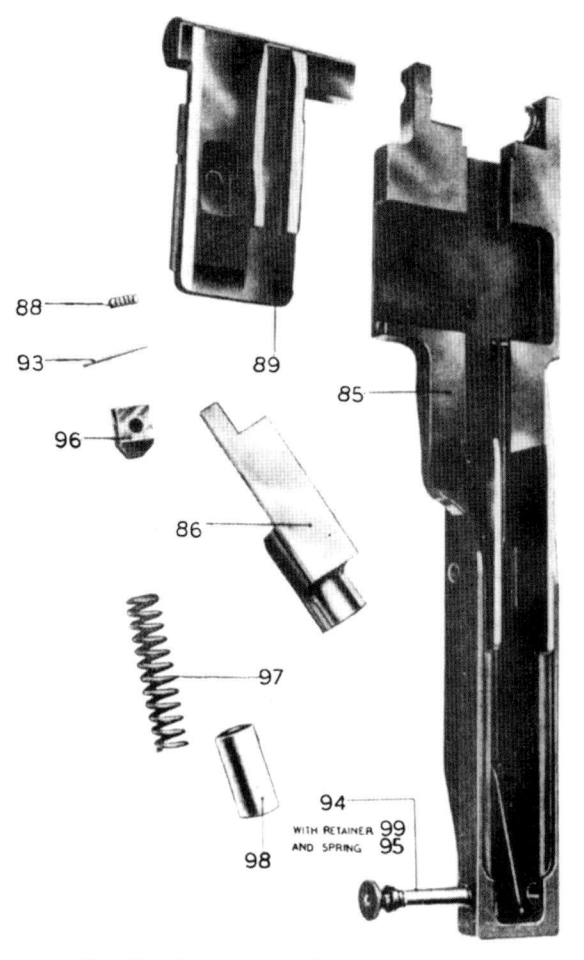

Fig. 37. Cover group—Besa 7.92 mm. M.G.

7.92 mm. BESA M.G.

and 41 (75)) mounted in the pistol grip. There are a number of minor constructional differences between the several marks, to simplify the construction and modifications arising due to redesigning.

Mk. II* embodies components of simplified pattern, but all are fully interchangeable with those of the Mk. II gun. In addition, the following components and their associated parts are omitted from the Mk. II*:

    Cover catch (Fig. 39).
    Feed pawl depressor (Fig. 40 (11)).
    Safety catch (Figs. 31 (54, 75), 41 (57, 75)).
    Accelerator (Fig. 38).

The components omitted from the Mk. II* are also omitted from the Mk. III gun. Mk. II belt guides (Fig. 33 (5)) are fitted without a catch. Mk. I belt guides and Mk. II gas cylinders will assemble to a Mk. III gun.

The Mk. III gun has no safety-catch and associated components, and the gas regulator has two ports only. No accelerator is fitted, but in its place two buffer springs (Fig. 31 (102 and 103)) are fitted in the return spring guide block, to speed the forward movements of the working parts and maintain a high fixed rate of fire of 750 rounds per minute.

Due to the fitting of inner and outer springs and a sleeve (Fig. 31 (104)) in the return spring guide, a shorter return spring is necessary, *i.e.* the Mk. II (free length 485 mm.—19⅛ in. approx.).

Mk. III* has the same modification as the Mk. III except for a reduced rate of fire, obtained by fitting a new return spring guide (Fig. 31 (105)), having no accelerator sleeve and springs.

OPERATION (see Fig. 31)

Forward stroke

When the trigger (56) is pressed, the sear (76) is disengaged from the piston extension (26) which is then driven forward by the return spring (33). The breech block (31) also rides forward by engagement with the piston extension. As the breech block moves forward, the feed projection drives a round out of the belt into the chamber. The rear of the breech block is lifted by ramps on the sides of the block riding over studs inside the barrel extension (27), to be finally engaged with the resistance face of the barrel extension. During the final closing movement of the breech block the extractor (30) grips the groove of the case. The continued movement of the piston extension actuates the firing pin (38).

Backward stroke

Expansion of the cartridge on firing, seals the breech. The force of the explosion forces the breech block, piston extension, barrel extension and barrel (41), all locked together, to the rear, compressing the recoil spring (97) which, upon expansion, drives the barrel and barrel extension forward.

Some of the gases produced on explosion escape

Fig. 38. Accelerator—Besa 7.92 mm. M.G.

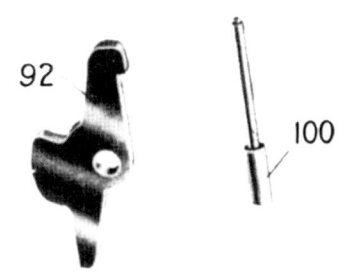

Fig. 39. Cover catch components— Besa 7.92 mm. M.G.

7.92 mm. BESA M.G.

through the gas vent into the gas cylinder (48) and force the piston extension to the rear. The rearward movement of the piston extension precedes the unlocking of the breech, which is effected when the inclined ramp on the piston post pulls down the breech block out of engagement with the barrel extension.

After the breech block has been carried to the rear the empty case is gripped by the extractor, withdrawn from the chamber and ejected by striking the ejector on the belt guide, passing through the piston extension and out of the ejection opening.

Compression of the return spring is effected during backward movements of the parts.

Action of the accelerator (when fitted)

With the accelerator set at "LOW" the gun fires at the normal rate, which is increased when the accelerator is set at "HIGH." The backward stroke of the piston extension is limited by contact with the accelerator (1), thereby compressing the springs (20) and (23), the additional action of which speeds the forward stroke of the piston extension and increases the rate of fire.

Action of feed (*see Fig.* 42)

During forward stroke

As the piston extension moves forward, the stud (1) on the lower arm of feed lever (2) engaged in the bottom of the piston extension, causes the upper arm feed slide (3) and feed pawl (4) to move to the right, so that the feed pawl is depressed by the next round in the belt until it rises and engages behind a link, the belt being held in position by the retaining pawl (5) during the action.

During the backward stroke

The piston extension acting on the lower arm of the feed lever (2) moves the upper arm and feed pawl (4) to the left, whereby the belt moves to the left due to its engagement with the feed pawl. During this movement, the front of the round is deflected downwards by the cartridge guide ramps, with the bullet pointing towards the breech. The retaining pawl (5) engages the upper surface of the link which is held by the feed pawl.

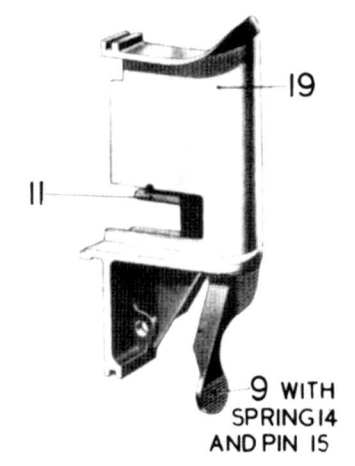

Fig. 40. Feed block body and components—Besa 7.92 mm. M.G.

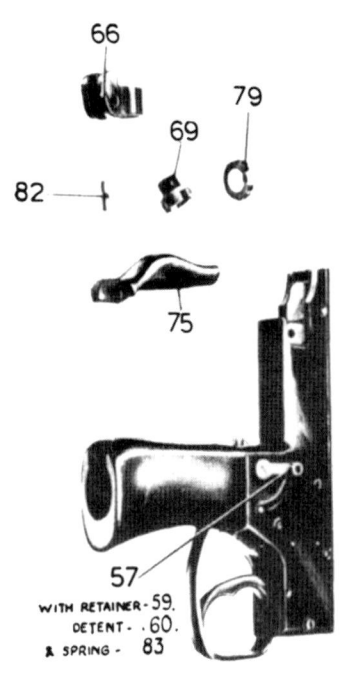

Fig. 41. Trigger guard, Mk. II—Besa 7.92 mm. M.G.

COVER, MUZZLE, BESA 7.92 MM. M.G.

No. 1, Mk. I.—Of waterproof canvas, tubular in shape and closed at the front end. It fits over the flash eliminator of the gun, and is secured by a cord.

No. 2, Mk. I.—Of waterproof canvas, fits over the barrel and the front part of the

VEHICLE HISTORY AND SPECIFICATION

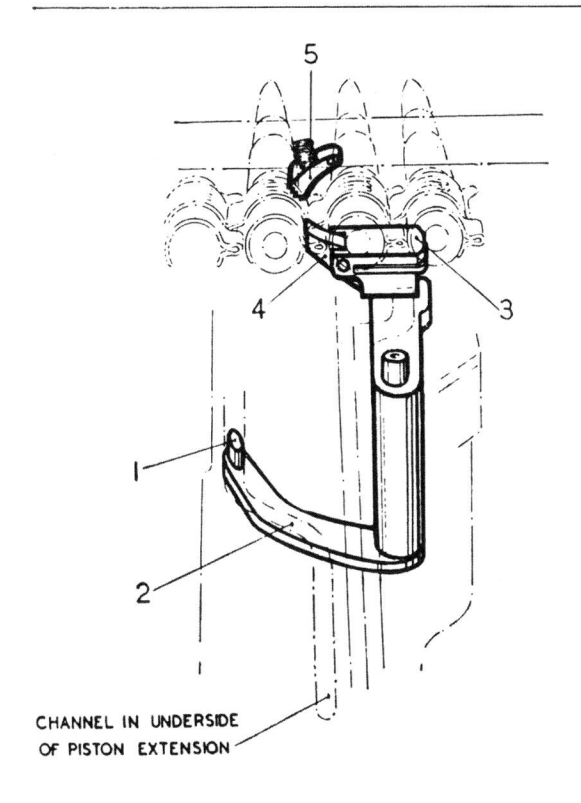

7.92mm. BESA M.G.

COCKED POSITION

PISTON EXTENSION TO THE REAR.
ROUND READY TO BE CARRIED
INTO CHAMBER & FIRED.

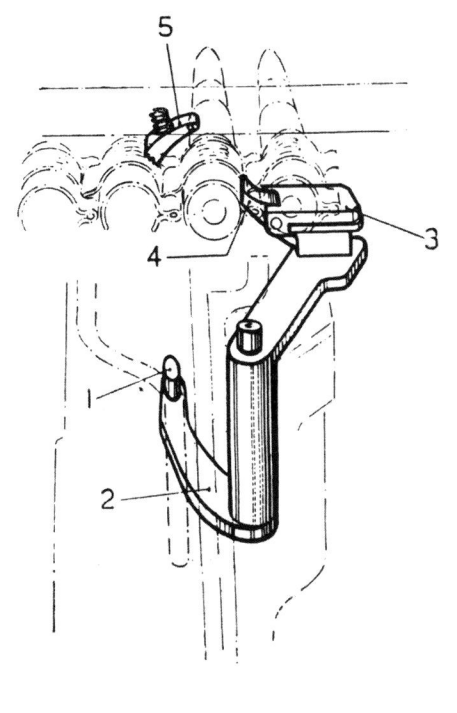

CHANNEL IN UNDERSIDE
OF PISTON EXTENSION

ROUND FIRED

FEED PAWL READY TO BRING FORWARD
THE NEXT ROUND.
PISTON EXTENSION FORWARD.

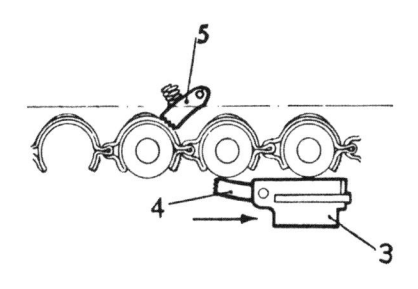

PISTON GOING FORWARD TO FIRE.

FEED PAWL RIDES UNDER NEXT ROUND

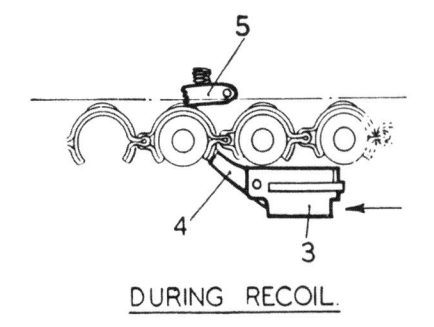

DURING RECOIL.

FEED PAWL BRINGING NEW ROUND INTO POSITION
RETAINING PAWL OVER RIDING THE ROUND

Fig. 42. Action of feed—Besa 7.92 mm. M.G.

7.92mm. BESA M.G.

body of the gun. The front part is tubular, with a closed end, and the rear part of rectangular cross-section. It is secured at the front and rear by cords.

The No. 1 cover is used in cases where only the barrel protrudes from the mounting, and the No. 2 where the front of the body is also exposed.

DEFLECTOR, CARTRIDGE CASE, BESA, 7.92 MM. M.G. No. 1, MK. I

The deflector consists of a canvas tube, at the top end of which are two metal attachments, the forward one fitting the front end of the ejection opening in the gun body and the rear one having two spring-loaded catches which engage the two studs on either side of the fore end of the trigger guard body. On the left side is a rectangular hole fitted with a metal chute, designed to pass the spent belt into the deflector after leaving the belt guide. At the lower end are four studs for the attachment of the mouth of the spent cartridge bag, by means of quick release fasteners. The top end is stiffened by means of spring cord sewn into the hem.

AMMUNITION

Cartridge, S.A., 7.92 mm.

The 7.92 mm. Besa M.G. takes a rimless cartridge comprising case, cap, charge and bullet. The base of the cartridge is stamped with the mark, contractor's initials or recognised trade mark, and the last two figures of the year of manufacture. The annulus is coloured to indicate the character of the cartridge.

The following marks of cartridge are issued :—

>Cartridge S.A. Ball 7.92 mm.
>>Mark I.Z and Mark II.Z annulus coloured purple.
>
>Cartridge S.A. Armour-piercing 7.92 mm.
>>Mark I.Z and Mark II.Z annulus coloured green.
>
>Cartridge S.A. tracer 7.92 mm.
>>Mark I.Z and Mark II.Z annulus coloured red.
>
>Cartridge S.A. incendiary 7.92 mm.
>>Mark I. annulus coloured blue.
>
>Blank and drill cartridges are available.

The cartridges are carried in belts holding 225 rounds, the filled belts being stored in wooden boxes, holding two tinned-plate boxes or liners from which the gun is fed direct. Each liner holds one belt which may be loaded, with ball, ball and tracer, A.P., or incendiary or a combination in definite proportions.

The boxes and liners are labelled to state the contents.

DESCRIPTION

Cartridge, S.A., Ball, 7.92 mm.

MK. I.E.—The cartridge consists of a brass case containing a charge of approximately 45 gr. N.C., a percussion cap and a bullet.

The case is of the rimless type, tapering slightly towards the mouth and bored out at the base to form an anvil and a chamber for the percussion cap. Two fireholes connect the cap chamber to the interior of the case. The cap may be secured in its chamber by " ringing in."

The cap is of brass and contains about 0.5 gr. of cap composition covered by a lead-tin foil disc.

7.92mm. AMMUNITION

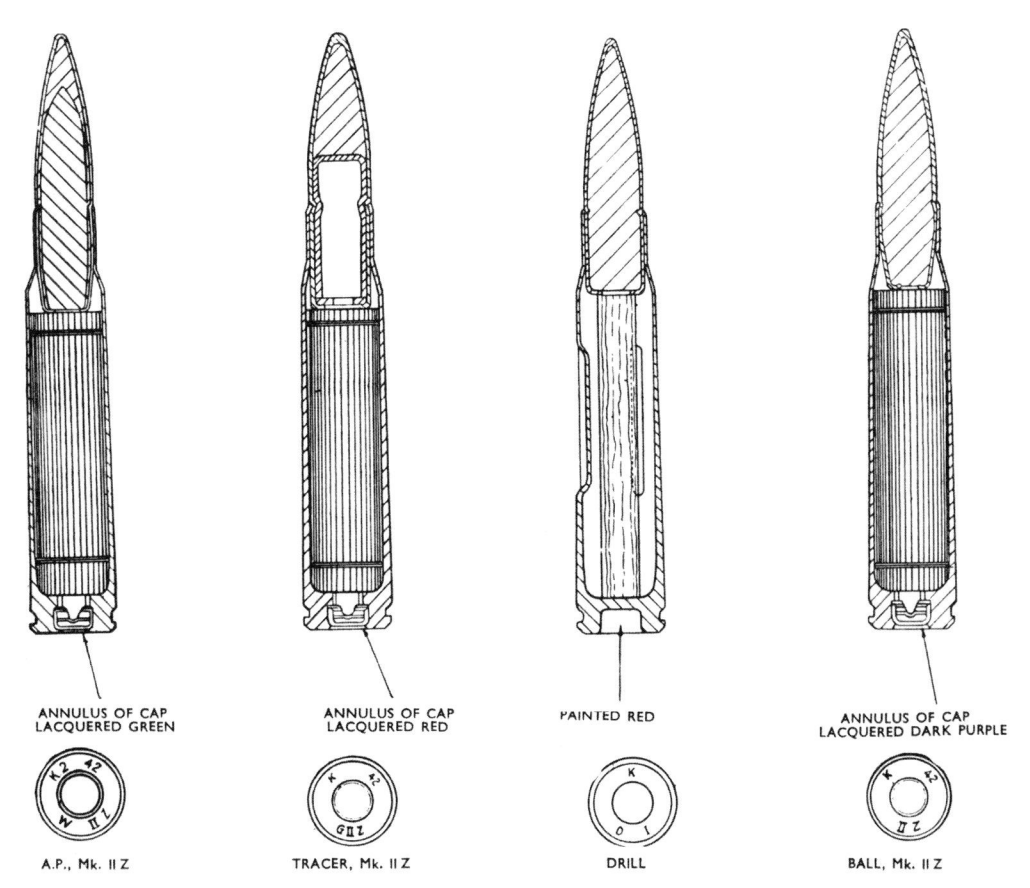

Fig. 43. Cartridges, S.A., 7.92 mm.

The bullet is streamlined and has a steel envelope coated with gilding metal or cupro-nickel, and lead-antimony core. The base of the bullet is stamped with the contractor's initial or trade mark.

The bullet is secured in the mouth of the case by coning or crimping the latter into a groove formed round the bullet.

The annulus of the cap is lacquered dark purple. This lacquering was omitted from cartridges of early manufacture.

The base of the cartridge is stamped with the Mark, contractor's initials or trade mark and the last two figures of the year of manufacture.

MK. II.Z.—Similar to the Mk. I.Z cartridge, except that it has the Mk.II bullet, as this has been found to give greater accuracy in worn barrels, and therefore a longer barrel life.

The Mk. II bullet is similar to the Mk. I, except that the nose is somewhat flatter and the parallel portion, which is engraved by the rifling, is longer.

The markings are similar to the Mk. I.Z, except for the Mark. Early Mk. II.Z cartridges are stamped " IS," but the boxes are labelled " MK. II BULLETS."

7.92mm. AMMUNITION

Cartridge, S.A., Armour-piercing, 7.92 mm., W.

Mk. I.Z.—The cartridge consists of a brass case, containing a charge of approximately 46 gr. N.C., cord or granules percussion cap and an armour-piercing bullet.

The case and cap are similar to those of the ball cartridge.

The armour-piercing bullet consists of a special hard steel core with a lead-antimony sleeve in an envelope of steel, coated with cupro-nickel or gilding metal, and is secured in the mouth of the case by coning or crimping the latter on to the bullet. The annulus of the cap is lacquered green.

Mk. II.Z.—Similar to the Mk. I.Z cartridge, except that it has the Mk. II bullet, which is slightly longer than the Mk. I, and has a flatter tip.

Cartridge, S.A., Tracer, 7.92 mm., G.

Mk. I.Z.—The cartridge is generally similar to the ball cartridge, but differs in being assembled with a tracer bullet.

The tracer bullet is not streamlined. It has a steel envelope, coated with gilding metal or cupro-nickel, and contains a lead-antimony tip, a copper tube filled with red tracer composition and a brass washer. The length of trace is 900 yards approximately. The annulus of the cap is lacquered red.

Mk. II.Z.—Similar to the Mk. I.Z except that it has a Mk. II bullet.

Cartridge, S.A., Incendiary, 7.92 mm., B.

The annulus of the cap is lacquered blue.

Cartridge, S.A., Drill, 7.92 mm., D.

Mk. I.—The cartridge is made up with a brass case, a bullet consisting of a cupro-nickel envelope with an aluminium core and a wood distance-piece. The bullet is not streamlined.

The distance-piece is placed inside the case and the bullet is secured in the mouth of the case by crimping or coning the latter into a groove formed round the bullet.

The case is chromium-plated and has a recess in the base and three longitudinal indents in the side, which are painted red in order to show definitely that the cartridge is for drill.

The letter "D," the Mark and contractor's initials or recognised trade mark are stamped on the base of the cartridge.

These cartridges are liable to break up with repeated use. When unserviceable, they should be exchanged and not repaired. Use of the D.P. return spring in the gun for instruction and demonstration will prolong the life of the cartridges. Drill cartridges must be kept separate from service ammunition.

BELT, 7.92 MM., 225-ROUND

The cartridges for the 7.92 mm. Besa M.G. are fed into the gun by means of a 225-round belt.

Mk. I. (Fig. 44)—Consists of 225 metallic links with a tag and eyelet, connected together by 225 pins. The links are pressed from spring steel sheet, folded to shape and spot-welded. They fit round the cartridges, which are retained by the small bulge at the rear projecting into the extractor groove in the cartridge case. The pins are a tight fit in the twin loops at the right of the link and slack in the single loop on the left, thus allowing the belt a certain degree of flexibility. The part of the link below

7.92mm. AMMUNITION

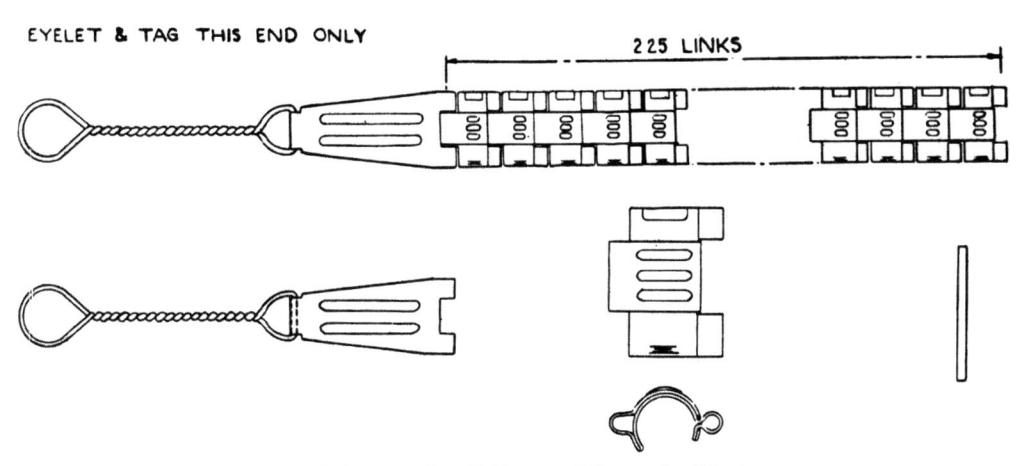

EYELET & TAG THIS END ONLY — 225 LINKS

Fig. 44. Belt, cartridge, 7.92 mm., 225 rounds, Mk. I.

the twin loops is serrated on the surface to assist the grip of the feed pawl. The tag is of sheet steel with two loops at one end for attachment to the link and one loop at the other for the eyelet. The eyelet is of twisted wire with a finger ring at the end. The tag and eyelet are passed through the feed block on loading the gun to enable the belt to be pulled into position and to lead the belt into the metal chute on the side of the cartridge case deflector.

MK. I*—This differs from the Mk. I pattern by the fitting of a flexible extension with a wire loop in place of the metal tag and eyelet. Mks. I and I* are surface-treated against corrosion.

These belts are commonly known as " Metal " belts. They are used both for factory-packed ammunition and also for instructional and demonstration purposes. For the latter, fired belts from factory-packed ammunition, shortened to about 50 links, are most suitable.

MK. II., 225-ROUND (Fig. 45)—This belt differs from the Mk. I and Mk. I* in the length of canvas webbing used to carry the clips. The belt comprises 226 clips each formed by top and bottom members which are locked together to clamp the canvas webbing, the last clip having a wooden plug to prevent the belt jamming upon leaving the gun. The entry end of the belt is riveted to a steel tab by two brass eyelets, and linked to a rectangular wire handle of mild steel or brass. The tab is marked with the manufacturer's initials or trade mark, month and last two figures of the year of manufacture, number of rounds (225), calibre 7.92 mm. and Mk. II.

The cartridges are retained by a small bulge in the bottom clip, which engages the extractor groove in the cartridge case.

Filling belts

To load a cartridge into the belt, enter the nose of the bullet into the rear of the link and press forward until the small retaining bulge in the link " clicks " into the

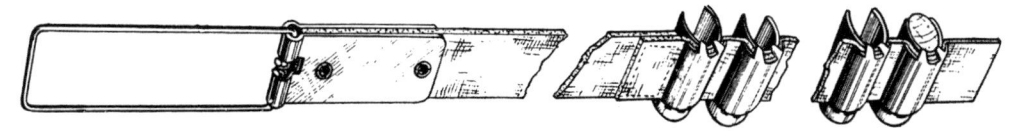

Fig. 45. Belt, cartridge, 7.92 mm., 225 rounds, Mk. II.

7.92mm. AMMUNITION

extractor groove in the cartridge case. The base of the cartridge should be flush with the rear edge of the link. There is no belt-filling or cartridge-positioning machine issued, and since ammunition is supplied factory-filled it is seldom that belts have to be filled by units, the chief exception being the preparation of belts of drill cartridges.

To remove a round from the belt

Twist the nose of the round downwards out of the link. Take care not to tear Mk. II belts when doing this.

AMMUNITION BOXES AND LINERS

Filled ammunition belts are packed and stored in belt boxes, from which the gun is fed direct.

Boxes, ammunition, S.A., H.29 (*Fig. 46*)

These are made of wood, and each contain two Mk. I tinned-plate boxes (*i.e.* 450 rounds in two belts).

MK. I.—The sides and ends are nailed together and the bottom secured to them by screws. The lid is battened and secured to the body at each end by an iron clamp. One clamp is a fixture, and the other can swing, the latter being secured in position by a split pin passing through the clamp, lid and end of the box.

A length of cotton webbing secured in position by vertical end battens is provided to form handles at each end of the box. The box is stained bluish-green and on each lower end is nailed a V-shaped piece of wood indicating belted ammunition, to assist identification at night. Raised metal figures and/or letters are also screwed on to each end of the box for the same reason, the indications being :—

7 ...	Ball
G7	Tracer
M7	Mixed
X	Special ammunition or packing

Examine labels carefully.

Stowage dimensions (maximum) :—

Length	16.9 in.
Width	10.75 in.
Depth	9.25 in.

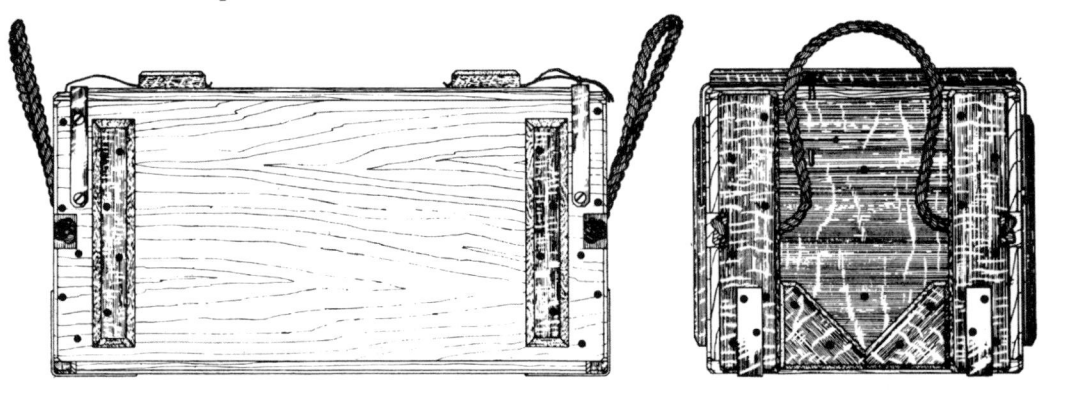

Fig. 46. Box, ammunition, S.A., H.29.

7.92mm. AMMUNITION

Weights :—
    Empty ... 18 lb.
    Filled ... 53½ lb.

MK. I.E.—Differs from the Mk. I pattern in being of a simpler form of manufacture for emergency use.

    Storage dimensions (maximum) :—
        Length ... 16.55 in.
        Width ... 10.1 in.
        Depth ... 8.9 in.

Weights :—
    Empty ... 14¼ lb.
    Filled ... 50¼ lb.

Boxes, Tinned-plate, Mk. I
(*Fig.* 47)

Known also as "Expandable liners" or "linings." The box is provided at the top with a central bridge-piece, and a tear-off lid on each side. Each lid is fitted with an iron or steel handle and a third handle is fitted to one end of the box for carrying purposes.

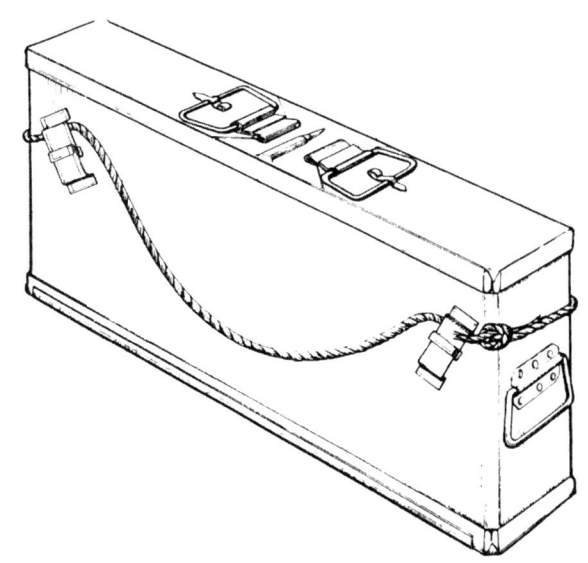

Fig. 47. Box, tinned-plate, Mk. I.

To facilitate removal from the packing box, a handle is formed at each side by a length of sisal twine joined to form a continuous loop which passes through four guides, located two on each side of the box. The bridge is embossed with the outline of a cartridge, and at one end is stamped the contractor's initials or recognised trade mark and year of supply.

The box, which is filled from the bottom, contains a belt of 225 rounds, folded into layers, each layer being separated from the next by a felt strip. There are also two felt packing pieces, one at the top and one at the bottom of the box. The box is hermetically sealed at the factory.

The belt may be filled with one of the following combinations :—
    Ball.
    Ball and tracer.
    Ball, tracer and A.P.
    Ball, tracer, A.P., and incendiary.

The actual proportions vary.

BOMB-THROWER, 2-INCH, MARKS I* AND IA*

A two-inch bomb-thrower is fitted to fire smoke emitting bombs from inside the A.F.V. It is mounted in the roof of the turret to the right of the co-axial mounting, and held by four bolts. Range is governed by a gas regulator valve fitted to the side of the rear barrel of the bomb-thrower. Three positions are provided for the valve, short, medium and long, giving respective ranges of 20 yards, 70 yards, and 110 yards approximately.

Except when being loaded or unloaded, *the bomb-thrower must always be kept in the closed position.*

OPERATION
To load

Grasp the handle portion of the junction nut so as to release the locking catch, rotate the nut in a counter-clockwise direction and lower the rear barrel. Insert the bomb in the front barrel. Raise the rear barrel, allow the bomb to slide back and rotate the junction nut until the locking catch re-engages.

To fire

Squeeze the trigger.

To unload

Open the bomb-thrower and lift out the smoke bomb by the lifting strap on the nose cap. Close the bomb-thrower.

CARE AND PRESERVATION

All working parts should be thoroughly clean, oiled and free from burrs. Before new lubricant is applied, the old should be removed to prevent grit being retained.

After lubricating, *operate the mechanism.*

No parts will be burnished.

Keep the bomb-thrower free from rust and the bore slightly oiled.

Remove fittings to check operation, but do not use unnecessary force.

Inspect for flaws and cracks.

Soda is harmful to the bore.

All spare parts should be tested for interchangeability.

LUBRICANTS

Purpose	Normal 20°F. to 90°F.	Severe Winter 0°F. to 20°F.	Arctic Below 0°F.	Tropical Above 90°F.
Mechanism and cleaning bright parts	C. 70 or oil A	Oil, low cold test, No. 2	Oil, low cold test, No. 2	C. 70 or oil A
General preservative	Mineral jelly			
Removing clogged oil	Kerosene (Grade 2)			

2-in. BOMB-THROWER

DESCRIPTION
BOMB-THROWER, 2-INCH, MARKS I* AND IA*

The Mark I* bomb-thrower is generally similar to the Mark IA* which differs from it in having certain details fabricated and others simplified in design to facilitate manufacture.

CONSTRUCTION

The bomb-thrower is made of steel and has a total length, with breech-piece, of 23-24 ins., a front barrel of 10.5 ins. and a rear barrel of 9.7 ins. The firing mechanism is percussion.

The bomb-thrower is illustrated in Fig. 48 and its various components are made up as follows :—

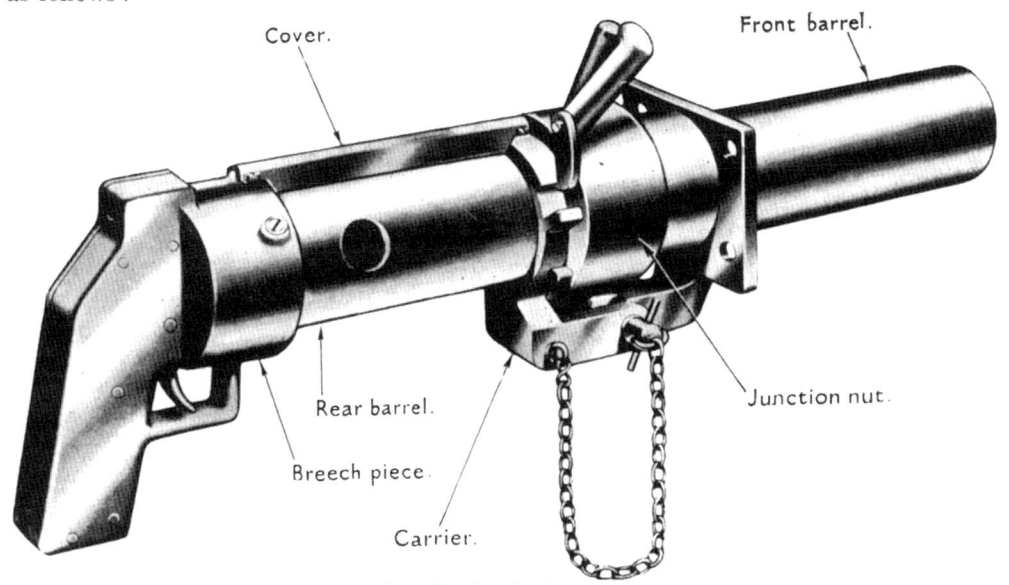

Fig. 48. Bomb-thrower, 2-in.

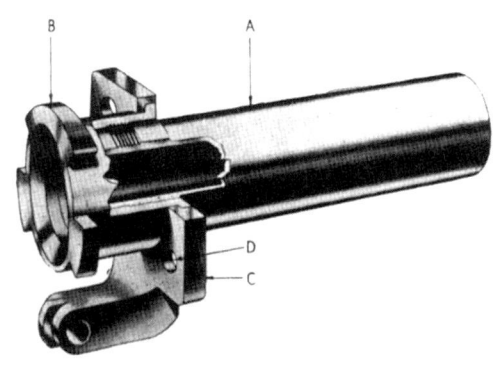

Fig. 49. Front barrel—2-in. Bomb-thrower.

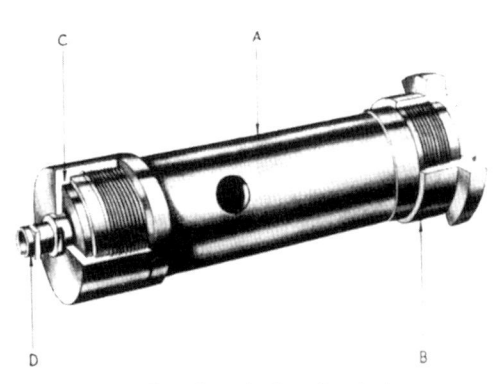

Fig. 50. Rear barrel—2-in. Bomb-thrower.

CHURCHILL TANK

2-in. BOMB-THROWER

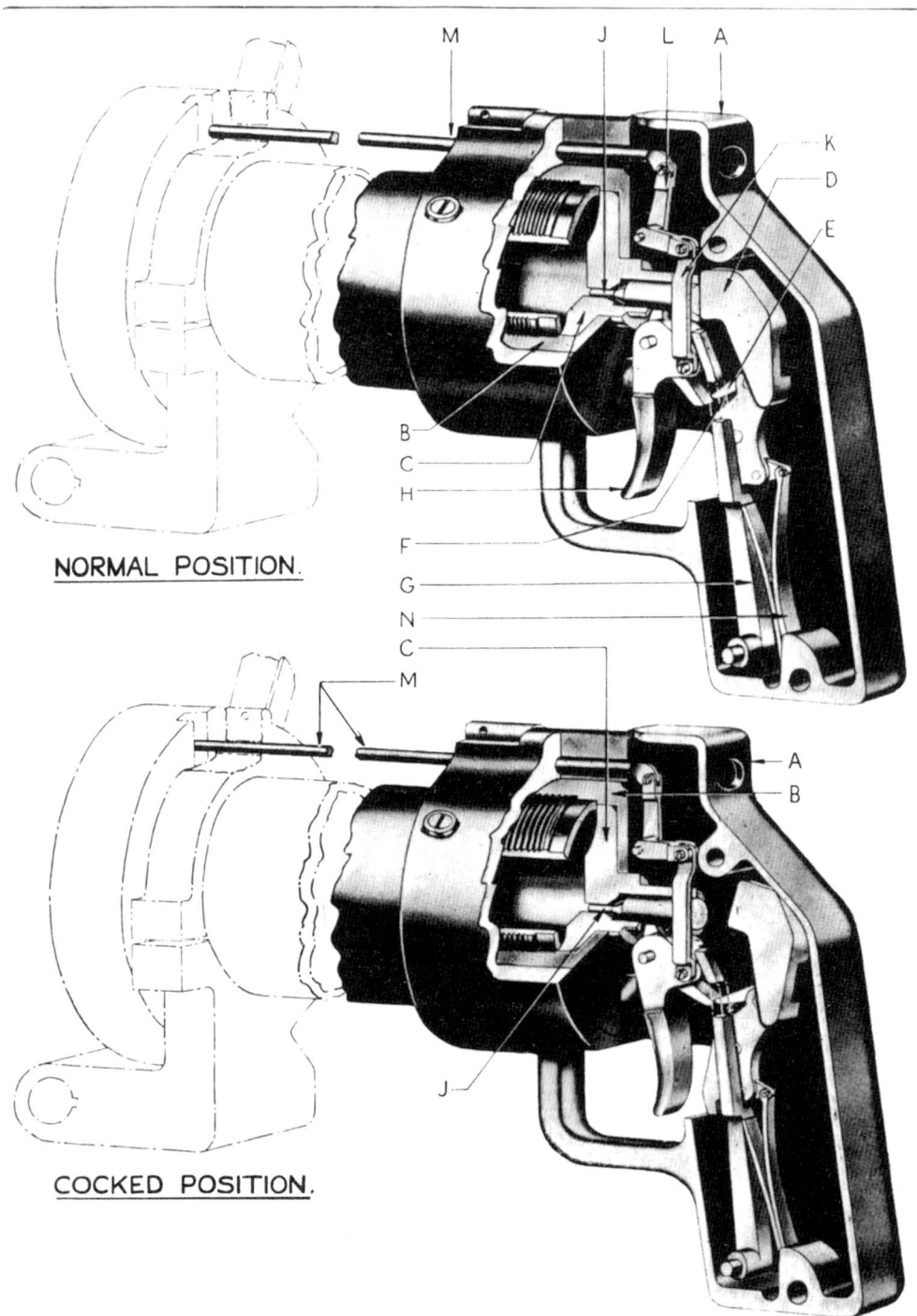

NORMAL POSITION.

COCKED POSITION.

Fig. 54. Breech piece—2-in. Bomb-thrower.

2-in. BOMB-THROWER AMMUNITION

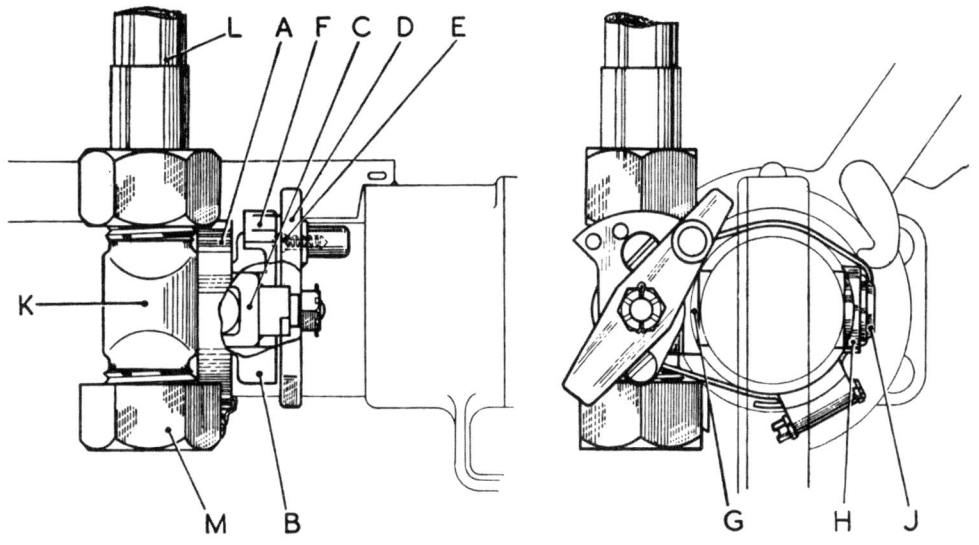

Fig. 55. Gas regulator—2-in. Bomb-thrower.

AMMUNITION, 2-INCH BOMB-THROWER

The ammunition for the 2-inch bomb-thrower consists of two types of smoke bomb :—

Bomb, Smoke, 2-in. Bomb-thrower, Marks I and II.

Bomb, Smoke, Bursting, 2-in. Bomb-thrower, Mark III.

using as a propellant either a

Cartridge, 2-in. Bomb-thrower (18 grain Ballistite) Mark I ; or a Cartridge, 2-in, Bomb-thrower (42 grain G.20).

The cartridges fit into the tail tubes of the smoke bomb.

Both bombs and cartridges have the usual markings, as have also the boxes and packages. The boxes hold eighteen rounds in packages of six and are painted green to denote smoke ammunition.

The body of the smoke bombs are painted green, with a red band around the head to denote that they are filled, and a white band if they contain white phosphorus.

The Mk. II smoke bomb differs from the Mk. I in that a short delay occurs in the emission of smoke.

The Mk. III contains as a smoke composition white phorphorus and is assembled with a D.A. percussion fuze covered with a safety cap, which must be removed before firing.

The Smoke Bomb, Mk. I (*See Fig.* 56)

Known as the Bomb, Smoke, 2-in. Bomb-thrower, Mk. I or Mk. II, consists of a tinned steel body (A) closed by a riveted and welded nose cap (B), to which a lifting strap (C) is riveted. The bottom is closed by an adapter (D). The upper end of the adapter is closed by a brass disc (E), while the bottom end screws into a central tube (F) being positioned by a grub screw. Four smoke escape holes are drilled in the neck of the adapter.

2-in. BOMB-THROWER AMMUNITION

The tail unit of the bomb is formed by the central tube (F) which has eighteen holes for even gas distribution around the bomb when fired, and is closed by a cartridge retaining cap (G), screwed on its lower end. Vanes (J) are welded to the central tube, and the cartridge (H) is placed inside.

The bomb is filled with smoke composition (K) and loose priming (L) in a muslin disc (M) above two millboard washers (N). On firing, the flash from the cartridge fuses the closing discs (E) in the adapter, passes to the primed muslin disc and loose priming, thence to the smoke composition.

THE MK. II SMOKE BOMB differs from the Mk. I in that a slight delay occurs before smoke emission.

Bomb, Smoke, Bursting, 2-in. Bomb-thrower, Mk. III (See Fig. 57)

The Bomb, Smoke, Bursting, 2-in. Bomb-thrower, Mk. III is somewhat similar in appearance to the Mk. I, but differs primarily in being assembled with a " Fuze, percussion D.A. No. 151 or 151A, Mk. I " for igniting the charge

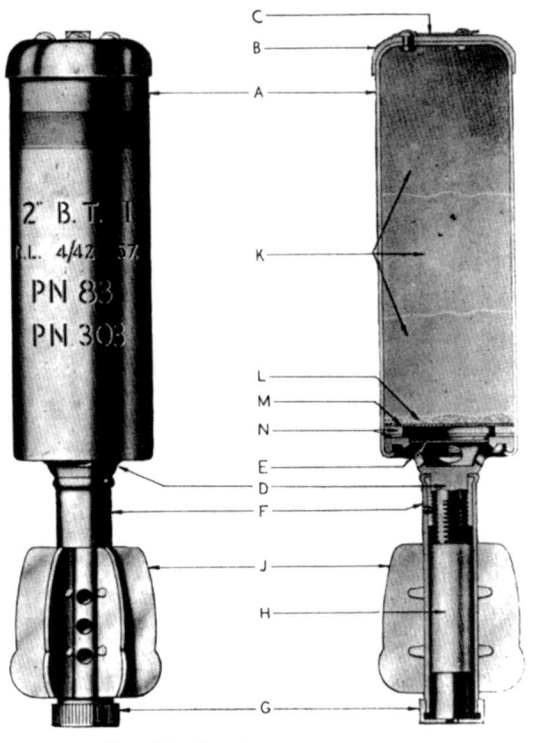

Fig. 56. Smoke bomb, Mk. I.

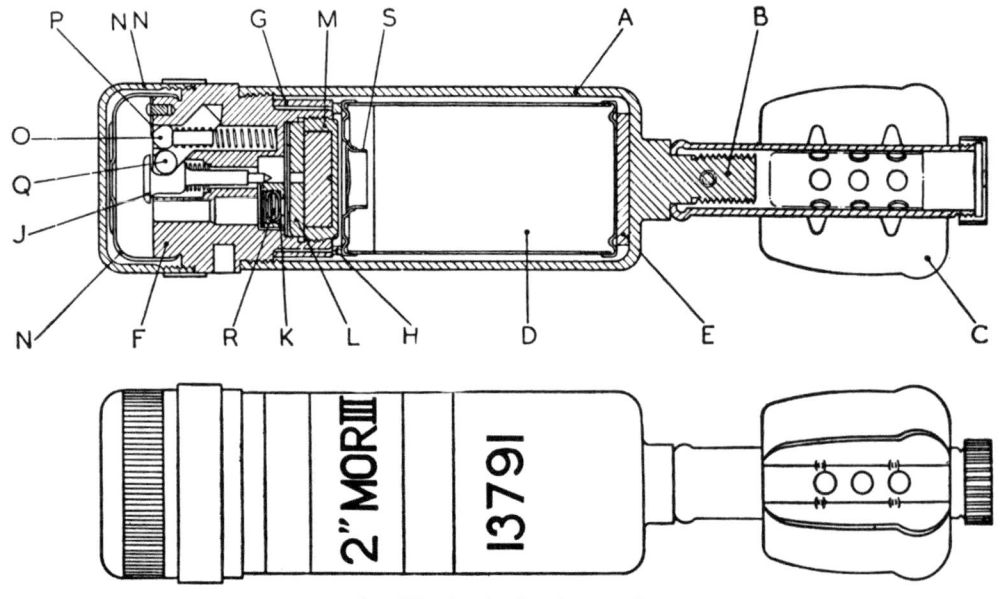

Fig. 57. Smoke bomb, Mk. III.

2-in. BOMB-THROWER AMMUNITION

of smoke composition (W.P.) filled into a container known as the "Container, Smoke, Mortar Bomb, No. 4, Mk. I." The smoke bomb is fired by a "Cartridge, 2-in. Bomb-thrower (18 grain Ballistite) Mk. I."

A safety cap, marked "Remove before firing" is fitted to the smoke bomb.

The smoke bomb comprises a hollow metal body (A) open at one end and having a screw-threaded spigot (B) at the other end, to which is attached a tail unit assembly (C) similar to that of the Mk. I smoke bomb. The body receives the container (D), which holds the smoke composition, a millboard disc (E) being interposed between the base of the container and the inner end of the body with a collar (G) and one or two spacing washers (H).

The percussion fuze body is bored axially and prepared for the striker (J) and recessed at the base for housing the spring pressed pivoted shutter (K),

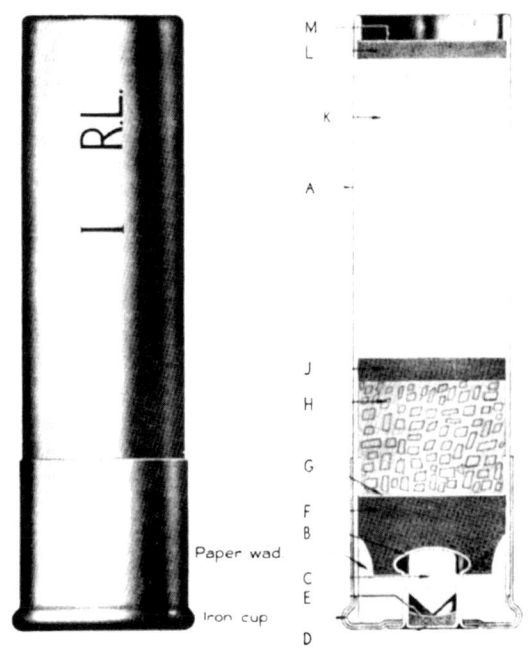

Fig. 58. Cartridge, 2-in. Bomb-thrower.

disc (L) and magazine (M), the latter being screwed into place. The top of the fuze is fitted with a cap (N), secured by canneluring, and a safety cap (NN) screwed over the body and knurled externally to facilitate its removal before firing the smoke bomb. A strip of adhesive tape covers the join. A longitudinal recess, displaced laterally to the boring for the striker, receives the detent (O) and detent spring, the detent being retained in place by a detent stop (P). An angularly disposed boring is provided for a loose ball (Q) which co-operates with a recess formed in the head of the striker to act as a latch and retain the striker in the inoperative position, with the striker spring in compression, and the fuze "safe."

The shutter is recessed for the reception of a percussion cap (R) and the disc (L) centrally apertured for stemmed C.E.; the magazine (M) is filled with C.E. or Pentalite.

The container (D) is of cylindrical form closed at each end and provided at the upper with a cap (S) which is blown in to enable the smoke composition to be ignited by the flash resulting upon the explosion of the charge in the magazine (M). An air space is left at the top of the container.

Action of Fuze

In the static condition of the fuze the shutter (K) is held inoperative against the action of the spring by the end of the striker (J), the striker in turn being held down by the latching action of the ball (Q) in the recess, the striker spring being compressed. The ball is held in the latching position by the detent (O) locked by the detent stop. Upon discharge of the smoke bomb, by means of the cartridge in the tail, the detent sets back, due to inertia, against its spring, thus allowing the ball to travel back in the angular boring, also due to inertia. The detent spring in due course reasserts itself and retains the ball out of action at the base of the angular boring. This action allows the

2-in. BOMB-THROWER AMMUNITION

striker to be forced upward under the action of its spring, thereby freeing the shutter (K). The shutter is moved by the action of its spring to bring the percussion cap (R) into a position below the striker.

When the smoke bomb strikes, the thin metal cap is forced in together with the head of the striker, the point of which detonates the percussion fuze. The resultant explosion of the charge in the magazine bursts the body of the smoke bomb and ignites the smoke composition in the container.

The safety cap (NN) must be removed prior to loading.

The Cartridge, 2-inch Bomb-thrower (18-Grain Ballistite), Mk. I (*See Fig.* 58)

Consists of a body (A) made of varnished cardboard with a brass cap and rim. In the rim there is a chamber (B) fitted with an anvil (C) and copper cap (D).

In the cap is 0.5 of a grain of " A " mixture, covered by a tinfoil disc (E) and above this is a gunpowder priming (F) retained by a celluloid cup (G). Above this the charge (H) of 18 grains of ballistite is retained by a cardboard disc (J) which is covered by a wad of felt (K). The whole assembly is covered by a cardboard disc (L) to which a paper disc (M) is shellaced, the mouth of the case being turned over to retain the cardboard disc (L).

The Cartridge, 2-inch Bomb-thrower (42-Grain G.20) (*See Fig.* 58)

Is the same as the Mk. I, except that there is no priming in the cap chamber (B), the charge has 42 grains of G.20 gunpowder and the felt pad (K) may be in one or more pieces.

THE GUN MOUNTINGS

INTRODUCTION

This section of the book covers the Mounting, 6-Pr/75-mm. and Besa M.G. No. 2, Mark II, fitted to the Churchill VII and the Mounting, 95-mm. Howitzer and Besa M.G., No. 2, Mark I, fitted to the Churchill VIII.

In view of the interchangeability, components and assemblies common to the mountings are described first, followed by those peculiar to the particular mounting.

FOREWORD

The type of gun mounting fitted to the vehicle may be determined by reference to the inscription plate fixed to the top of the ordnance cradle, on which is given the nomenclature, mark and serial number of the mounting. This data must always be quoted in any written reference to the mounting.

The ordnance and Besa machine gun co-axial mountings provide for the main armament of the vehicles and consist of a mantlet pivotally mounted on trunnions secured in the turret, to which is secured the ordnance cradle, the machine gun cradle and the sighting gear. The other components of the mounting are attached to the ordnance cradle.

Movement of the mounting in azimuth is obtained by an elevating gear. On the Churchill VII the maximum elevation obtainable is 20 degrees above the horizontal and the maximum depression $12\frac{1}{2}$ degrees below. On the Churchill VIII, the machine gun is in 7 degrees depression when the howitzer is horizontal, being due to the seatings on the mantlet for the howitzer and machine gun cradles being 7 degrees out of alignment with each other. This mal-alignment allows a maximum elevation for the howitzer of 25 degrees above the horizontal and a depression of 3 degrees below, and a maximum elevation for the machine gun of 18 degrees and a maximum depression of 10 degrees. Positive elevation and depression stops are fitted in the splash guards.

Foot firing gears are provided which operate through a selector mechanism so that either the ordnance or machine gun may be fired from the one control.

CHURCHILL TANK

GUN MOUNTINGS

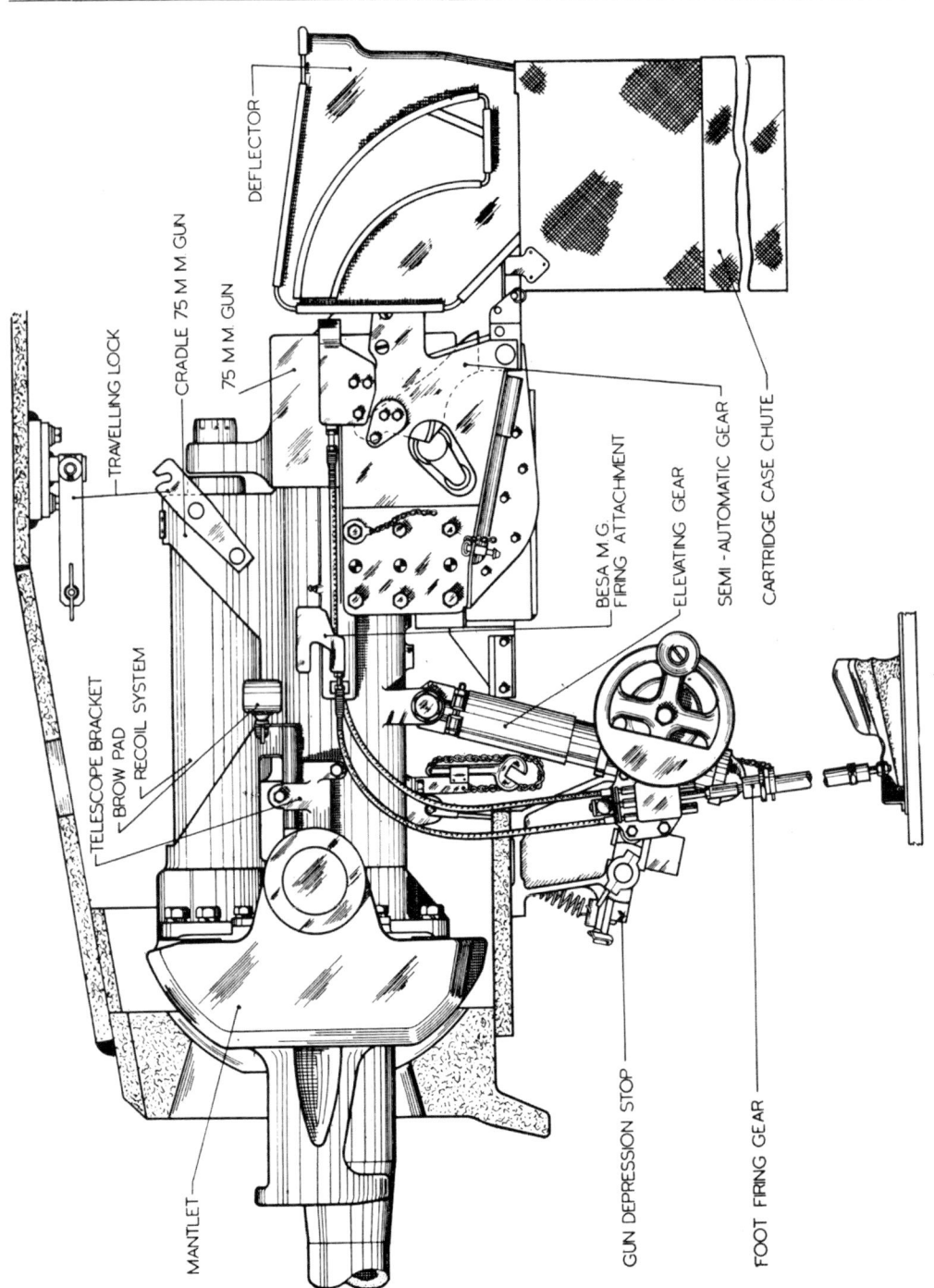

Fig. 59. Mounting, 6-pr./75-mm. and Besa M.G. No. 2: Mk. II.

GUN MOUNTINGS

Fig. 60. Mounting, 95-mm. Howitzer and Besa M.G. No. 2, Mk. I.

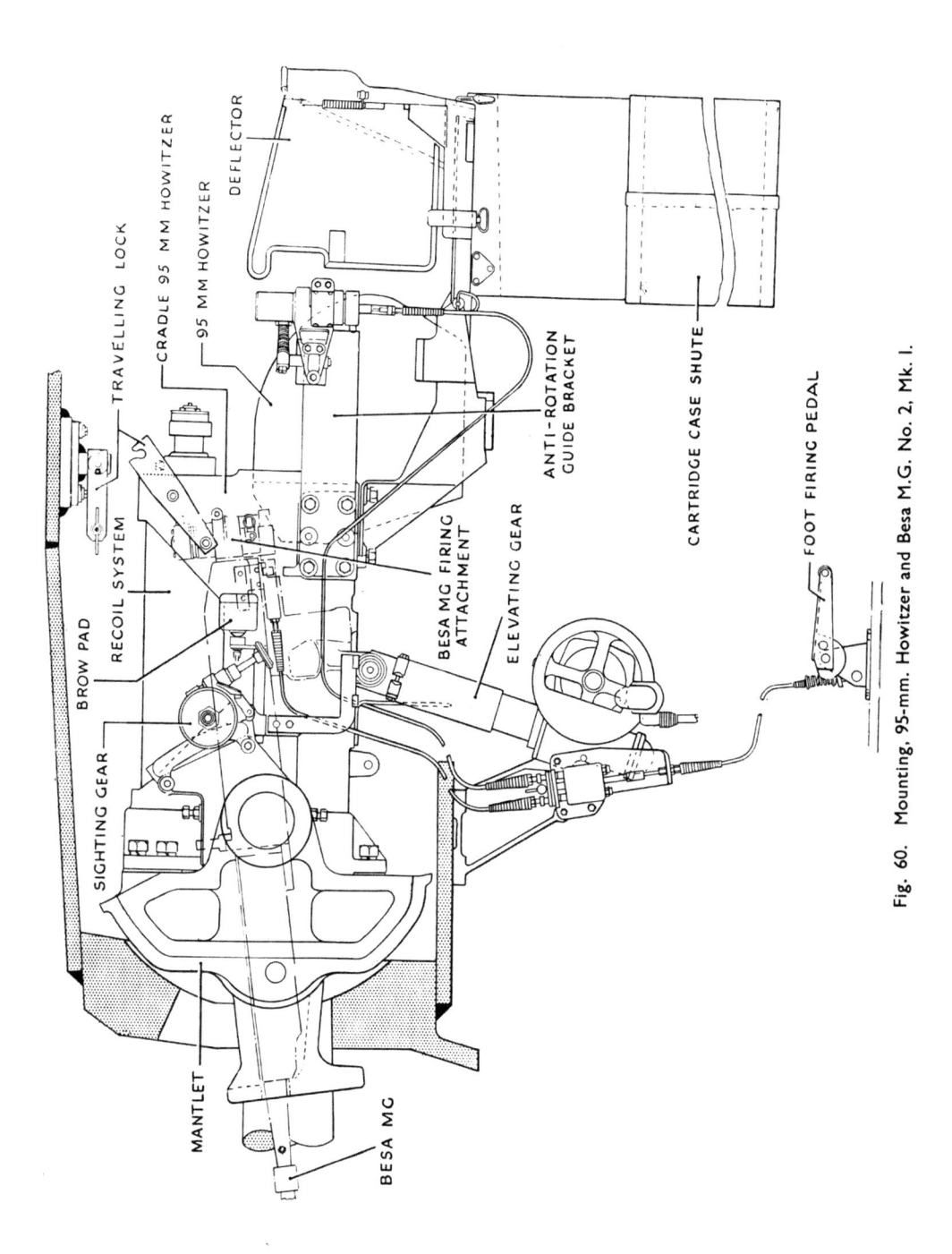

GUN MOUNTINGS

LUBRICANTS

Purpose	Normal 20°F. to 90°F.	Severe Winter 0°F. to 20°F.	Arctic Below 0°F.	Tropical Above 90°F.
Buffer	Oil, mineral, hydraulic buffer C.S.1117B	Oil, mineral, hydraulic buffer C.S.1117B	Oil, mineral, hydraulic buffer C.S.1117B	Oil, mineral, hydraulic buffer C.S.1117B
Cradle guides and gun slides	C.600	Hypoid 80	Hypoid 80 + Kerosene (C.V.O.)	C. 600
Oil-can lubrication	30 H.D.	10 H.D.	10 H.D. + Kerosene (C.V.O.)	50 H.D.
Elevating gear	C.600	Hypoid 80	Hypoid 80 + Kerosene (C.V.O.)	C.600
Forced feed lubrication	C.600	Hypoid 80	Hypoid 80 + Kerosene (C.V.O.)	C.600
Removing clogged oil	Kerosene	Kerosene	Kerosene	Kerosene

INSTALLING AND REMOVING A BESA MACHINE GUN

To Install (*See Fig. 63*)

Slacken the clamping strip retaining bolt (E) with the spanner attached to the mounting and turn the recoil bolt (G) until the flat (H) on its diameter is flush with the face of the cradle. Slide the gun into the cradle and secure it by turning the recoil bolt. Lock the gun in position by tightening down the clamping strip. Keep the spanner in the clip provided when not in use.

To connect the remote control firing gear, lift the plunger and slide the cable attachment into the guide on the right side of the gun. Release the plunger which will locate the attachment, then tighten the securing screw.

To Remove the Gun

Reverse the procedure.

DESCRIPTION
RECOIL SYSTEM
fitted to
CHURCHILL VII & VIII

The recoil is known as the H.P. No. 1, Mk. I and comprises a hydraulic buffer to regulate the recoil and springs to return the gun to its run-out position and retain it there. The buffer cylinder (A) is encased by the run-out springs, one a left hand spiral (B), the other a right hand spiral (C), working in series, supported and separated by a washer (D) fitting loosely over the buffer cylinder. The whole assembly is enclosed by a tubular spring case (E) and held in the cradle directly over the ordnance.

The object of the buffer is to dissipate recoil energy by forcing liquid in the buffer

VEHICLE HISTORY AND SPECIFICATION

GUN MOUNTINGS

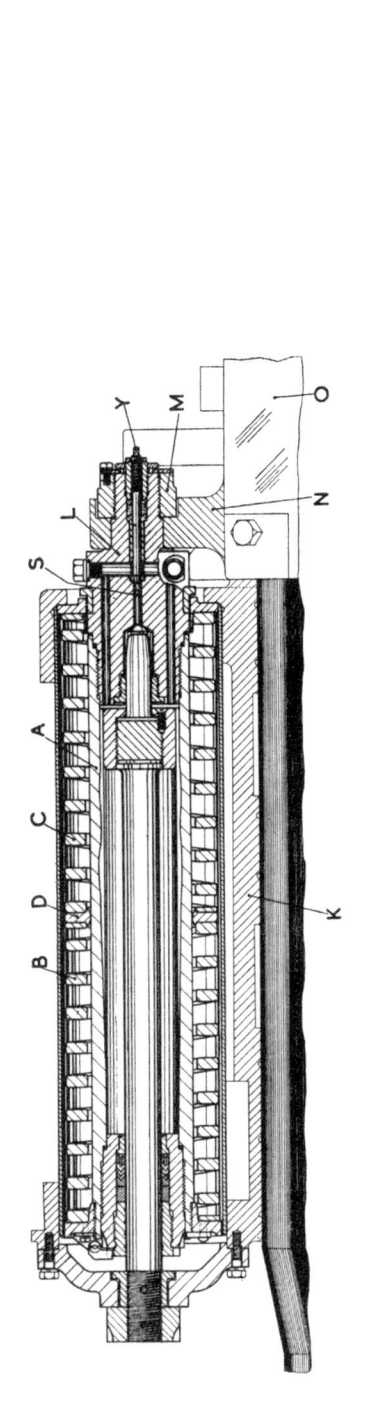

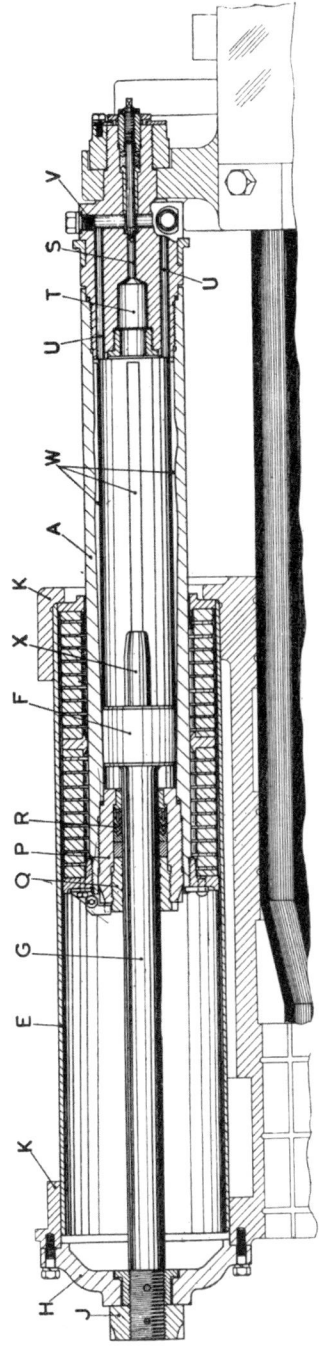

Fig. 61. The recoil system.

139

GUN MOUNTINGS

past the piston (F). The piston rod (G) is secured to the cradle (K) by the cap (H) and nut (J), and the springs held by the cradle against compression. The cylinder head (L) is secured by the nut (Z) to the gun lug (M) formed on the breech ring (N) of the gun. To seal the cylinder, a stuffing box (O) is screwed into it at the piston rod end and a head (L) at the other end. The stuffing box, closed by the gland (P), is packed with chevron packings (R). In the cylinder head (L) three holes are drilled longitudinally. The centre one (S) is a port which controls oil flow from a recess (V) in the cylinder head, the outer ones (T) are ports allowing liquid to enter the cylinder from the filler plug hole (U) and the ejected liquid from the recess to pass back to the cylinder. In the cylinder wall four grooves (W) are cut, varying in depth over the length of the cylinder. The depth of the grooves is varied so that the reacting force set up in the buffer is in proportion to the force of the recoil and as a result the gun is brought to a stop steadily.

When recoil takes place, the gun pulls the cylinder out, compressing the run-out springs and forcing the liquid in the cylinder through the four grooves from one side of the piston to the other. The control of the flow of liquid by the grooves, maintains an equal pressure over the whole length of recoil, thereby giving stability and distribution of stress. Near the beginning of the recoil, the grooves being deeper, allow a freer passage to the liquid to counter the maximum recoil velocity, but as this is progressively reduced, the shallower part of the grooves restrict the flow of liquid proportionately until the recoil energy is overcome by the energy absorbed by the run-out springs. The springs then reverse the action and return the gun and buffer to the run-out position.

To bring the gun to rest gently, the piston rod is so made that a part (X) projects through the piston and enters a recess in the cylinder head. Liquid trapped in the recess can only escape through the centre port (S) where its rate of flow is controlled by a spindle valve (Y) screwed through the cylinder head and adjusted to eliminate any hammering when the gun comes to rest.

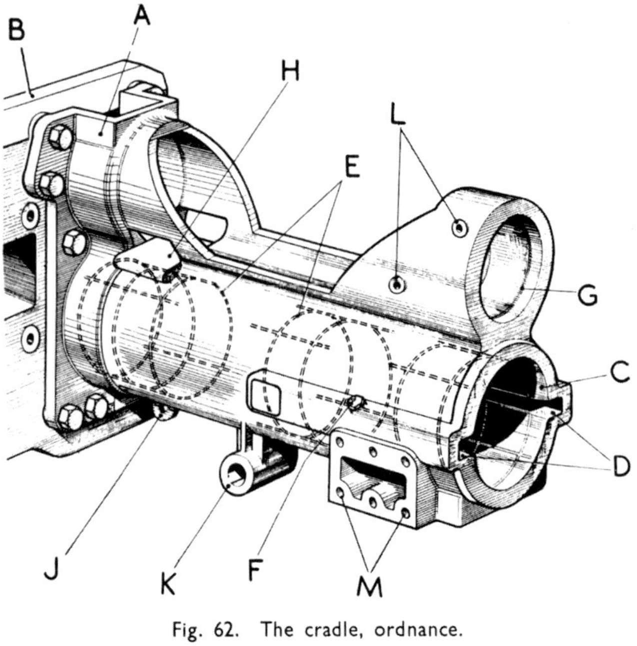

ORDNANCE CRADLE
fitted to
CHURCHILL VII AND VIII

The cradle (A) is a casting in which is carried the ordnance and recoil system. It is bolted on its front face to the mantlet (B). The lower bore (C) is machined to fit the outside diameter of the ordnance and has two guideways (D), chamfered at the entry to give a "lead in" to the guides on the gun. Oil grooves (E), cut over its length, are fed from lubricating nipples (F), one connecting with each guideway and another with the body of the cradle. The upper part where the buffer is held, is cast so that the spring case is held at its ends only. The buffer and spring case is inserted from the

Fig. 62. The cradle, ordnance.

GUN MOUNTINGS

front of the cradle, the spring thrust ring abutting the stop face (G) in the bore and the piston rod held by the end cap bolted to the cradle. Through the forward part of the casting between the buffer and the ordnance is a slot (H) through which the ammunition belt passes to the M.G. The lug (J) on the underneath of the cradle connects with the cable of the gun depression stop on the 75 mm. gun mounting and the lug (K), with the elevating gear. Two tapped holes (L) in the rear upper part, are for securing the travelling lock bracket and the holes (M) in the lower part for the semi-automatic gear bracket on the 75mm. gun mounting or the anti-rotation bracket on the howitzer mounting.

MACHINE GUN CRADLE
fitted to
CHURCHILL VII & VIII

The cradle (A) is a gun-metal casting bolted with an interposed packing piece (B) to the mantlet and machined internally to form a slide for the gun. One side of the slide is a detachable strip (C) which is retained by a bolt (D) extending through the cradle and mounted on springs (E) so that the strip is raised as the retaining bolt is slackened and the gun given free withdrawal. When the gun is in position, the retaining bolt is tightened. The gun is located in the cradle by the recoil bolt (F), the shank of which engages a groove in the base of the gun body, a flat (G) machined on it, allowing entry or withdrawal of the gun when turned to a position flush with the face of the cradle slide.

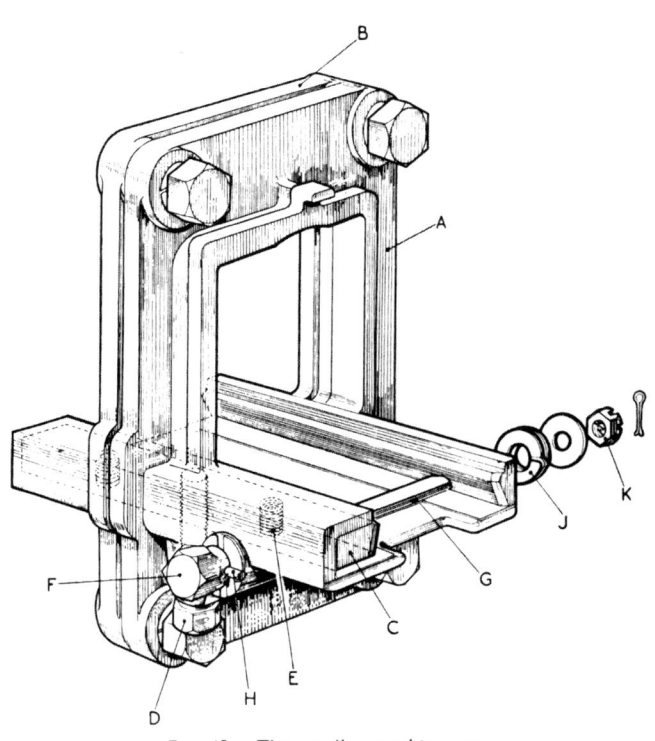

Fig. 63. The cradle, machine gun.

A snug (H) fitted under the head of the recoil bolt and held in a notch in the cradle by the spring (J) and nut (K) retaining the bolt, allows the flat to be positioned.

ELEVATING GEAR
fitted to
CHURCHILL VII & VIII

A geared elevating mechanism is fitted to control the elevation and depression of the gun by swinging the mounting on its trunnions. The elevating screw (A) is raised or lowered by a nut (B) rotated by a spiral gearing housed in a gear case (C) supported by trunnions in the bracket (D) in which is also supported the gun depression stop. The elevating screw is connected to a lug on the underside of the ordnance cradle to pivot on the fulcrum pin (E). To allow for misalignment between the fulcrum pin and the supporting bracket (D), a spherical bush (F) is fitted in the cap (G) of the elevating

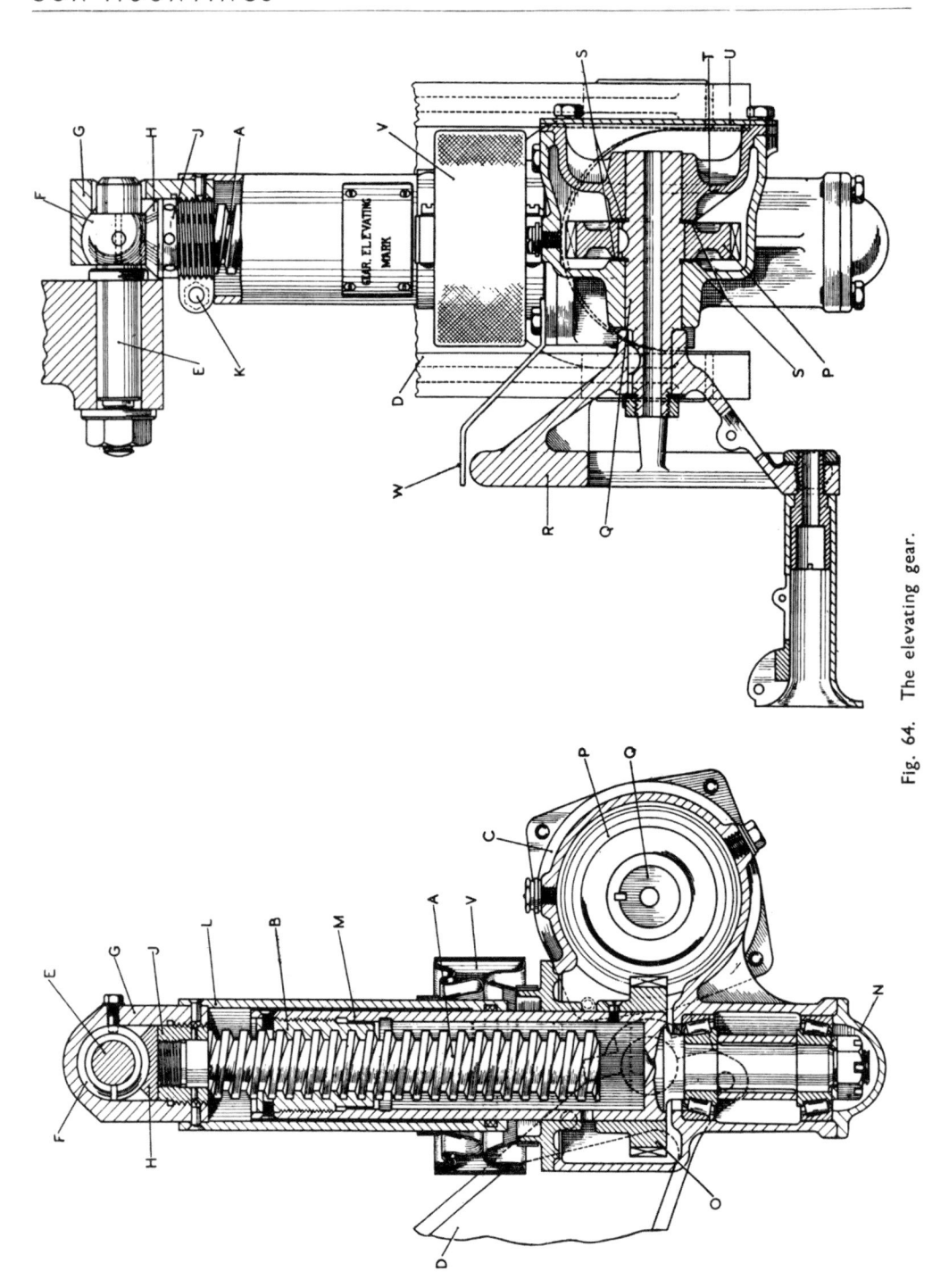

CHURCHILL TANK

GUN MOUNTINGS

Fig. 64. The elevating gear.

142

GUN MOUNTINGS

screw and retained by the cup (H). The spherical bush is split by a sawcut at one place and partly cut through opposite and positioned in the cap by a locating screw. The adapter (J) is screwed and taper pinned to the elevating screw, having six holes drilled radially for adjusting with a tommy bar, the holes being accessible through the cut-away part of the cap (G). The elevating screw with the adapter is screwed into the cap until the spherical bush is held without slack and the screw (K) tightened to clamp the adapter and lock it in position.

The end cap is secured to the sleeve (L) by three steel plugs welded in position. In the lower end of the sleeve a bronze ring is sprung into a groove and acts as a bearing surface when the sleeves telescope.

The inner sleeve (M) holds the elevating nut (B) which is screwed into it and secured by three countersunk screws tack welded in position. The stem at the lower end of the sleeve is machined for two Timken roller bearings which are retained by a castellated nut, washer and split pin with a distance piece between. Shims fitted under the cap (N) of the gear case allow the bearings to be adjusted. The driving pinion (O) of the sleeve is fitted over the sleeve and secured by three countersunk screws.

The elevating screw is lubricated from the gear case, the oil passing through a hole drilled through the sleeve just above the pinion. The pinion is driven by the gear (P) which is keyed to the shaft (Q) and to which is also keyed the handwheel (R), the handwheel being retained on the shaft by a nut and tab washer. The gear is positioned on the shaft by shims (S) inserted between the gear and casing, the end of the shaft being supported in the bearing plate (T) and the casing enclosed by the cover plate (U).

The periphery of the handwheel is graduated into sixteen divisions numbered one to sixteen, and each division sub-divided. A reader (W) attached by the top cover screws, gives an indication of the movement of the handwheel.

A lubricating nipple fitted in the top of the gear case provides for filling with oil and a plug underneath for draining. A name plate fixed to the outer sleeve gives the nomenclature of the elevating gear.

A dustproof fabric cover (V) is fitted over the telescoping part of the sleeve (L, M) and held by " Jubilee " clips.

DESCRIPTION
FIRING GEAR
CHURCHILL VII
(if fitted)

The firing gears for both the ordnance and the Besa M.G. are foot operated. The pedal consists of a plate (A) with a hinged flap (B) shaped to fit a boot and edged with strip metal to stop the boot from slipping off. Between the plate and flap is a compression spring (C) to hold the flap up. The space between the flap and plate is enclosed with canvas to exclude any object which might get between and stop the flap being pressed downward. An instep guard (D), to position the foot on the pedal, is fixed with the plate to the floor of the turntable.

Riveted laterally across the flap is a metal strip (E) to which is secured by a Simmonds nut and a lock nut the ball pin (F) of the connecting rod (G). The ball pin is a threaded pin with a spherical head fitting into a socket cap (H), retained by a cup (J) screwed into the cap and secured by a back nut (K). The stem of the cap is fitted into the end of the tubular connecting rod (G) and secured by a bolt (L) through the stem and rod and riveted over into the nut after final assembly. At the other end of the connecting rod is a similar socket cap and cup receiving a ball pin (M) screwed into a

CHURCHILL TANK

GUN MOUNTINGS

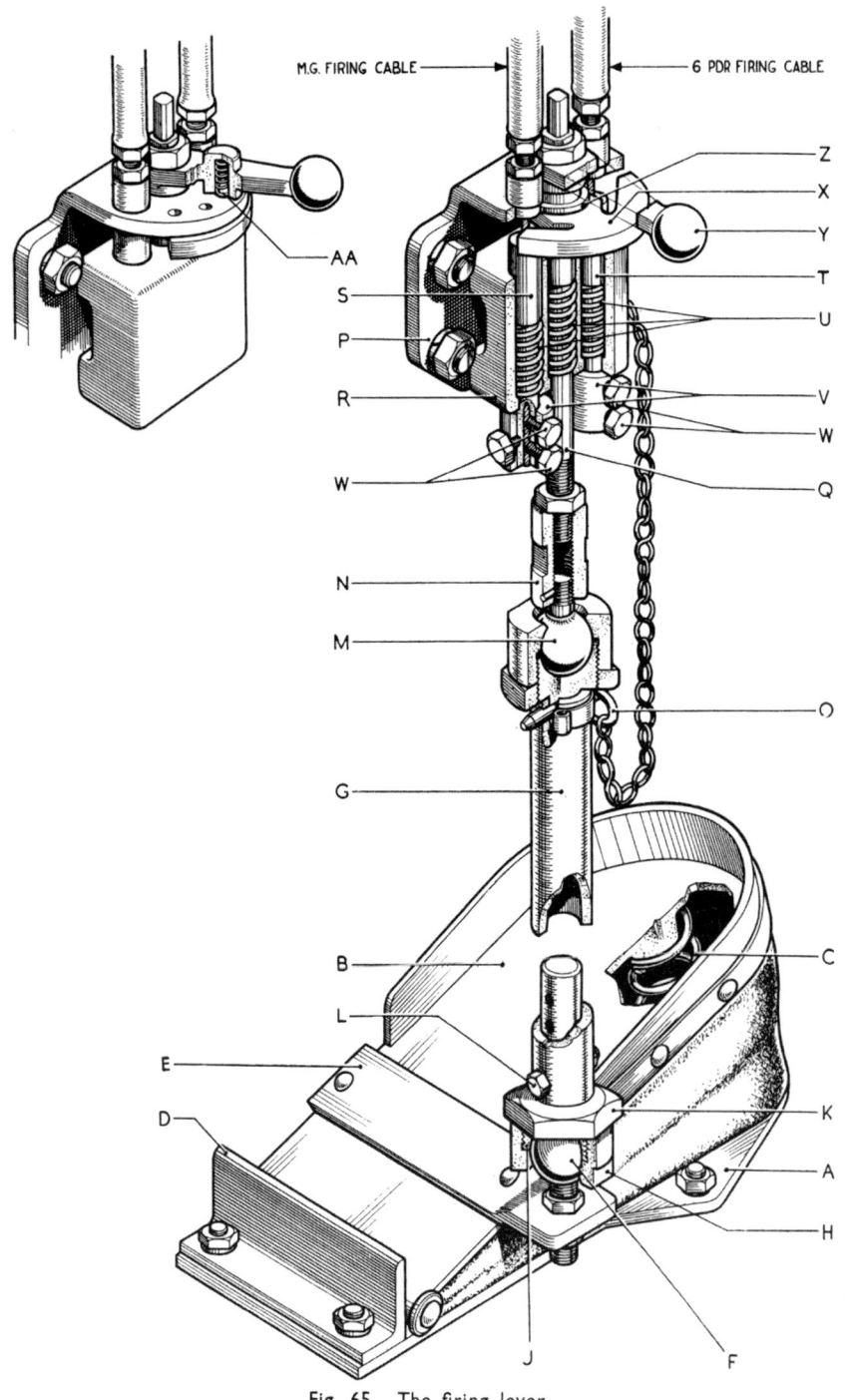

Fig. 65. The firing lever.

144

GUN MOUNTINGS

turnbuckle (N) and pinned on assembly. The upper end of the connecting rod is connected to the stem of the socket cup by a quick release fastener (O), consisting of a pin passing through the connecting rod and stem and retained by a spring circlip, the pin being chained to the backplate (P) of the selector to ensure against its loss. The other end of the turnbuckle is screwed to a shaft (Q) welded to the selector plate.

The selector consists of a back plate (P) to which is bolted a box (R) housing two push rods (S, T), one connected to the howitzer firing cable, the other to the M.G. firing cable and between them the selector shaft (Q). The push rods and the selector shaft are spring loaded, the springs (U) reacting between shoulders formed in the housing and shoulders formed on the rods. The push rods are positioned by a collar (V) fixed to each rod by a set screw and abutting the underside of the housing. Two screws (W) are provided in each collar to clamp the inner firing cables which pass through a hole drilled longitudinally in each push rod, to the collars.

The selector plate (X) is flat and cut away on two sides to form slots sufficiently wide to clear the inner cables. When the selector is rotated in either direction an inner cable enters the slot and the face of the selector plate covers the top of the push rod.

When the pedal is operated, whichever push rod is covered is forced downward by the selector plate and the firing cable of the selected gun thereby pulled. The selector plate is operated by a spherical knobbed lever (Y) pivoting on a bush (Z) through the back plate of the selector housing, the top part of which is bent at right-angles to the plungers. The upper part of the selector shaft is squared to fit the selector lever bush thus allowing it to slide up and down when the pedal is operated. A spring-loaded ball (AA) in the selector lever fitting into one of three notches in the back plate holds the lever in position to operate the ordnance or M.G. or in the intermediate " safe " position.

The upper end of the ordnance firing cable is connected to one arm of a bell crank lever held in a fork bracket on the anti-rotation guide bracket or the semi-automatic gear bracket, the end of the arm being slotted to allow the cable to be inserted and the nipple on the cable seating in a counterbore at the root of the slot. The other arm of the lever is fitted with a roller which makes contact with the firing lever on the breech of the gun. A spring through which the cable is passed actuates between the bell crank lever and the root of the fork formed on the bracket, to hold the roller away from the firing lever on the gun. A set bolt screwed through the fork bears on the bell crank lever to act as a stop and prevent more movement of the arm than is nceessary to fire the ordnance.

An alternative firing control bracket may be fitted in which the cable is attached to a wedge-shaped piece. On one side it is supported by a roller and on the other in contact with a roller fitted to a lever which is secured in the bracket so as to pivot about the middle of its length. A plate on the back of the lever contacts the firing lever of the breech mechanism, and the other end of the lever seats a compression spring tending to hold the lever away. When the firing cable is pulled, the roller on the lever runs up the slope on the wedge piece and forces the pivoting lever over and in turn the firing lever on the ordnance.

The upper end of the M.G. firing cable is connected to the attachment which slides into a guide on the body of the M.G. where it is located by a spring loaded plunger and retained by a bolt. The attachment consists of an arm protruding from a slotted sleeve which permits it to slide when pulled by the cable. The arm is in contact with the trigger shaft of the M.G. which actuates the firing mechanism of the gun when pressed.

Churchill VIII and later Churchill VII vehicles will be fitted with electrical firing gear and emergency foot-firing gear, details of which will be published when available.

GUN MOUNTINGS

MOUNTING, M.G., No. 22, MARK I
fitted to
CHURCHILL VII & VIII

The No. 22 M.G. mounting is primarily similar to the No. 23 described below, differing in the manufacture of the protector assembly and the splash shield and arm assembly. Balance weights are not fitted on the forward part of the protector, the holes provided for fitting an F.T. unit being each plugged with a bolt. The splash shield is strengthened at the lower part by a stiffening plate, and has welded to it the pistol grip supporting arm. The arm is not removable as on the No. 23 mounting.

MOUNTING, M.G., No. 23, MK. I
CHURCHILL VII & VIII
(if fitted)

The Mounting, M.G., No. 23, MK. I carries a 7.92 mm. Besa machine-gun and is mounted in a compartment to the left of the driver. The mounting is free to be moved in any direction within its limits, being built up on a spherical bearing (A) fitting into a housing in the front plate of the hull where it is retained by a housing ring (B) bolted to the outside of the front plate. The spherical bearing is lubricated through a nipple (C) screwed into the inner face of the housing and connecting with the cavity for the spherical bearing.

The spherical bearing is shrunk on to the machine-gun protector (D) to the rear face of which is bolted the cradle (E) carrying the machine-gun so as to allow the muzzle to project through the protector. To the left of the machine-gun aperture in the protector is an aperture for sighting through, fitted with a plug shaped to give maximum protection and vision. The side of the protector is gouged to clear the line of sight.

The machine-gun is held in the cradle in a similar way to that in the co-axial mounting, the recoil bolt (F) positioning and retaining it and the clamping strip (G) locking it.

The telescope mounting bracket is formed as part of the machine-gun cradle. The telescope is inserted and clamped in position by the two wing nuts (H). A lug on the top of the mounting bracket towards the rear holds the brow pad (J) which is clamped in position by the bolt (K), and a lug towards the front is bored to receive the elevating and traversing control handle (L) which is inserted and secured by a nut and spring washer.

The brow pad is similar to those in general use, and is adjustable by means of a socket joint clamped by the wing nut (M).

Secured to the rear face of the cradle by two countersunk screws is a splash shield (N) in the top part of which is fitted a shutter (O) capable of being slid up and down to allow the cover of the machine-gun to be raised. The shutter is located by a flat spring. The splash shield is further secured by a bolt (P) screwed into the machine-gun protector, a distance piece on the bolt permitting it to be tightened without distorting the splash shield.

Welded to the lower part of the shield is a stiffening plate and boss into which is fitted and secured by bolts a pistol grip supporting arm (Q), the arm being cranked and made in two parts to bring the pistol grip (R) into position. The pistol grip consists

VEHICLE HISTORY AND SPECIFICATION

GUN MOUNTINGS

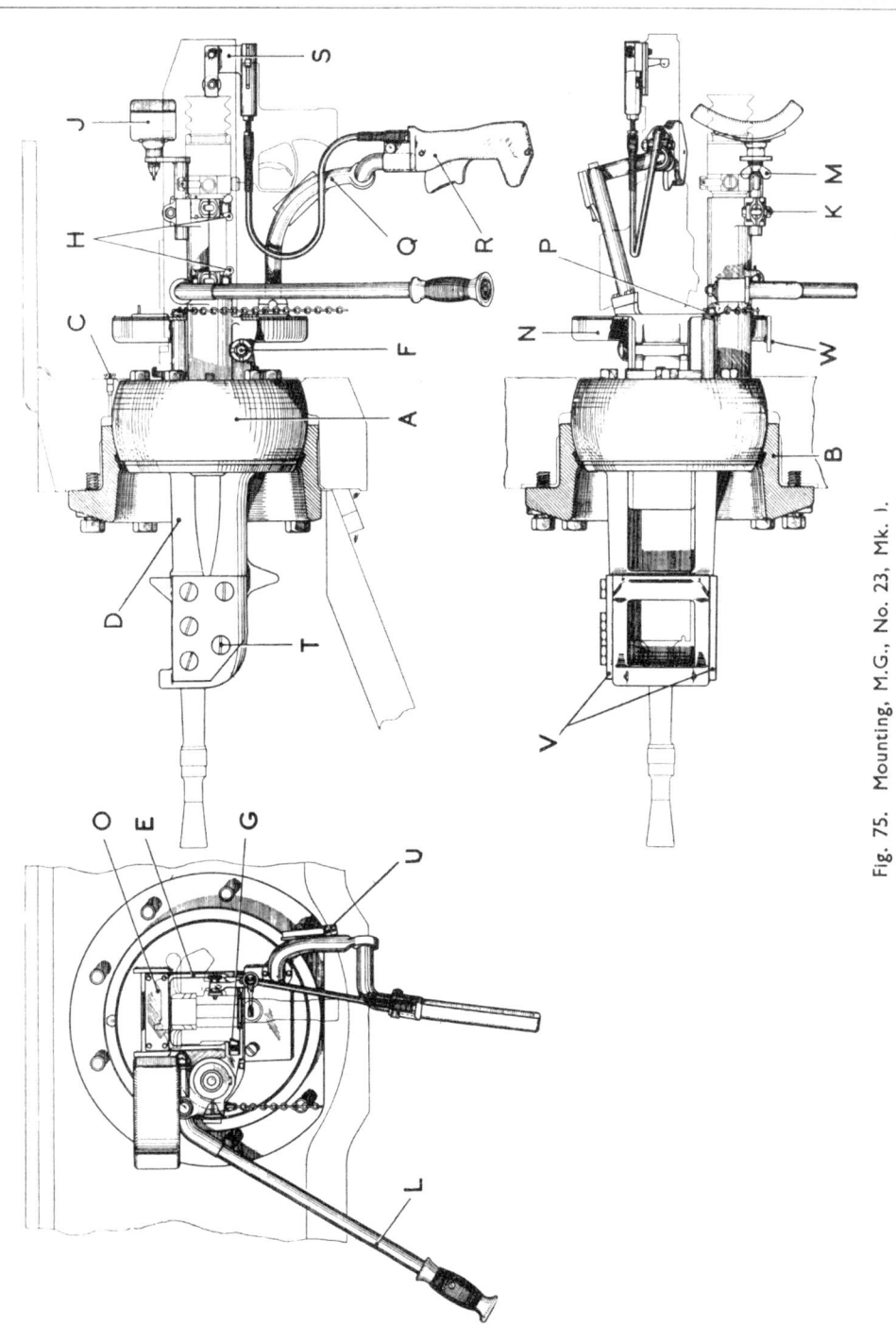

Fig. 75. Mounting, M.G., No. 23, Mk. I.

GUN MOUNTINGS

of a body clamped to the cranked arm, in the body being fitted the trigger, trigger spring and pivot pins, retained by a cover plate. The trigger is a bell crank lever having one arm inside the body connected to the firing cable and the other protruding from the body to form a finger piece. A tension spring holds the trigger in position for firing. When the trigger is pressed, a pulling force is exerted on the cable which actuates the arm in the firing attachment (S) to bear on the trigger shaft in the gun.

Welded to the pistol grip supporting arm is an accommodation housing (U) for the firing attachment when disconnected from the gun.

The forward part of the protector (D) is machined parallel and provided with tapped holes for the attachment of balance weights (V), the left weight being secured by countersunk bolts (T). The holes also provide for the attachment of a shroud for use with an F.T. unit when required.

Traverse of the mounting to the right is limited by a stop (W) which is welded to the splash shield and abuts the hull front plate when the safety limit is reached.

VEHICLE HISTORY AND SPECIFICATION

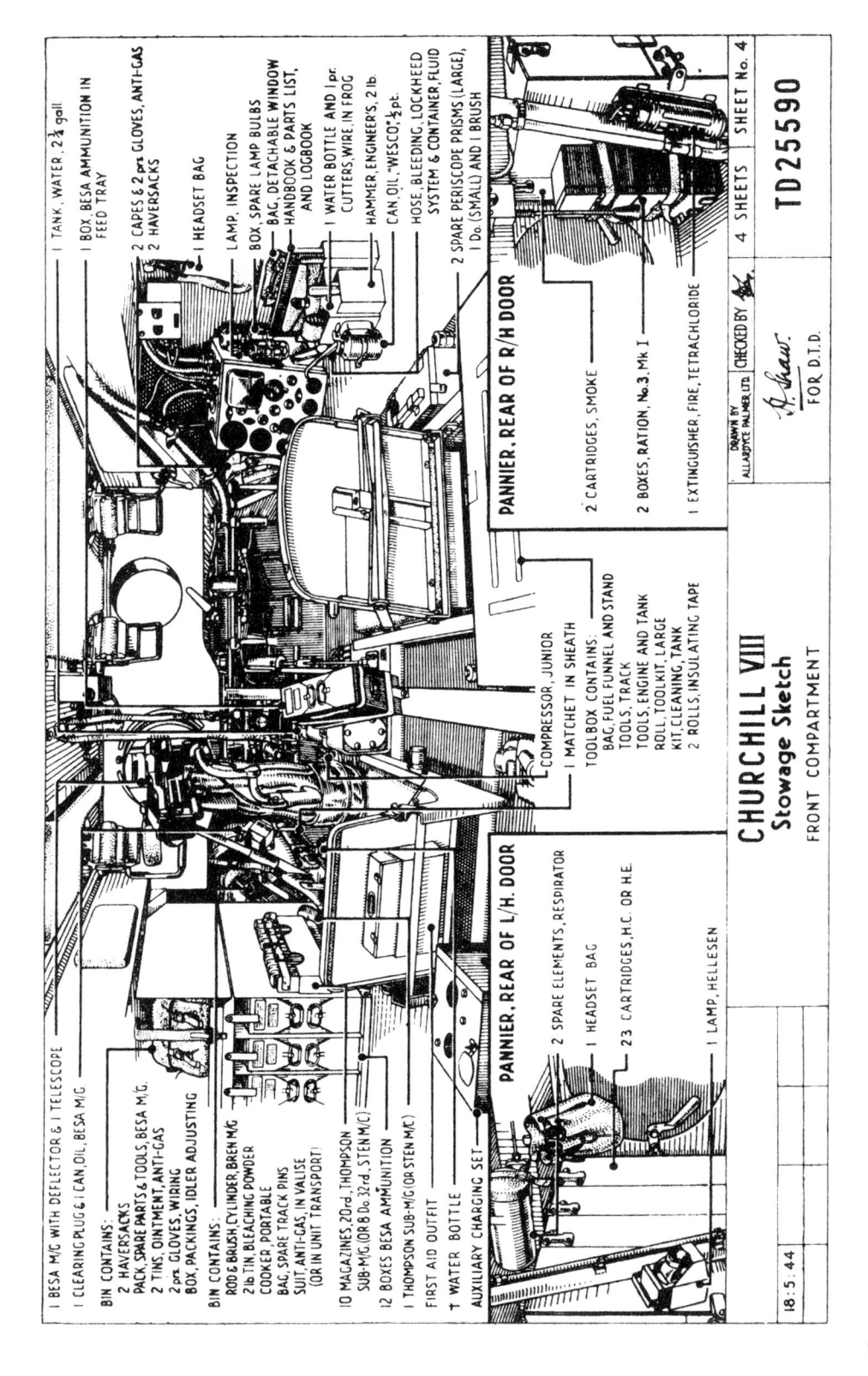

CHURCHILL VIII Stowage Sketch
FRONT COMPARTMENT

1 BESA M/C WITH DEFLECTOR & 1 TELESCOPE
1 CLEARING PLUG & 1 CAN, OIL, BESA M/C
BIN CONTAINS:
 2 HAVERSACKS
 PACK, SPARE PARTS & TOOLS, BESA M/G
 2 TINS, OINTMENT, ANTI-GAS
 2 prs. GLOVES, WIRING
 BOX, PACKINGS, IDLER ADJUSTING
BIN CONTAINS:
 ROD & BRUSH, CYLINDER, BREN M/G
 2 lb. TIN, BLEACHING POWDER
 COOKER, PORTABLE
 BAG, SPARE TRACK PINS
 SUIT, ANTI-GAS, IN VALISE
 (OR IN UNIT TRANSPORT)
10 MAGAZINES, 20-rd., THOMPSON SUB-M/G (OR 8 Do. 32-rd. STEN M/C)
12 BOXES BESA AMMUNITION
1 THOMPSON SUB-M/G (OR STEN M/C)
FIRST AID OUTFIT
1 WATER BOTTLE
AUXILIARY CHARGING SET

1 TANK, WATER, 2½ gall
1 BOX, BESA AMMUNITION IN FEED TRAY
2 CAPES & 2 prs GLOVES, ANTI-GAS
2 HAVERSACKS
1 HEADSET BAG
LAMP, INSPECTION
BOX, SPARE LAMP BULBS
BAG, DETACHABLE WINDOW
HANDBOOK & PARTS LIST, AND LOGBOOK
1 WATER BOTTLE AND 1 pr. CUTTERS, WIRE, IN FROG
HAMMER ENGINEER'S, 2 lb.
CAN, OIL, 'WESCO', ½ pt.
HOSE, BLEEDING, LOCKHEED SYSTEM & CONTAINER, FLUID
2 SPARE PERISCOPE PRISMS (LARGE), 1 Do. (SMALL) AND 1 BRUSH

PANNIER, REAR OF R/H DOOR
2 CARTRIDGES, SMOKE
2 BOXES, RATION, No. 3, Mk I
1 EXTINGUISHER, FIRE, TETRACHLORIDE

PANNIER, REAR OF L/H DOOR
2 SPARE ELEMENTS, RESPIRATOR
1 HEADSET BAG
23 CARTRIDGES, H.C. OR H.E.
1 LAMP, HELLESEN

COMPRESSOR, JUNIOR
1 MATCHET IN SHEATH
TOOLBOX CONTAINS:
 BAG, FUEL FUNNEL AND STAND
 TOOLS, TRACK
 TOOLS, ENGINE AND TANK
 ROLL, TOOLKIT, LARGE
 KIT, CLEANING, TANK
 2 ROLLS, INSULATING TAPE

18:5.44

DRAWN BY ALLADYCE PALMER LTD. CHECKED BY A. Shaw FOR D.T.D.

4 SHEETS SHEET No. 4
TD25590

CHURCHILL TANK

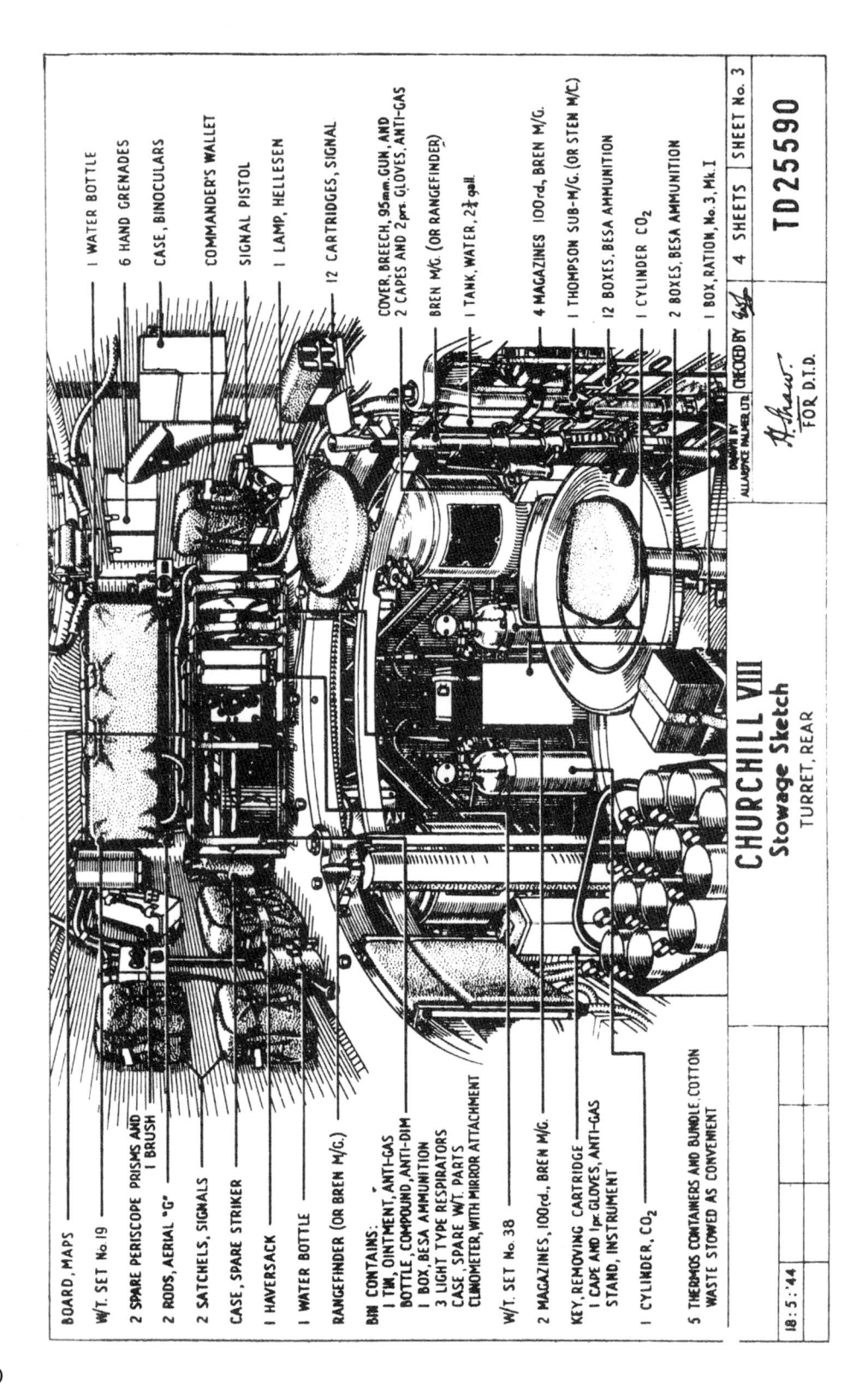

CHURCHILL VIII Stowage Sketch — TURRET, REAR

Labels (left side):
- BOARD, MAPS
- W/T. SET No. 19
- 2 SPARE PERISCOPE PRISMS AND 1 BRUSH
- 2 RODS, AERIAL "G"
- 2 SATCHELS, SIGNALS
- CASE, SPARE STRIKER
- 1 HAVERSACK
- 1 WATER BOTTLE
- RANGEFINDER (OR BREN M/G.)
- BIN CONTAINS:
  1 TIN, OINTMENT, ANTI-GAS
  BOTTLE, COMPOUND, ANTI-DIM
  1 BOX, BESA AMMUNITION
  3 LIGHT TYPE RESPIRATORS
  CASE, SPARE W/T. PARTS
  CLINOMETER, WITH MIRROR ATTACHMENT
- W/T. SET No. 38
- 2 MAGAZINES, 100rd., BREN M/G.
- KEY, REMOVING CARTRIDGE
- 1 CAPE AND 1 pr. GLOVES, ANTI-GAS
- STAND, INSTRUMENT
- 1 CYLINDER, CO₂
- 5 THERMOS CONTAINERS AND BUNDLE, COTTON WASTE STOWED AS CONVENIENT

Labels (right side):
- 1 WATER BOTTLE
- 6 HAND GRENADES
- CASE, BINOCULARS
- COMMANDER'S WALLET
- SIGNAL PISTOL
- 1 LAMP, HELLESEN
- 12 CARTRIDGES, SIGNAL
- COVER, BREECH, 95mm. GUN, AND 2 CAPES AND 2 prs. GLOVES, ANTI-GAS
- BREN M/G. (OR RANGEFINDER)
- 1 TANK, WATER, 2¼ gall.
- 4 MAGAZINES 100rd., BREN M/G.
- 1 THOMPSON SUB-M/G. (OR STEN M/C.)
- 12 BOXES, BESA AMMUNITION
- 1 CYLINDER, CO₂
- 2 BOXES, BESA AMMUNITION
- 1 BOX, RATION, No. 3, Mk. I

18:5:'44 | DRAWN BY ALLIANCE PALMER LTD. | CHECKED BY / FOR D.I.D. | 4 SHEETS | SHEET No. 3 | TD25590

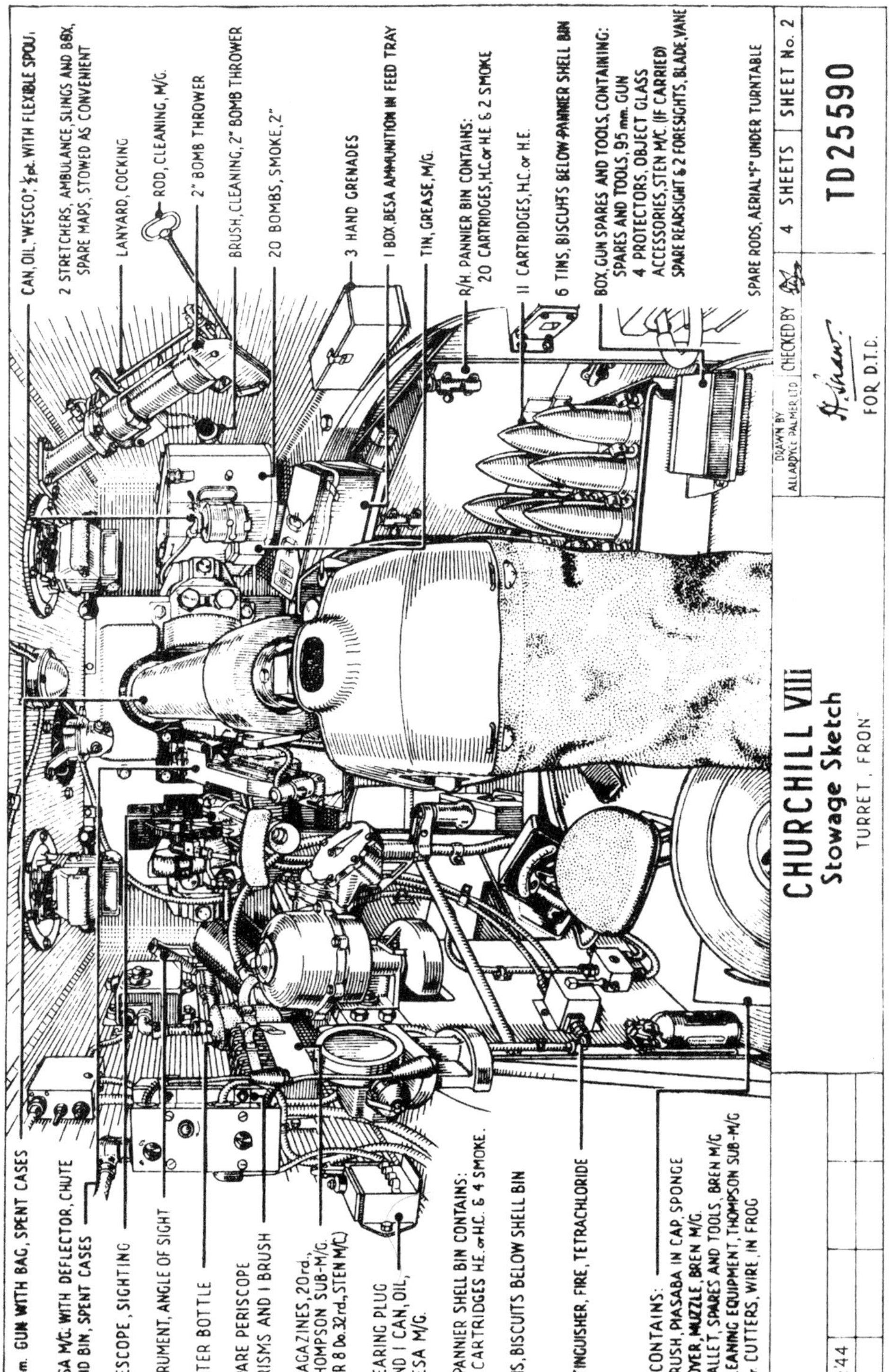
95 mm. GUN WITH BAG, SPENT CASES
1 BESA M/C. WITH DEFLECTOR, CHUTE AND BIN, SPENT CASES
TELESCOPE, SIGHTING
INSTRUMENT, ANGLE OF SIGHT
1 WATER BOTTLE
2 SPARE PERISCOPE PRISMS AND 1 BRUSH
10 MAGAZINES, 20rd., THOMPSON SUB-M/G. (OR 8 Do. 32rd., STEN M/C)
1 CLEARING PLUG AND 1 CAN, OIL, BESA M/G.
L/H. PANNIER SHELL BIN CONTAINS: 23 CARTRIDGES H.E. or H.C. & 4 SMOKE.
9 TINS, BISCUITS BELOW SHELL BIN
1 EXTINGUISHER, FIRE, TETRACHLORIDE
BIN CONTAINS: BRUSH, PIASABA IN CAP, SPONGE COVER, MUZZLE, BREN M/G. WALLET, SPARES AND TOOLS, BREN M/G CLEANING EQUIPMENT, THOMPSON SUB-M/G 1pr. CUTTERS, WIRE, IN FROG
CAN, OIL, "WESCO"; ½pt. WITH FLEXIBLE SPOU
2 STRETCHERS, AMBULANCE, SLINGS AND BOX, SPARE MAPS, STOWED AS CONVENIENT
LANYARD, COCKING
ROD, CLEANING, M/G.
2" BOMB THROWER
BRUSH, CLEANING, 2" BOMB THROWER
20 BOMBS, SMOKE, 2"
3 HAND GRENADES
1 BOX, BESA AMMUNITION IN FEED TRAY
TIN, GREASE, M/G.
R/H. PANNIER BIN CONTAINS: 20 CARTRIDGES, H.C. or H.E. & 2 SMOKE
11 CARTRIDGES, H.C. or H.E.
6 TINS, BISCUITS BELOW PANNIER SHELL BIN
BOX, GUN SPARES AND TOOLS, CONTAINING: SPARES AND TOOLS, 95 mm. GUN 4 PROTECTORS, OBJECT GLASS ACCESSORIES, STEN M/C. (IF CARRIED) SPARE REARSIGHT & 2 FORESIGHTS, BLADE, VANE
SPARE RODS, AERIAL "F" UNDER TURNTABLE
4 SHEETS
SHEET No. 2
TD25590
DRAWN BY ALLARDYCE PALMER LTD
CHECKED BY
FOR D.T.D.
CHURCHILL VIII
Stowage Sketch
TURRET, FRON
18:5:44

CHURCHILL TANK

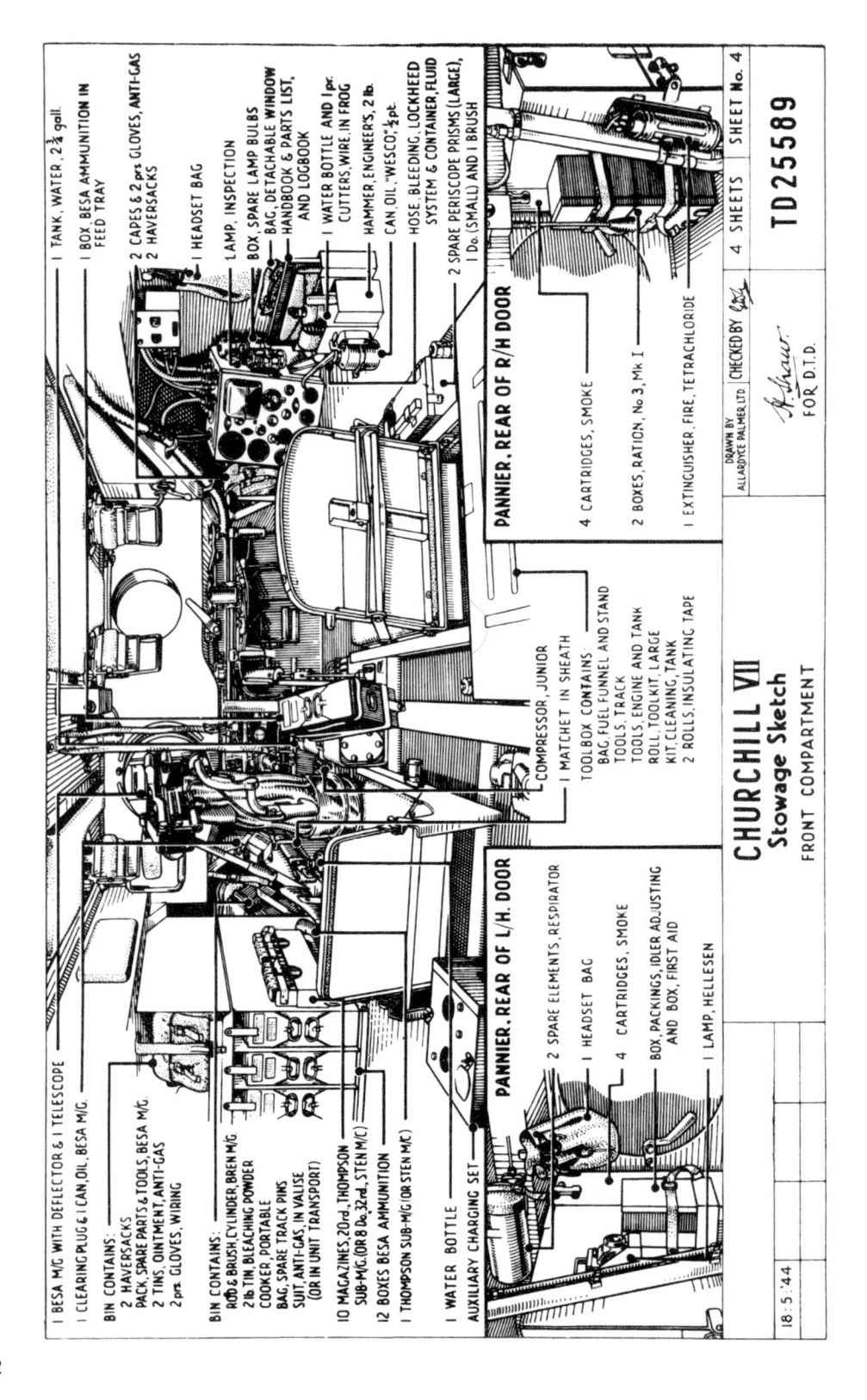

CHURCHILL VII
Stowage Sketch
FRONT COMPARTMENT

Labels (left side):
- 1 BESA M/G WITH DEFLECTOR & 1 TELESCOPE
- 1 CLEARING PLUG & 1 CAN, OIL, BESA M/G.
- BIN CONTAINS:
  2 HAVERSACKS
  PACK, SPARE PARTS & TOOLS, BESA M/G.
  2 TINS, OINTMENT, ANTI-GAS
  2 prs GLOVES, WIRING
- BIN CONTAINS:
  ROD & BRUSH, CYLINDER, BREN M/G
  2 lb. TIN, BLEACHING POWDER
  BAG, SPARE TRACK PINS
  COOKER, PORTABLE
  SUIT, ANTI-GAS, IN VALISE
  (OR IN UNIT TRANSPORT)
- 10 MAGAZINES, 20rd., THOMPSON
  SUB-M/G, (OR 8 Do, 32rd., STEN M/C)
- 12 BOXES BESA AMMUNITION
- 1 THOMPSON SUB-M/G (OR STEN M/C)
- 1 WATER BOTTLE
- AUXILIARY CHARGING SET

PANNIER, REAR OF L/H. DOOR
- 2 SPARE ELEMENTS, RESPIRATOR
- 1 HEADSET BAG
- 4 CARTRIDGES, SMOKE
- BOX, PACKINGS, IDLER ADJUSTING AND BOX, FIRST AID
- 1 LAMP, HELLESEN

Labels (right side):
- 1 TANK, WATER, 2¾ gall.
- 1 BOX BESA AMMUNITION IN FEED TRAY
- 2 CAPES & 2 prs GLOVES, ANTI-GAS
- 2 HAVERSACKS
- 1 HEADSET BAG
- 1 LAMP, INSPECTION
- 1 BOX, SPARE LAMP BULBS
- BAG, DETACHABLE WINDOW HANDBOOK & PARTS LIST, AND LOGBOOK
- 1 WATER BOTTLE AND 1 pr. CUTTERS, WIRE, IN FROG
- 1 HAMMER, ENGINEERS, 2 lb.
- 1 CAN, OIL, "WESCO", ½ pt.
- HOSE, BLEEDING, LOCKHEED SYSTEM & CONTAINER, FLUID
- 2 SPARE PERISCOPE PRISMS (LARGE), 1 Do. (SMALL) AND 1 BRUSH

PANNIER, REAR OF R/H. DOOR
- 4 CARTRIDGES, SMOKE
- 2 BOXES, RATION, No. 3, Mk I
- 1 EXTINGUISHER, FIRE, TETRACHLORIDE
- 1 COMPRESSOR, JUNIOR
- 1 MATCHET IN SHEATH
- TOOLBOX CONTAINS:
  BAG, FUEL FUNNEL AND STAND
  TOOLS, TRACK
  TOOLS, ENGINE AND TANK
  ROLL, TOOLKIT, LARGE
  KIT, CLEANING, TANK
  2 ROLLS, INSULATING TAPE

18·5·'44

DRAWN BY ALLARDYCE PALMER LTD.
CHECKED BY
FOR D.T.D.
4 SHEETS SHEET No. 4
TD 25589

VEHICLE HISTORY AND SPECIFICATION

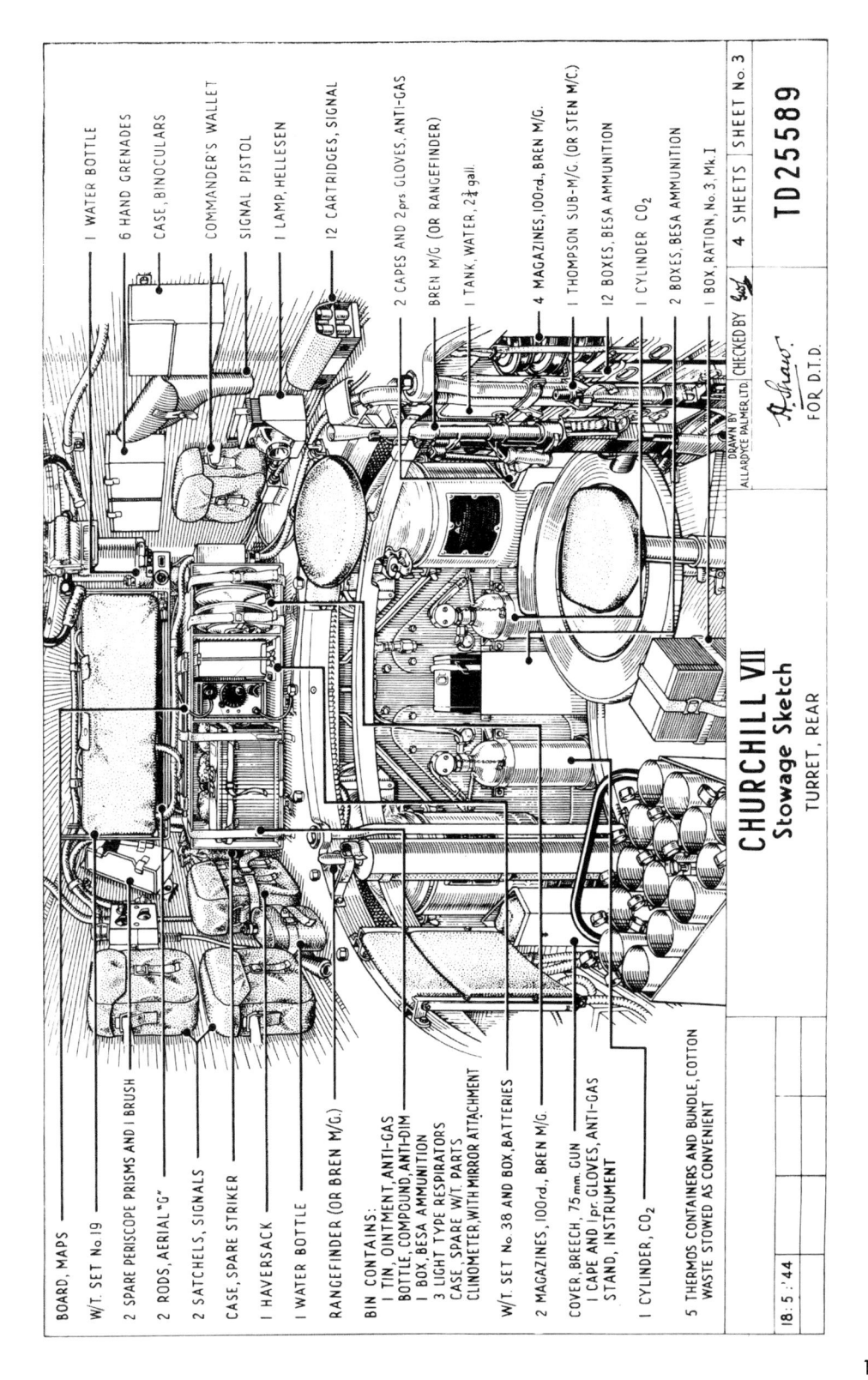

CHURCHILL VII Stowage Sketch
TURRET, REAR

TD25589 — 4 SHEETS, SHEET No. 3
18:5:'44
DRAWN BY ALLARDYCE PALMER LTD.
CHECKED BY A. Shaw FOR D.T.D.

Labels (top, left to right):
- 1 WATER BOTTLE
- 6 HAND GRENADES
- CASE, BINOCULARS
- COMMANDER'S WALLET
- SIGNAL PISTOL
- 1 LAMP, HELLESEN
- 12 CARTRIDGES, SIGNAL
- 2 CAPES AND 2 prs GLOVES, ANTI-GAS
- BREN M/G (OR RANGEFINDER)
- 1 TANK, WATER, 2¼ gall.
- 4 MAGAZINES, 100rd, BREN M/G
- 1 THOMPSON SUB-M/G (OR STEN M/C.)
- 12 BOXES, BESA AMMUNITION
- 1 CYLINDER CO₂
- 2 BOXES, BESA AMMUNITION
- 1 BOX, RATION, No.3, Mk.I

Labels (bottom, left to right):
- BOARD, MAPS
- W/T. SET No 19
- 2 SPARE PERISCOPE PRISMS AND 1 BRUSH
- 2 RODS, AERIAL "G"
- 2 SATCHELS, SIGNALS
- CASE, SPARE STRIKER
- 1 HAVERSACK
- 1 WATER BOTTLE
- RANGEFINDER (OR BREN M/G.)
- BIN CONTAINS:
  1 TIN, OINTMENT, ANTI-GAS
  BOTTLE, COMPOUND, ANTI-DIM
  1 BOX, BESA AMMUNITION
  3 LIGHT TYPE RESPIRATORS
  CASE, SPARE W/T PARTS
  CLINOMETER, WITH MIRROR ATTACHMENT
- W/T. SET No 38 AND BOX, BATTERIES
- 2 MAGAZINES, 100rd, BREN M/G.
- COVER, BREECH, 75 mm. GUN
  1 CAPE AND 1 pr. GLOVES, ANTI-GAS
  STAND, INSTRUMENT
- 1 CYLINDER, CO₂
- 5 THERMOS CONTAINERS AND BUNDLE, COTTON WASTE STOWED AS CONVENIENT

153

CHURCHILL TANK

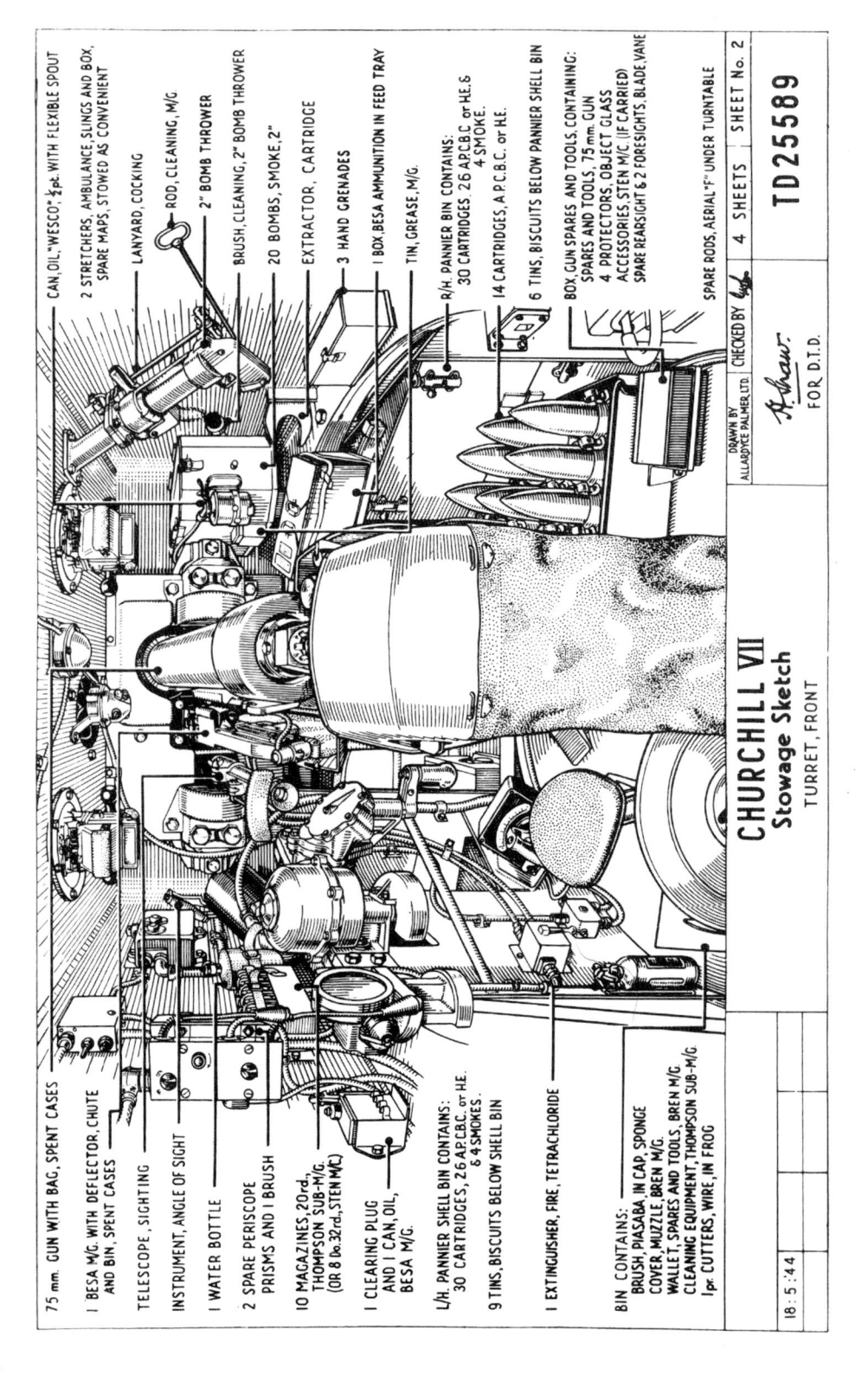

VEHICLE HISTORY AND SPECIFICATION

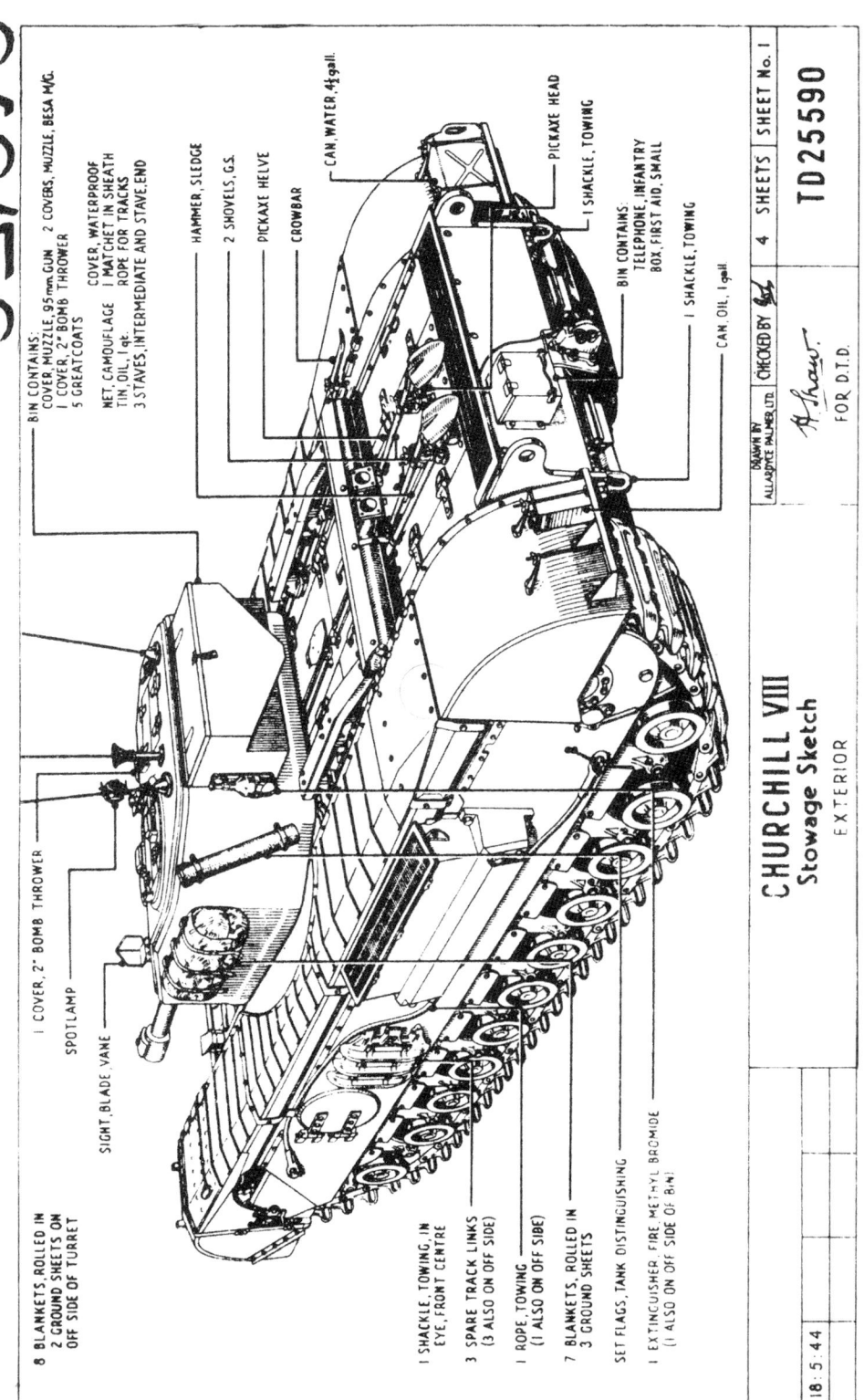

CHURCHILL TANK

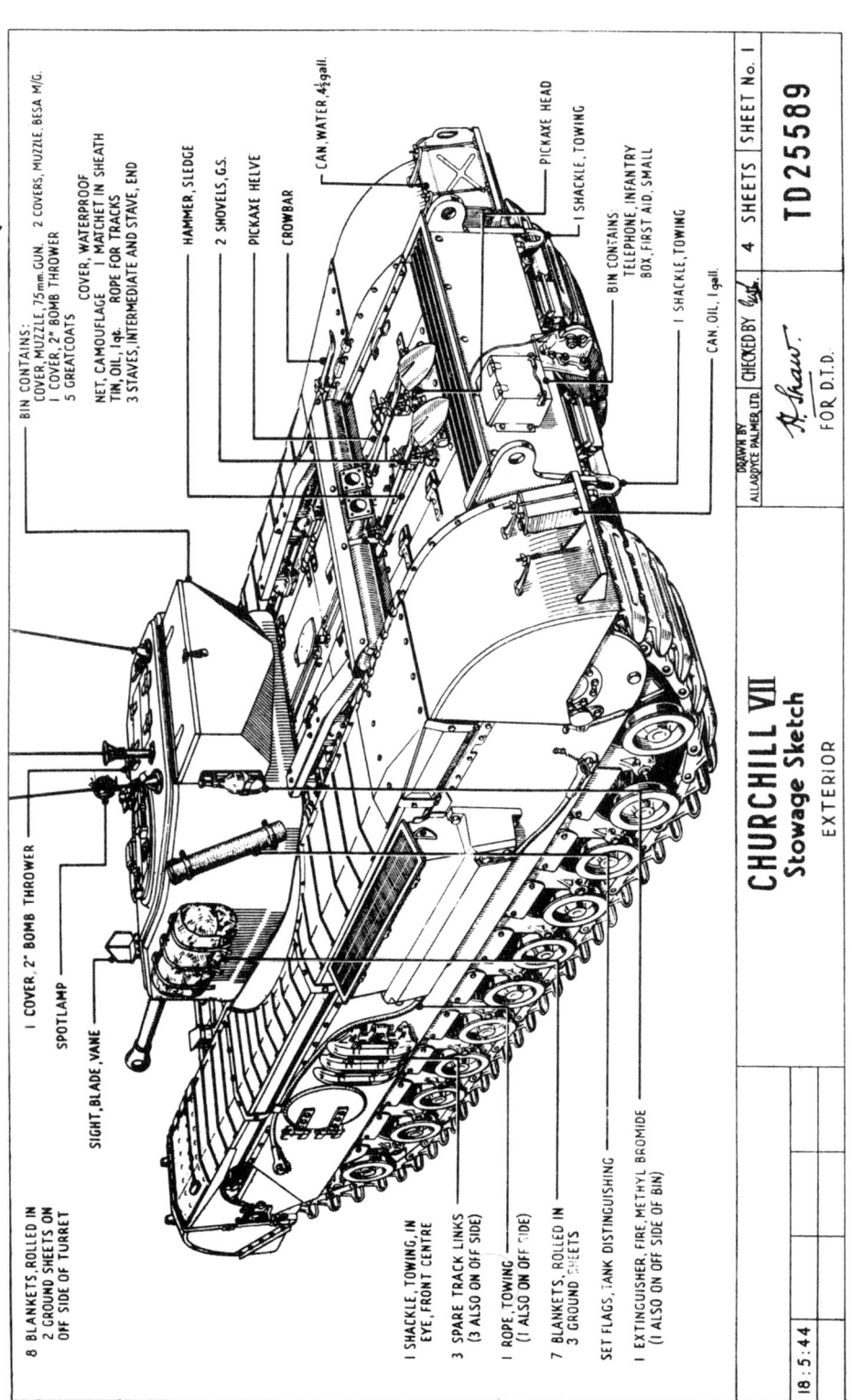

VEHICLE HISTORY AND SPECIFICATION

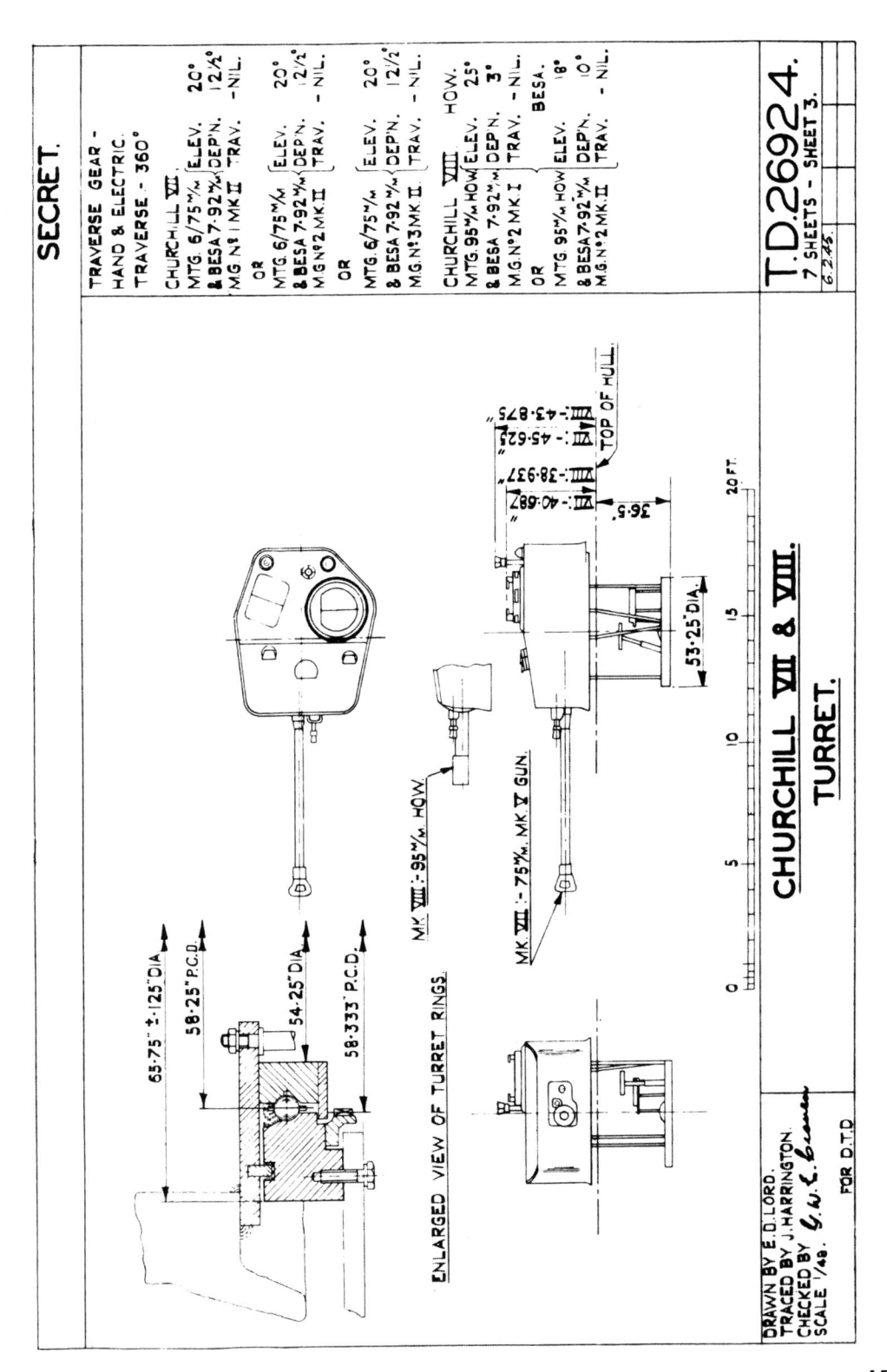

CHURCHILL VII & VIII.
TURRET.

T.D.26924. 7 SHEETS – SHEET 3.

CHURCHILL TANK

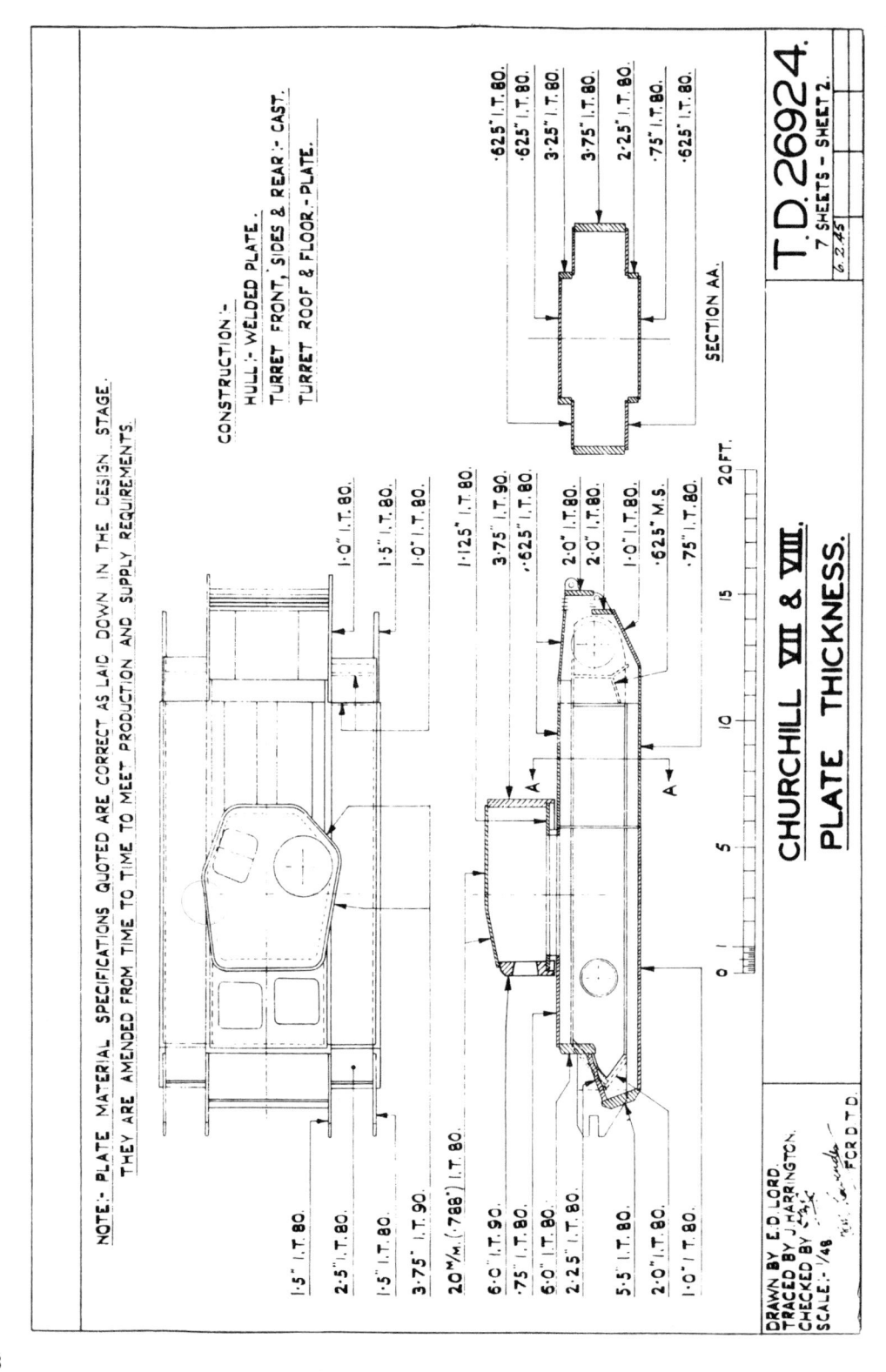

VEHICLE HISTORY AND SPECIFICATION

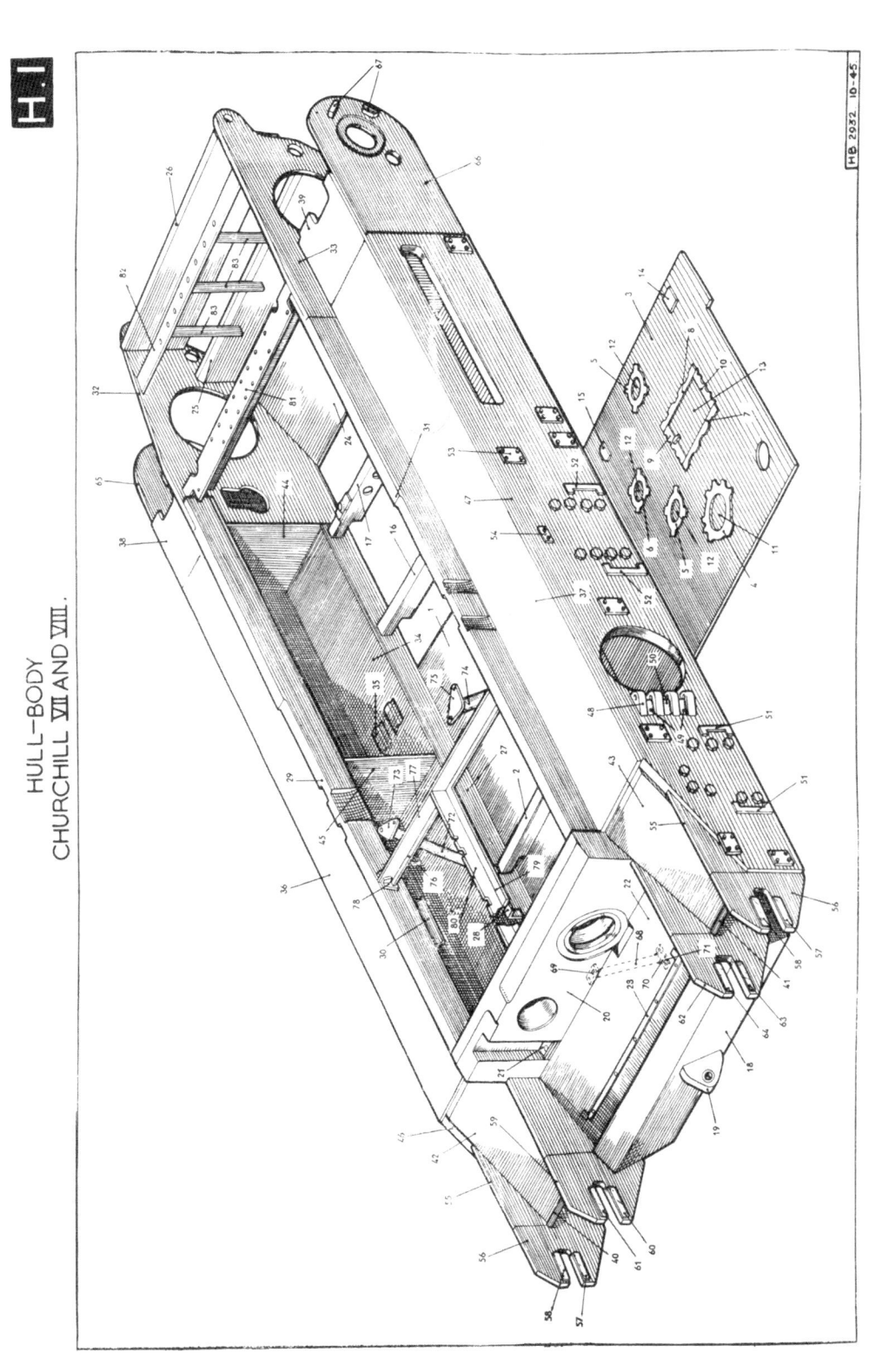

H.1

HULL—BODY
CHURCHILL VII AND VIII.

CHURCHILL TANK

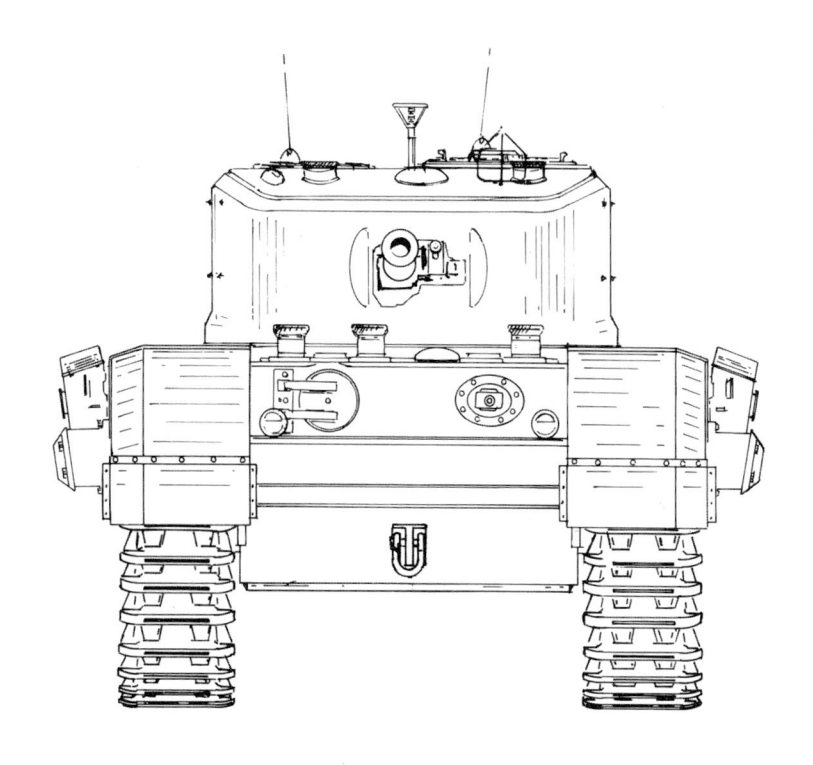

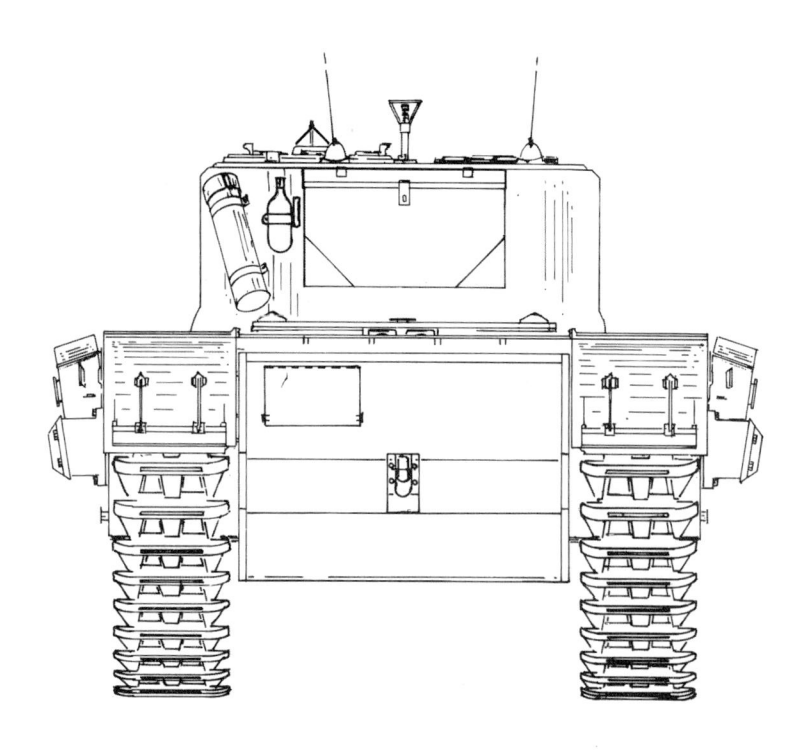

VEHICLE HISTORY AND SPECIFICATION

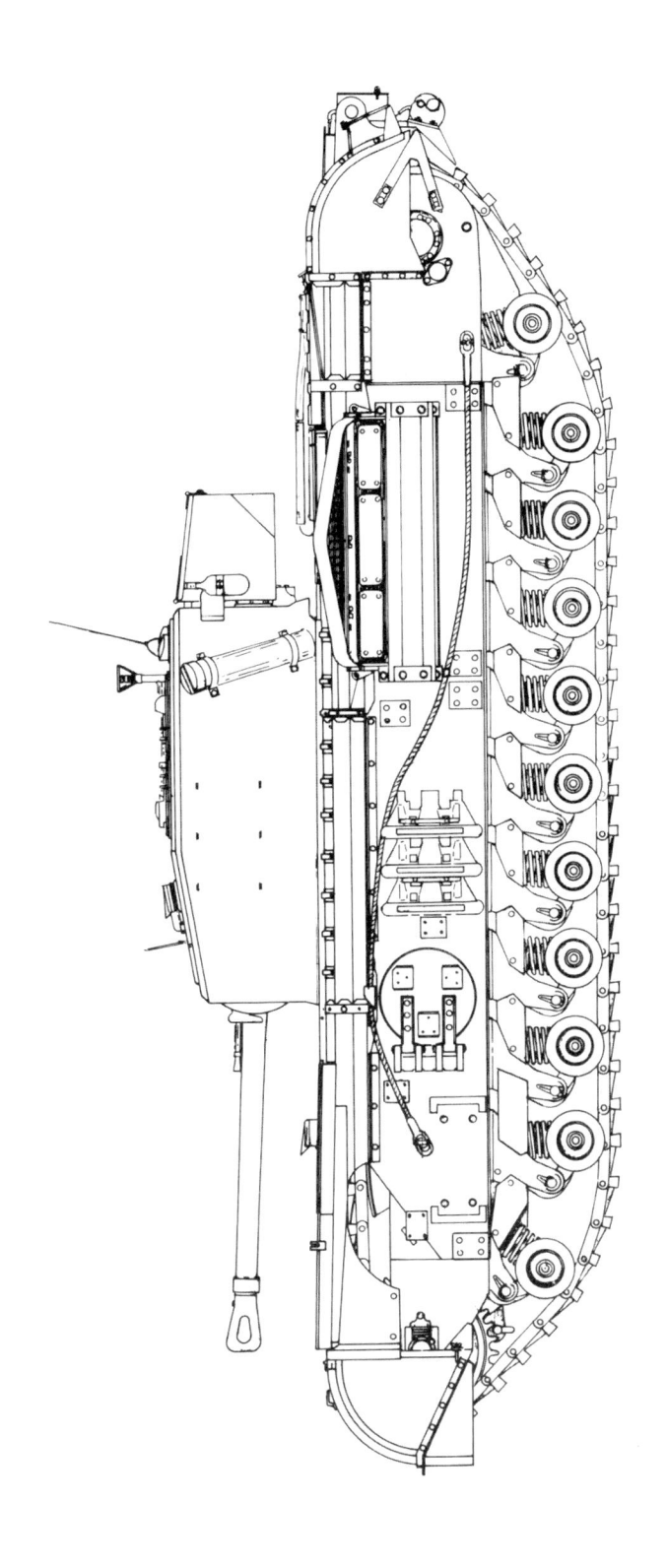

CHURCHILL TANK

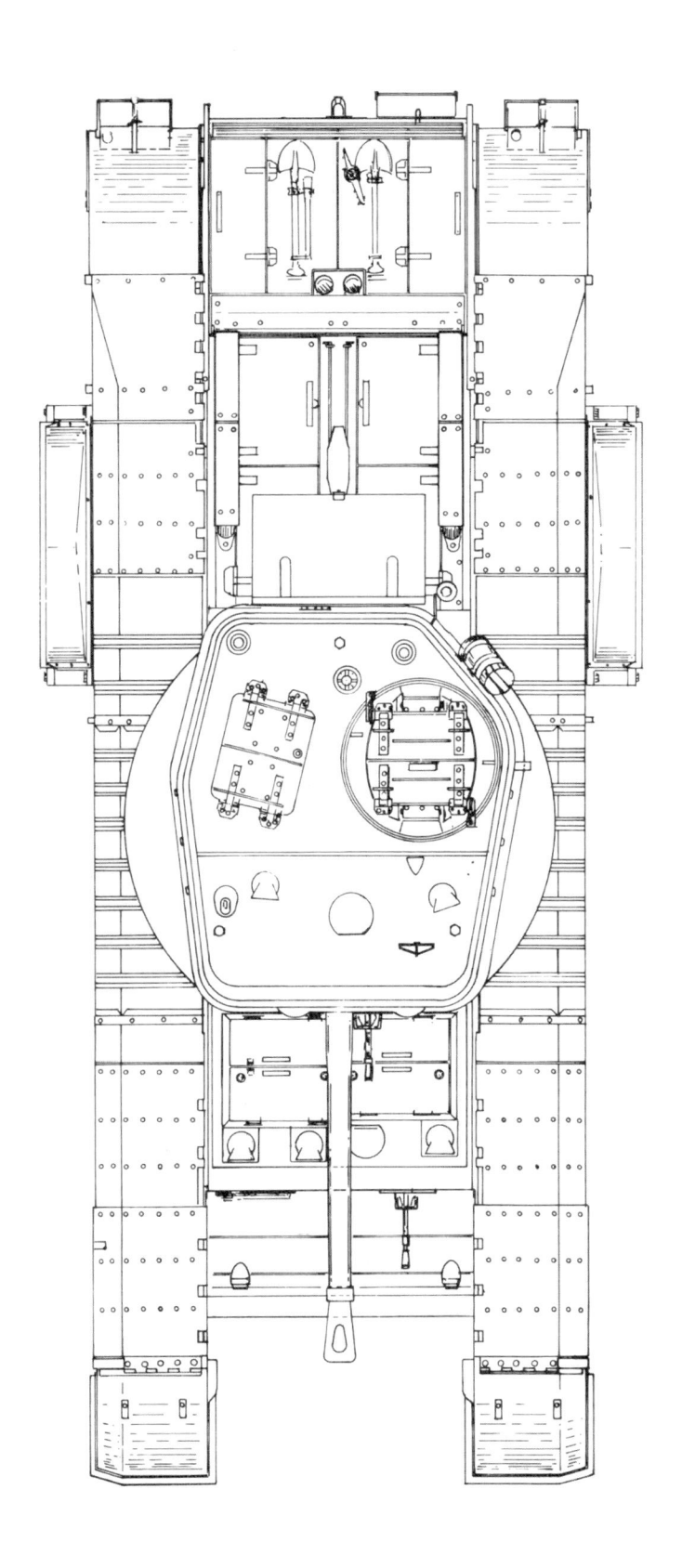

THANKS TO

The Tank Museum wishes to thank and acknowledge the following who kindly supported the crowdfunding campaign, which enabled this title to be republished in 2022.

Bradley Mitchell
Scott Parkinson
David Tabner
Andrew Smurthwaite
Frederick Brown
Stephen Birch
Kelvin Zhang
Jerald Marquardt
Trevor Wilson
Hans Johansson
Andrew Cadel
Steve Ellis
Bob Andrews
MSG Eddie M. Redfearn
Theo Hercules
Luigi Naruszewicz
Aaron Somerville
John Doyle
Howard Mitchell
Martin Jones
James J.G. Griffiths
Terry Hall
Steve Ellis
Ichikawa Tetsurou
Martyn Keen
Kirk Grainger
Chris Potter
Chris Swindells
Damian Brooks
John Kasawan
M.G.A. Weers
Andrew Downs
John Reeve
Peter Wilson
Philip Taylor
John Stanger
Edward Preston
Julian Davies
To Luka
Charles Taylor
Tancred Cassar
Ryan Allen
Joseph Jolley
Joanne Baker
Tom Achard
Andrew Speechley
Tom Grindall

Steven Bannister
Russ Spence
Peter James
Brendan Healy
WOII Bob Teasdale
R Hamps
Uwe Springhorn
Rocco Plath
Daniel Standen
Anthony J. Bird
Kieron Weller
Adrian Harris
Mark Rogers
Rob Brunton
Andrew Morley Wilkinson
Niclas Lindberg
Gary Draper
Liam Young
Rhys Fouracre
Andrew Dickey
Kenneth Lilley
Kevin Dyke
Rick Williams
Richard Beale
Mark Osborne
Mark Guttag
Marcus Mosley
Elliot Wade
William Pointing
Brian Page
Peter Smith
Ralph Hart
Ashley Garrison-Brown
Andrew Philpott
Esler Jim
P.S. Waugh
Peter White
Robert Cousin
Stuart Butterfield
Mark Ryan
Joe Bristoll
Benjamin T. Richter
Paul James
Steve Stuart
For Oliver
Sean Harper
David Corran

Joseph Searles
Stephen Dickens
Steven Howes
Dr Stephen Pannell
Norman Salmon
Nigel Chappell
Mark Edmands
Penni Elton
Richard Curren
Michael Townsend
Chris Clements
Cok Martijn
Robert Harwood
Keith Dallimore
Rebecca Mill-Wilson
Jack Levai
Rasmus Rex
Andreas Kowald
Ben Lawrence
Tyler Steele
Sam Barratt
Oliver Austin
Matthew Walker
Connor Cane
John Wright
Mike Pratt
Paul Middleton
Martin Littlecott
David Woodside
Sean Day
David Makinson
David Byrne
Rodney Anderson
Warren Mason
Mark Reynolds
John Beck
Michael Hobbs
Anthony Roberts
Nick Hodges
Andrew Desborough
Brian Hitch
Simon Smith
Kieran Hall
Timothy Hills
Keith Terry
Connor Storey
Ben Williams

Andrew Ray
Anthony Fletton
Matthew Carn
Charles Paddick
Tizian Dähler
Adrian Chorlton
Leonard Decant
George S. Harbinson
Michael Patey
Steven Thornton
Richard Purvis
Nathanael Wood
James Cooke
Glenn Rose
David Pope
Andrew Tomlinson
Richard Lucas
Steven Blackburn
Simon Ashcroft
Steve Bastable
John Hunt
Keith Olding
Ian Creasy
Brendan Quinlan
Giles Morley-Loft
Paul Goffin
Carter Birchfield
Jack Porter-Lindsey
Clemens Doll
Matthew Charles Gray
Steve Hocking
Peter Marshall
Andrew Woodward
Ian McLaughlin
Alan Baxter
Fiona Kendall
Eddie King
Herman du Preez
Carl Doran
Marcel Tromp
Wayne Davison
Jordan Weaver
Andrew Gilbert
Lowell Wong
Adrian Pethick
Terence Plant
Michael Cooper

THANKS TO

Kenneth Goss
Chris Fitzsimmons
Russell Barnes
Gordon Chrisp
David Cole
Cameron Moeller
Paul Button
Richard Gibbon
Jeremy Double
Chris Naden
Adam Gilliver
Clive Bower
Keith Meachem
Connor Storey
Percy D. Boyles
Steven Dyer
Richard Featherstone
Paul Willms
Maurice Andrews
Chris Matson
Charlie Barker
Graham Green
Craig Smith
Robin McEwen
Nigel Heather
Simon Day
Gerald Pierson
Neil Illingworth
Stuart Greenhalgh
Mark Etheridge
Shaun Leeks
Shaun Poller
Mark Powell
Ryan Tennant
Jack Yates
John Hill
Christopher Thompson
Chris Mackay
Mark Paines
Phil Gray
Mark Jennings
Andrew Paul Cook
Quinten van Kasteel
Martin Campbell
Christopher Noble
Don More
Adrian Symonds
Jay Kaelin
Mark Brooking
Andrew David
Michael Green
Raymond Wong

Andrew Eatock
Paul Kerr
Lauren Child
Huw Williams
Oliver-Emil Pedersen
Geoff Housego
Neil Cooper
James Cutts
Luke Culley
Michael Schweizer
Scott Gill
Owen Fitzpatrick
Richard Brown
Jakub Masařík
Richard Burdett
David Crosbie
Matt Faiers
David Clark
Peter Paterson
Bradley Cameron
Andrew Peck
David Peck
Connor Coolbaugh
Winston Gould
Bryan Davis
Ian Hambelton
Robin van Dijk
Stephen Burkwood
Daniel House
Teresa Fletcher
Terry Drewett
Tim Wrate
M. Simpelaar
Paul Mutton
Christopher Pilags
Trevor Povey
Eero Juhola
Terry Marsh
David Cruickshank
James Hulme
Anthony Boyce
Paul Charlwood
Devon Spears
Jason Singleton
Nathan Schlehlein
Sean Morrison
Jason Hofer
Esker McConnell
Dave Batten
Anthony Grayson
Brian Silver
George G. Hill

Sarah Woodcock
Daniel J. Parker
Joshua Gibbons
Peter Patrick
Mark Barnett
Juha Honkanen
Stuart Mackenzie
Henry Tornetta
Robert Peach
Michele Petriello
Richard Tugwell
Ian Tong
Chris Saulpaugh
Carl Pfutzenreuter
Barry Curtis
James Smith
Alexander Ridler
Sven Soderberg
John Wells
Jeroen van Dijk
T. Hoult
Deverne Jones
Scott Harwood
Philip Kaye
John Allgood
Sander Vreuls
Bence Juhász
Paul Spandler
Andrew Osborne
Christopher Winkels
Colin Gibson
Ray Young
Philip McCarty
Ben Dummer
Michael Woong
Jonathan Nielsen-Moore
Robert Dickinson
Norman Jaffe
Eivind Helgetun
Matt Klotz
Eddie Jackson
Paul Bradley
Arron Chiswell
Thomas Stromberg
Alexander Carr
Edric Chang
Christopher Skelton
Steven Adams
Dougie Smith
Alan Mincher
Mark Ambridge
Friedrich Klett

Andrew Down
Chris Bridgman
Alan Hall
Graeme Bates
Paul Hachey
Mark Niblett
Robert Smith
Steven Parkes
Andrew Reilly
Alastair Boyles
John Tripi
Stewart Garnett
Stephen Booth
Tom Davidson
Robert Pilling
Brad Dunleavy
Keith Major
Ewan Spence
Mark Hook
Dafydd Lyons
Constantin Schreiber
Danny Hin
James Sherman
James Scrivener
Paul Baker
Richard Lunson
Graham Duff
Matthew Bell
Hannah Lightowler
Andrew Lind
Michael Carroll
David Corboy
David Howling
Steven Bromley
Gary Miller
Michael Gerus
Carson Thomas
Lance Garwood
Mark Arnold
Neil Smith
Paul Schoeman
Mark Hiles
Gert De Cuyper
Kevin Pennycook
Jacob Tierney
Paul Mullaney
Ian Reeves
Stephen Chopping
Mark Bolger
Harold Rutten
John Conran
Steve Sanders

165

THANKS TO

Pawel Czarnocki
James Flint
Robert Elder
Eric Hollis
Terence Brewer
Thomas Ruiz
Barry Canning
Erik Miller
Harry Grosvenor-Collis
Gordon Brown
Connor Green
James Taggerty
Ben Davies
Keith Stafford
Daniel Jerbi
Harry McKnight
Stephen Ayres
Bernard Wylie
Adam Mathwig
David Pyle
Mark Collins
Keith Walker
Tim Wisehart
Keith Dray
Alan Johnson
Colin Smith
Glenn Wilson
Graham Mellis
Alexander Delf
Mark Pugh
Adam Pascuzzo
Alexander Burnett
Nick Brown
Jake Martin
David Mason
Charles Walker
Alex Winchell
Stephen White
Philip Bateman
Richard Evans
David Leatherdale
Ashley Smyth
John Johnston
Justin De Lavison
David Lynch
Colin Avern
Rob Shipman
Jack Hewson
Mark Lechmere
Samuel Picardo
Aaron Ashbrooke
Jonathan Bordell

Darren Rolfe
Mark Towner
Diane Dowling
Simon Hodson
Jack Denley
David Pengilly
Nigel Ashcroft
David Preston
Christian Wall
David Julien Griebel
Richard Burdett
Steve Thomas
Dave Mylett
Harry Hennessey
Eoghan Jones
Michael Brydges
Mark Dorsett
Guillaume Galy
Hugh Thomas
Darren Baker
Paul Jones
John Bradshaw
Salvador Cadengo
Jacob Cain
Paul Turner
Josephine Drew
Richard Bradley
Steven Browning
Tony Kear
Nick House
Philip Moor
Howard Lindsay
John Gathercole
Andy Sacha
Annie And Michael
Martin Smith
Adrian Hampton
Per Ove Sekse
Christian Bieletzki
Grahame Bebb
Richard Stevens
Alan Batten
Stuart Gunner
Stuart Armstrong
Sam Vincent
Jürgen Hammann
Barry Richardson
Adam Rich
Johan Van der Bruggen
Liam Cooney
Ramsay Fergal
Cameron Van Den Hoek

Ian Raine
Jim Pascoe
Terry Veal
Derek Brown
Philip Newitt
Piers Burwell
Nigel Pollard
Chris Apletree
Nick Payne
David & Jill Mears
Martin France
Graeme Whiting
John Drover
Martin Reynell
Ian Clarke
Steve Percy
Mark Baird
James Dack
Paul Wilcox
Guy Walker
Simon Tankard
Josh Mounter
Stuart Marshall
Jonathan Vickers
Ildefonso Gómez Yáñez
Christopher Stokes
Hugh Maguire
George Price
Tracy Wood
David Adams
John Hodgkinson
Richard Palmer
Maj Gen D.H. Crook
Stuart Bestford
Thomas Williams
Julian Loewenthal
David Fraser
Peter Edmondson
Bã‚Rge
Andre Arild
Paul Perry
James Neal
Martyn Clark
Matthew M. Smith
Chris Payne
Shane Dale
David Alexander
Bruno Valerio
Sal Castellana
Matthew Hynett
David Adams
Nigel Walker

Rodolfo G. San Agustin Jr
Simon Barnes
Patrick Crelly
Louis Mcafoos
António Castelo
Mr Passfield
Steve Murphy
Cammie Lamont
Charles Odell
Gage W. Smith
Siyu Fu
Anthony Witham
Herminio Ramirez
Alan Marks
Joe Szul
Martin Killick
Craig McRobbie
John Parr
Mike Smith
Matt Davies
Debbie Thompson
Syd Coleman
Aaron Hutson
David Battson
Ian Merriman
David O'Reilly
Dwight Luetscher
Kevin Hopwood
Michael Woodcock
Colin Baddeley
Nathan Parker
Jake Owen
Hanqiu Jiang
Richard Morris
Douglas Wade
Steve Richard
David Ford
David Wright
Samuel A. Grant
Vlastimil Tkacik
Matthew Hadnum
Lindsay Turner
Stuart Humphries
Stuart Woods
Stephen Barber
Aaron Brown
Martin Tuck
Leslie Stephenson
Stuart Carter
Dave Malott
Stephen Brown
Lee Smith

THANKS TO

Andrew Shelley
Nick Goffin
Daniel Ogles
Chris Brook
James Turner
Harry Wilding
Eric Hede
Christopher Budd
Stephan Zadziuk
Vivian Symonds
Aaron Jackson
Andrew Robert Bevan
Christopher Wood
Alan Willcock
Glyn Lewis
Warren Fenner
Michael Corser
Alan Rhodes
Juergen Schaaf
James Glendinning
Albert Squires
Jeremy Witt
Andrew Dixon
Roy Griffiths
Jonathan Jones
David Shaw
Jeroen Vantroyen
Laurence Behan
Michael Earnshaw
Geoffrey Stobbart
Leonard Thomson
Mike Grant
Nigel Titchen
Anjan Saikia
Jack Rimmer
Andy Macrae
Jonathan Ireland
Martyn Sime
Alex Horton
Axel Lohmann
Gary Richardson
Stephen Laccohee
Malcolm McEwan
Krzysztof A. Edelman
Ian Appleby
Charles Jones
Iori Hicks
Chris Bill
Stephen
Steven Devlin
Steven Randall
Clough Derek

John White
William Allen
Phil Puddefoot
Anthony Antilles
Stephen Wilcox
Christopher Smith
Christopher Worsley
Martin Bürgisser
Michael Ball
Ian Williams
Rob Treen
Adam Crew
Jacob Grove
Gary Dhillon
Brian Siela
Kenneth Teeter
Benjamin Puricelli
Scott Atchison
David Butterfield
Louis Devirgilio
Kurt Zwick
Gary Stewart
Louis Powell
Nicholas Brodar
Michael Sanchez
Daniel Cosier
Martin Frost
Sam Lockwood
Keith Matthews
Ashley Connor
Chris Alexander
Michael Billings
John Tapsell
Andrew Penman
Justin Fischer
William Bradley
Jorrian Dorlandt
Gavin Bryant
George Warne
Kristian Wicks
Christopher Maher
Paul Gerrard
Steve Kummerfeldt
Chris Blackler
Richard Davies
Paul V. Scourfield
Sam Wild
Joe Seaman
Paul Cramer
Gavin Steff
Alan Long
Paul Wallis

Ian Sims
Jake Holden
Mark Cheyney
Christopher Clarke
Campbell Harris
Stephen Squirrell
Anthony Gaughan
Jennifer Maydon
Jeremy Budd
Patrick Bailey
Ron Blackman
Graham Mellis
Lachlan Harris
Felix Stiessen
James Peacock
Gary Coates
William Calvert
David Woodrow
Paul Watts
Göran Löwkrantz
Chris Heath
Alastair Monk
Andy Musgrove
Robert Pews
Tamila McMullan
Paul Newman
Jeffrey Moots
Michael Gettings
Bruce Ghent
Peter Kuonen
Tony Poulter
Jack Sharpe
Andrew Kenny
Elliot Goddard
John Patrick Doran
Jan Meyer-Kamping
Arran Hartley
Gordon Matthews
Derek Smith
Paul Turrell
Stuart Purvis
John Turner
John Kent
Robert Bayliss
Matthew Wassell
David May
Stuart Cooper
Timothy Stevenson
Shirley Stedman
Tony Edwards
Simon Cannon
Paul Flanary

Scott Batchlor
Steve Cartwright
Alexander Amini
Eleanor Billinghurst
Philip Castle
Steven Hopwood
Raymond King
Israel S. Gibson
Nick Jones
David Bottomley
Steven Marley
Nigel Chandler
Thomas Costall
Martin Deacon
Simon Paterson
Garry Bailey
Dr Lynn Gareze
Adrian Knight
Heidi Smith
Steven Boddy
Sean Ogden
Matthew Muraska
Michael Bishop
Daniel John Bright
Peter Dawson
Steven Harker
Jason Parfitt
Gary Davis
Matthew Dawson
Alex Tucker
Ben Couldwell
Stuart Shaw
Robert Parker-Bowen
David Young
James Underwood
David Britten
Jon Howes
Tony Waterhouse
Brian Smith
Graham Croft
David Cohen
Alfie Higgins
James Upton
Stephen Harvey
Catherine Chapman
David Evans
John Bateman
Shade Kelly
Richard St Cooper
Chris Standen
Anthony Meyers
Emily M. Hamilton

CHURCHILL TANK

Kevin Page
Peter Frost
Rob Nichols
Peter Turner
James Stewart
Alexander Gibson
Ronald Lofthouse
Ian Crooks
Richard Lewis
Steven East
Matt Magee
Ian Kelly
Jeff Connolly
Paul Driscoll
Darren Hopkins
Robin Karpeta
Christopher Halford
Katy Moore
Carl Brodie
Mark Yates
Andrew Lowe
Dylan Ross
Aleksander Williams
Timothy Gray
Scott Liddell
Barry Walser
Kieran Caley
Neil Wiffen
Joyce West
Ian Griggs
Graeme Campsie
George Exon
Jeremy Bond
Simon Rilot
Rebecca Green
Chris Bray
Mark Meredith
Simon Gumbley
Robin Hardcastle
Ka Wo Au
Peter Piper
Dean Clark
Ashley Forster
Simon Jackson
Gary Burns
David Pepper
Glen Andrews
Maj R.D.B. Burgess HAC
Richard Bradley
Peter Everitt
Jolene Turner
Earl Nordgren
Jen Wilson
Andrew Butler
Robbie Macauley
Mark Jeffery
Kevin Bradley
Brian Burdette
Mike Howlett
Ian Clarke
Kevin Hazard
Tim Jones
Alistair Goodwin
Thomas Beck
Isaac Boots
Greg Kotecha
David Dibben
Dave Mitchell
Dominic Collins
Lee Greenwood
Deborah Schouten
Min Jung
David Reeves
Andrew Grayman
Clive Eastwood
Mark Knibbs
Zack Wright
Richard Mounstephen
Joe Taylor
Jeremy Fenby-Taylor
Tracy Gresty
Vance Chambers
Jean Grieten
Andrew Wood
Barclay Caras
Anthony Stewart
Joe Skinner
Chris Weston
Stuart Dobson
Joshua Bettinelli
David Crompton
Martin Clouder
Nik Johnson
Alastair Macfarlane
Mark Collins
Barry Sulliva
Kevin Mcalinden
 Gdsn 2665727
John Collier Coldstream
 Guards
Nicholas Ridley
Keith Skelhorne
Miller Watson
Matt Dawson
Thomas Foster
Cameron Liddle
Graeme Rigg
Nigel Fairhurst
Nicholas Nurden
Stuart Beaton
Matthew Sinn
Damian Van Velzen
David Shackleton
Brian Monument
Nathan Shine
Ian Price
Iain Longford
John Robertsom
Christopher Dunmill
Darren Partridge
Jan Schijff
Tim Marsh
Alan J. Brown
Steve Barnes
Alec James
Neil Kedney
Mark Abbott
Jamie Goodridge
Andrew Noble
Paul Isles
Reuben Bale
Martin J. Quinn
Gareth Davies
Nick Crabb
Sebastian Shimmings
William Donnelly
Robert Rodden
Nick Vaughan
Phil Loder
Jacob Burnett
Stephen Rothwell
Mark Moore
Alec Graham
Gary Major
Graham Hurst
Mears Richard
Chris Reynolds
Matthew Perry
Charlie Trumpess
Andrew Hopkin
Ceri Thomas
John Harris
Mike Potter
Gary Hewings
Stephen O'Connor
Simon Harper
Wayne Symons
Jonathan Vardy
Roy Saylors
Clive Laws
Jesus Escudero
Ian McCormack
Chris Holt
Robert Dicken
Anthony Simmons
Steven Reid
Rodney Marshall
Ian Robinson
Tristan A Cooper
Mark Smith
Phillip Heron
Anne Waite
Bruce Fritz
Nick Wood
James Killala-Ringwood
Panithi Itthithammaboon
Annabella McKenna
Werner Peters
Mark West
John Blackmore
Douglas Swanson
Kjell Arne Randen
Phil Jones
Bernard Pire
Daniel Ford
Alan Gould
Robert O'Connor
Richard Robson
Thomas Myers
Ramon Solar
Richard Bishop
Geoff White
Jyue Lim
Ian Uttridge
Melvin Avery
Huw Davies
Stephen Fleming
and Joel Fulcher.